Word-to-word (Bilingual)
DICTIONARY

ENGLISH-ARABIC
ARABIC-ENGLISH

Word-to-word Dictionaries

English-Urdu / Urdu-English (compiled by Dr Khurshid Alam)
English-Hindi / Hindi-English (compiled by Joseph W. Raker)
English-Punjabi / Punjabi-English (compiled by Prakash Singh Gill)
English-Farsi / Farsi-English (compiled by Maryam Zamankhani)
English-Arabic / Arabic-English (compiled by Abdulla Hasan Al-Jabre)
English-Somali / Somali-English (compiled by Mohamud Korshel)
English-Spanish / Spanish-English (compiled by Candido Sesma)
English-Gujarati / Gujarati-English (compiled by Nehal Mehta)
English-Chinese / Chinese-English (compiled by Weixuan Liao)
English-Korean / Korean-English (compiled by Mindy Kim Christlieb)
English-Russian / Russian-English (compiled by Ekaterina Strieby)
English-Portuguese / Portuguese-English (compiled by Suzana Santos)
English-Vietnamese / Vietnamese-English (compiled by Terry Gwenn)
English-German / German-English (compiled by Hella Bell)
English-Turkish / Turkish-English (compiled by Nagme Yazgin)
English-Bengali / Bengali-English (compiled by Prodip Kumar Dutta)
English-Tagalog / Tagalog-English (compiled by Norma Smith)
English-Haitian Creole / Haitian Creole-English (compiled by Karine Gentil)
English-Cambodian / Cambodian-English (compiled by Hak Sokleang)
English-French / French-English (compiled by Vanessa Munsch)
English-Pashto / Pashto-English (compiled by Sobia Kattak)
English-Romanian / Romanian-English (compiled by Ana Cristana Dobrin)
English-Thai / Thai-English (compiled by Kesorn Kawila)

More languages in print

STAR PUBLICATIONS PVT.LTD
New Delhi 110 002

Word-to-word (Bilingual) DICTIONARY

ENGLISH-ARABIC
ARABIC-ENGLISH

Compiled by
Moustafa Boudjerada

617357

Boudjerada, Moustafa
ENGLISH-ARABIC / ARABIC-ENGLISH
Word-to-word (Bilingual) Dictionary

© **Bilingual Dictionaries Inc, USA**

First Edition : 2009

Published in India by :
Star Publications Pvt. Ltd.
4/5B Asaf Ali Road
New Delhi- 110 002 (India)
(e-mail: starpub@satyam.net.in)

under arrangement with
Bilingual Dictionaries Inc, USA

Printed at: Star Print O Bind, New Delhi- 110 020

List of Irregular Verbs

present - past - past participle

arise - arose - arisen
awake - awoke - awoken, awaked
be - was - been
bear - bore - borne
beat - beat - beaten
become - became - become
begin - began - begun
behold - beheld - beheld
bend - bent - bent
beseech - besought - besought
bet - bet - betted
bid - bade (bid) - bidden (bid)
bind - bound - bound
bite - bit - bitten
bleed - bled - bled
blow - blew - blown
break - broke - broken
breed - bred - bred
bring - brought - brought
build - built - built
burn - burnt - burnt *
burst - burst - burst
buy - bought - bought
cast - cast - cast
catch - caught - caught
choose - chose - chosen
cling - clung - clung

come - came - come
cost - cost - cost
creep - crept - crept
cut - cut - cut
deal - dealt - dealt
dig - dug - dug
do - did - done
draw - drew - drawn
dream - dreamt - dreamed
drink - drank - drunk
drive - drove - driven
dwell - dwelt - dwelt
eat - ate - eaten
fall - fell - fallen
feed - fed - fed
feel - felt - felt
fight - fought - fought
find - found - found
flee - fled - fled
fling - flung - flung
fly - flew - flown
forebear - forbore - forborne
forbid - forbade - forbidden
forecast - forecast - forecast
forget - forgot - forgotten
forgive - forgave - forgiven
forego - forewent - foregone
foresee - foresaw - foreseen
foretell - foretold - foretold

forget - forgot - forgotten	**light** - lit * - lit *
forsake - forsook - forsaken	**lose** - lost - lost
freeze - froze - frozen	**make** - made - made
get - got - gotten	**mean** - meant - meant
give - gave - given	**meet** - met - met
go - went - gone	**mistake** - mistook - mistaken
grind - ground - ground	**must** - had to - had to
grow - grew - grown	**pay** - paid - paid
hang - hung * - hung *	**plead** - pleaded - pled
have - had - had	**prove** - proved - proven
hear - heard - heard	**put** - put - put
hide - hid - hidden	**quit** - quit * - quit *
hit - hit - hit	**read** - read - read
hold - held - held	**rid** - rid - rid
hurt - hurt - hurt	**ride** - rode - ridden
hit - hit - hit	**ring** - rang - rung
hold - held - held	**rise** - rose - risen
keep - kept - kept	**run** - ran - run
kneel - knelt * - knelt *	**saw** - sawed - sawn
know - knew - known	**say** - said - said
lay - laid - laid	**see** - saw - seen
lead - led - led	**seek** - sought - sought
lean - leant * - leant *	**sell** - sold - sold
leap - lept * - lept *	**send** - sent - sent
learn - learnt * - learnt *	**set** - set - set
leave - left - left	**sew** - sewed - sewn
lend - lent - lent	**shake** - shook - shaken
let - let - let	**shear** - sheared - shorn
lie - lay - lain	**shed** - shed - shed

shine - shone - shone
shoot - shot - shot
show - showed - shown
shrink - shrank - shrunk
shut - shut - shut
sing - sang - sung
sink - sank - sunk
sit - sat - sat
slay - slew - slain
sleep - sleep - slept
slide - slid - slid
sling - slung - slung
smell - smelt * - smelt *
sow - sowed - sown *
speak - spoke - spoken
speed - sped * - sped *
spell - spelt * - spelt *
spend - spent - spent
spill - spilt * - spilt *
spin - spun - spun
spit - spat - spat
split - split - split
spread - spread - spread
spring - sprang - sprung
stand - stood - stood
steal - stole - stolen
stick - stuck - stuck
sting - stung - stung
stink - stank - stunk

stride - strode - stridden
strike - struck - struck (stricken)
strive - strove - striven
swear - swore - sworn
sweep - swept - swept
swell - swelled - swollen *
swim - swam - swum
take - took - taken
teach - taught - taught
tear - tore - torn
tell - told - told
think - thought - thought
throw - threw - thrown
thrust - thrust - thrust
tread - trod - trodden
wake - woke - woken
wear - wore - worn
weave - wove * - woven *
wed - wed * - wed *
weep - wept - wept
win - won - won
wind - wound - wound
wring - wrung - wrung
write - wrote - written

Those tenses with an * also have regular forms.

English-Arabic

Abbreviations

a - article
n - noun
e - exclamation
pro - pronoun
adj - adjective
adv - adverb
v - verb
iv - irregular verb
pre - preposition
c - conjunction

A

a أداة تنكير *a*
abandon *v* يهجر
abandonment *n* التّرك
abbey *n* الكنيسة
abbreviate *v* اختصر
abbreviation *n* الاختصار
abdicate *v* يتخلى
abdication *n* التّنازل
abdomen *n* البطن
abduct *v* اخطف
abduction *n* خَطْف
aberration *n* الاضطراب
abhor *v* يمقُت
abide by *v* يلتزم
ability *n* القدرة
ablaze *adj* مشتعل
able *adj* قادر
abnormal *adj* شاذّ
abnormality *n* الشّذوذ
abolish *v* يُلغي
abort *v* اجهض , أحبط
abortion *n* إسقاط
abound *v* يَكْثُرُ
about *pre* بشأن
about *adv* حول

above *pre* أسمى من
abreast *adv* جنباً إلى جنب
abridge *v* يُقصّر
abroad *adv* خارجَ البلد
abrogate *v* يُبْطل , يُلغي
absence *n* غياب
absent *adj* غائب
absolute *adj* كامل
absolution *n* غفران
absolve *v* يَغْفِر
absorb *v* يمتص
absorbent *adj* ممتص
abstain *v* يُمسِك
abstinence *n* عِفّة
abstract *adj* مجرّد
absurd *adj* سخيف
abundance *n* وَفرَة
abundant *adj* وافر
abuse *v* يشتِم
abuse *n* إساءة استعمال
abusive *adj* اعتسافيّ
abysmal *adj* سَحِيق
abyss *n* هاوية
academic *adj* جامعيّ
academy *n* مَعْهَد
accelerate *v* يُعجِّل
accelerator *n* المُعاجِل
accent *n* لهجة

accept v يَقْبَل	achieve v يُنجز
acceptable adj مقبول	achievement n إنجاز
acceptance n قبول	acid n حَمْض
access n مَدْخَل	acidity n حُموضة
accessible adj في المُتَنَاوَل	acknowledge v يعترف بـ
accident n مصادَفة	acorn n البلّوطة
accidental adj عَرَضيّ	acoustic adj صَوْتيّ
acclaim v يصفّ	acquaint v يُطلِع
acclimatize v يؤقلم	acquaintance n معرفة
accommodate v يلائم , يكيّف	acquire v يحرز
accompany v يرافِق	acquisition n اكتساب
accomplish v يُنجز	acquit v يُعفي
accomplishment n إنجاز	acquittal n إعفاء
accord n اتفاق	acre n قَدّان , أكْر
according to pre طبقا	acrobat n بهلوان
accordion n الأكورديون	across pre عَبْر
account n حساب , محاسَبة	act v يمثّل
account for v يفسّر	action n فعلٌ
accountable adj مسؤول	activate v شغل
accountant n المحاسيب	activation n تَنْشيط
accumulate v يُكدّس	active adj عمليّ
accuracy n ضَبْط	activity n نشاط
accurate adj صحيح	actor n الممثّل المسرحيّ
accusation n اتهام	actress n الممثّلة المسرحيّة
accuse v يَتّهم	actual adj واقعيّ
accustom v يُعوّد	actually adv فى الواقع
ace n آص	acute adj حادّ
ache n ألم متواصل خفيف	adamant adj صُلْب

adapt v يُكيِّف	admire بـ v يُعجَب
adaptable adj متكيِّف	admirer n المعجَب
adaptation n تكييف	admissible adj مقبول
adapter n مُكيِّف	admission n تسليم بقضية
add v يُضيف	admit بـ v يسمح
addicted adj مُدْمِن	admittance n قبول
addiction n معاقرة	admonish v يلوم
addictive adj إدْمانيّ	admonition n لوم
addition n زيادة	adolescence n المراهقة
additional adj إضافيّ	adolescent n مُراهِق
address n عنوان	adopt v يتبنّى
address v عنون	adoption n تَبَن
addressee n المرسَل إليه	adoptive adj بالتَّبنّي
adequate adj كافٍ	adorable adj فاتن
adhere بـ v يتقيّد	adoration n توقير
adhesive adj لاصِق	adore v يوقر
adjacent adj مجاور	adorn v يزيّن
adjective n صفة	adrift adv طافٍ
adjoin v يحاذي	adulation n تزلف
adjoining adj مُجَاوِر	adult n بالغ , راشد
adjourn v يُؤجِّل	adulterate v يَمْذُق , يغشّ
adjust v يُسَوِّي	adultery n زناً
adjustable adj مُتَكيِّف	advance v تقدم
adjustment n تسوية	advance n تقدُّم
administer v يدير	advantage n أفضليّة
admirable adj رائع	Advent n حلول
admiral n أميرال	adventure n مغامرة
admiration n إعجاب	adverb n حال

adversary n خَصْم

adverse adj مُعادٍ

adversity n شدّة

advertise v يُعلِم

advertising n إعلان

advice n نصيحة

advisable adj مُسْتَصْوَب

advise v ينصح

adviser n الناصح ,

advocate v يدافع عن

aeroplane n طائرة

aesthetic adj جَمالِيّ

afar adv مِن بُعْد

affable adj أنيس

affair n مسألة , شأن

affect v يولَع بـ

affection n عاطفة

affectionate adj محبّ

affiliate v يَضُمّ إلى

affiliation n دمج

affinity n صلة

affirm v يُثْبت

affirmative adj ايجابى

affix v يُلصق

afflict v يُحْزن

affliction n حزن

affluence n وفرة

affluent adj وافر

afford v يتحمّل

affordable adj سهل المأخذ

affront v يُهين

affront n إهانة

afloat adv طافٍ

afraid adj خائف

afresh adv كرّة أخرى

after pre خَلف

afternoon n الأصيل

afterwards adv بعدئذ

again adv من جديد

against pre تجاه

age n عُمْر

agency n قوّة

agenda n برنامج

agent n عامل

agglomerate v يكتّل

aggravate v يفاقم

aggravation n إثارة ,

aggregate v يجمّع

aggression n عُدْوان

aggressive adj عُدْواني

aggressor n الباغي

aghast adj مشدوه

agile adj رشيق

agitator n المُهيِّج

agnostic n اللاأدري

agonize v يعذّب

agonizing adj موجع	**aisle** n ممشى
agony n كَرْب	**ajar** adj مفتوح جزئيًّا
agree v يتطابق	**akin** adj قريب
agreeable adj مقبول	**alarm** n إنذار بخطر
agreement n اتفاق	**alarm clock** n المُنَبِّه
agricultural adj زراعيّ	**alarming** adj مرعب
agriculture n زراعة	**alcoholic** adj سكّير
ahead pre متقدِّما	**alcoholism** n إدمان الكحول,
aid n معاونة	**alert** n يَقِظ
aid v يعاون	**algebra** n الجَبْر
aide n المعاون	**alien** n غريب ,
ailing adj معتل	**alight** adv مشتعلًا
ailment n اعتلال جسدي	**align** v يَصُفّ
aim v يسدِّد	**alignment** n رصف
aimless adj بلا هدف	**alike** adj سواء
air n هواء ,	**alive** adj حيّ
air v يهوّي , يعرّض للهواء	**all** adj كلّ
aircraft n مُنطاد أو طائرة	**allegation** n ادعاء ,
airfare n سلاح الطيران	**allege** v يدّعي
airfield n المَهْبط ,	**allegedly** adv ظاهِريًّا
airline n خط جوي	**allegiance** n ولاء
airliner n طائرة	**allegory** n مجاز
airmail n بريد جوّي	**allergic** adj استهدافي
airplane n طائرة	**allergy** n الاستهداف
airport n ميناء جوّي	**alleviate** v يخفِّف
airspace n مجال جوى	**alley** n مَمْشى
airstrip n مَهْبط طائرات	**alliance** n اتحاد
airtight adj سَدُوْدٌ للهواء	**allied** adj مُتّحد

alligator n تمساح إستوائي

allocate v يوزّع

allot v يحصّص

allotment n حصّة

allow v لـ يخصّص

allowance n نصيب

alloy n خليط معدني

allure n إغراء

alluring adj مُغْرٍ

allusion n تلميح

ally n دولة حليفة

ally v يصاهر بين

almanac n تقويم

almighty adj كلّي القدرة

almond n لوز

almost adv تقريباً

alms n صَدَقة

alone adj متوحّد

along pre على طول كذا

alongside pre بجانب

aloof adj متحفّظ

aloud adv ب جهاراً

alphabet n الألف باء

already adv الآن

alright adv حسناً

also adv أيضاً

altar n المَذْبَح

alter v يُبدّل

alteration n تبديل

altercation n مشاحنة

alternate v يُناوب

alternate adj متناوب

alternative n خيار

although c مع أنّ

altitude n ارتفاع

altogether adj تماماً

aluminum n الألومينيوم

always adv دائماً

amass v يكدّس

amateur adj هاوٍ ,

amaze v يُذْهِل ,

amazement n انذهال

amazing adj مُذْهِل

ambassador n سفير

ambiguous adj غامض

ambition n مَطْمَح

ambitious adj طموح

ambivalent adj متردد

ambulance n سيارة إسعاف

ambush v لـ يكمن

amenable adj مسؤول

amend v يعدّل

amendment n تعديل

amenities n لطافة

American adj أميركي

amiable adj أنيس

amicable adj حُبّي	**anatomy** n علم التشريح
amid pre وبينَ	**ancestor** n سَلَفٌ
ammonia n نُشادر	**ancestry** n سلسلة النسب
ammunition n ذخيرة حربيّة	**anchor** n مِرْساة
amnesia n فَقْد الذاكرة	**anchovy** n البَلَم
amnesty n عفو عام,	**ancient** adj قديم
among pre وسَط	**and** c واو العطف
amoral adj لا أخْلاقي	**anecdote** n حكاية
amorphous adj غير متبلور	**anemia** n الأنيميّة
amortize v يستهلك الدّين	**anemic** adj مصاب بفقر الدم
amount n مبلغ	**anesthesia** n تحذير
amount to v بلغ	**anew** adv بشكل جديد
amphibious adj برمائيّ	**angel** n مَلاك
amphitheater n مُدَرّج	**angelic** adj مَلائِكيّ
ample adj مُتّسع,	**anger** v يُغْضب
amplifier n المضخم	**anger** n غضبٌ
amplify v يوسّع	**angina** n خناق
amputate v يَبْترُ	**angle** n زاوية
amputation n بتر	**Anglican** adj الإنجليكاني
amuse v يُلْهي	**angry** adj غاضب
amusement n لهو	**anguish** n كَرْب
amusing adj مُسلٍّ	**animal** n حيوان
an a أداة تنكير	**animate** v يحيي
analogy n تشابه	**animation** n احياء
analysis n تحليل	**animosity** n حِقد
analyze v يُحلّل	**ankle** n الكاحل
anarchist n فوضوي	**annex** n مُلحَق
anarchy n فوضى	**annexation** n إلحاق

annihilate v يُبطِل

annihilation n تدمير

anniversary n ذكرى سنوية

annotate v يحشّي

annotation n حاشية، ملاحظة

announce v يُعْلِن

announcement n إعلان

announcer n مذيع

annoy v يُزعِج

annoying adj مزعج

annual adj سنويّ

annul v يلغي

annulment n فسخ

anoint v يدهن بمرهم

anonymity n إسم مستعار

anonymous adj مجهول

another adj آخر

answer v يجيب

answer n جواب

ant n نملة

antagonize v يخاصم

antecedent n سالف

antecedents n أسلاف

antelope n الظبي

antenna n هوائي

anthem n ترنيمة دينية

antibiotic n مضادّ للجراثيم

anticipate v يسبق

anticipation n سَبْق

antidote n تِرْياق

antipathy n كراهية

antiquated adj مهجور

antiquity n العصور القديمة

anvil n سِندان

anxiety n قَلَق

anxious adj قلق

any adj أيّ

anybody pro أيّ إنسان

anyhow pro بأية حال

anyone pro أيّ شخص

anything pro أيّ شيء

apart adv منفرداً

apartment n شقّة للسكن

apathy n فتور الشعور

ape n قِرد

aperitif n فاتح للشهية

apex n قمة

apiece adv لكلّ

apocalypse n رؤيا نبوئية

apologize v يعتذر

apology n اعتذار

apostle n رسول

apostolic adj رَسولي

apostrophe n الفاصلة العليا

appall v يُرْعِب

appalling adj مُرْعِب

apparel n كِساء	**appreciation** n تقدير قيمة
apparent adj مرئيّ	**apprehend** v يعتقل , يقبض على
apparently adv ظاهريّا	**apprehensive** adj سريع الفهم
apparition n شَبَحٌ	**apprentice** n المتمهّن
appeal n استئناف , استغاثه	**approach** v يدنو
appeal v يستغيث بـ =	**approach** n دنوّ
appealing adj جَذّاب	**approachable** adj مُمْكِنٌ بُلُوغُهُ
appear v يَظْهر للعيان	**approbation** n استحسان
appearance n ظهور	**appropriate** adj ملائم
appease v يهدّئ	**approval** n موافقة
appeasement v ترضية	**approve** v يوافق على
appendix n الزائدة الدودية	**approximate** adj تقريبيّ
appetite n شهية	**apricot** n المشمش
appetizer n مشهيات	**April** n أبريل
applaud v يصفّق	**apron** n مِئْزَر
applause n تصفيق	**aptitude** n قابلية
apple n تُفّاحة	**aquarium** n حوض السمك
appliance n استعمال	**aquatic** adj مائيّ
applicable adj ملائم	**aqueduct** n قناة
applicant n طالب الوظيفة	**Arabic** adj عربيّ
application n استعمال	**arable** adj مُنْزَرع
apply v يستعمل	**arbiter** n الحَكَم
apply for v قدم طلبا	**arbitrary** adj اعتباطيّ
appoint v يعيّن	**arbitrate** v يحكّم
appointment n تعيين , توظيف	**arbitration** n التحكيم
appraisal n تثمين	**arc** n قوْس
appraise v يثمّن , يقيّم	**arch** n قنطرة
appreciate v يُقَدّر شيئًا	**archaeology** n علم الآثار القديمة

archaic *adj* قديم

archbishop *n* مطران

architecture *n* فن العمارة

archive *n* أرشيف

ardent *adj* غيور

ardor *n* غَيْرَة

arduous *adj* شاقّ

area *n* منطقة

arena *n* حلبة, المجتلد

argue *v* يبرهن

argument *n* حجة

arid *adj* جافّ

arise *iv* برز للعيان

aristocracy *n* الأرستقراطية

aristocrat *n* الأرستقراطي

arithmetic *n* علم الحساب

ark *n* سفينة نوح

arm *n* ذراع

arm *v* يُسَلِّح

armaments *n* قوّات حربية

armchair *n* أريكة

armed *adj* مُسلَّح

armistice *n* هُدْنة

armor *n* دِرْع

armpit *n* إبْطٌ

army *n* جيش

aromatic *adj* عِطريّ

around *pro* حَوْل

arouse *v* يوقظ , يستحثّ

arrange *v* يرتّب , ينظّم

arrangement *n* ترتيب

array *n* عرض

arrest *v* يُوْقف

arrest *n* إيقاف

arrival *n* وصول

arrive *v* يَصِل

arrogance *n* تكبُّر

arrogant *adj* متكبّر

arrow *n* سَهْم

arsenic *n* زَرْنيخ

arson *n* إحراق المباني

arsonist *n* محرق المباني

art *n* فنّ

artery *n* شِريان

arthritis *n* التهاب المفاصل

artichoke *n* خُرْشوف

article *n* بَنْد

articulate *v* يَرْبط بمَفْصِل

articulation *n* الإرتباط بمفاصل

artificial *adj* اصطناعي

artillery *n* المِدفعيّة

artisan *n* الحِرَفي

artist *n* الفَنّان

artistic *adj* فنّي

artwork *n* قطعة فنية

as *c* كأن

as adv لكذا	**assemble** v يحشد , يجمع
ascend v يصعد	**assembly** n اجتماع ,مركب,
ascendancy n سطوة	**assent** v يوافق على
ascertain v تحقق من	**assert** v يؤكّد
ascetic adj زُهْديّ	**assertion** n توكيد
ash n رماد	**assess** v يَفرضُ ضريبة
ashamed adj خَجِل	**assessment** n تخمين
ashore adv إلى الشاطئ	**asset** n شيء نافع
ashtray n مرمدة	**assets** n موجودات
aside adv جانباً	**assign** v يتخلى عن
aside from adv فضلا عن	**assignment** n مهمة
ask v يسأل , يطلب	**assimilate** v يستوعب
asleep adj نائم	**assimilation** n تمثيل
asparagus n نبات الهِليون	**assist** v يُساعد
aspect n سيماء	**assistance** n مساعَدة
asphalt n زفت	**associate** v يُزامِل
asphyxiate v يَخْنق	**association** n جمعية
asphyxiation n خنق	**assorted** adj مصنّف
aspiration n تنَفُّس	**assortment** n تصنيف
aspire v يتوق	**assume** v يتولى
aspirin n الأسبرين	**assumption** n تولّ
assail v يهاجم	**assurance** n عَهْد
assailant n المُهاجِم	**assure** v يؤكّد
assassin n القاتل	**asterisk** n المُنجّمة
assassinate v يغتال	**asteroid** n سُيَّر
assassination n اغتيال	**asthma** n النّسَمَة
assault n اغتصاب	**asthmatic** adj رِبَوي
assault v يغتصب	**astonish** v يُدْهِش

astonishing adj مُدْهِش	**attached** adj مُلْحَق
astound v يَصْعَق	**attachment** n حَجْز
astounding adj مندهش	**attack** n مهاجمة
astray v ضالّ	**attack** v يهاجم
astrologer n المنجّم	**attacker** n مهاجم
astrology n علم التنجيم	**attain** v يحرز
astronaut n الفضائيّ	**attainable** adj سهل المنال
astronomer n الفَلَكيّ	**attainment** n التحقيق
astronomic adj فَلَكيّ	**attempt** n محاولة اعتداء
astronomy n علم الفَلَك	**attend** v اعتنى
astute adj ذكي	**attendance** n الحضور
asunder adv إرَباً	**attendant** n حاضر
asylum n الحرم المقدس	**attention** n انتباه
at pre عند	**attentive** adj يقظ
atheism n كفر	**attenuate** v يُنْحِل
atheist n الملحد	**attenuating** adj مُخَفّف
athlete n الرياضيّ	**attest** v يُظهر , يصدّق على
athletic adj رياضي	**attic** n عِلّية المنزل
atmosphere n الجوّ	**attitude** n سلوك ,
atmospheric adj جوّي	**attorney** n الوكيل
atom n ذرّة	**attract** v يجذب
atomic adj ذَرّيّ	**attraction** n جذب
atone v يعوّض	**attractive** adj جذّاب
atonement n تعويض	**attribute** v خاصيّة
atrocious adj أثيم	**auction** n مزاد علنيّ
atrocity n وحشية	**auctioneer** n الدلّال
atrophy v يَضْمُر	**audacious** adj جريء
attach v يحجز	**audacity** n جرأة

audible *adj* مسموع	availability *n* تيسير
audience *n* سماع	available *adj* قانونيّ
audit *v* يدقّق الحسابات	avalanche *n* التّيهُوْر
auditorium *n* قاعة المحاضرات	avarice *n* جَشَعٌ
augment *v* يزداد	avaricious *adj* جَشِيع
August *n* أغُسْطُس	avenge *v* ينتقم
aunt *n* عمة	avenue *n* طريق
auspicious *adj* ميمون	average *n* المعدل
austere *n* قاسٍ	averse *adj* كارةٌ
austerity *n* قسوةٌ	aversion *n* مقتَ
authentic *adj* موثوق	avert *v* يتجنّب
authenticate *v* يوثّق	aviation *n* الطّيَران
authenticity *n* أصالة ,	aviator *n* الطيّار
author *n* مؤلف,	avid *adj* طمّاع
authoritarian *adj* فاشِسْتِي	avoid *v* يتفادى
authority *n* سلطة	avoidable *adj* مُتفادي
authorization *n* ترخيص	avoidance *n* اِجتناب
authorize *v* يُفَوّض	avowed *adj* مُعْتَرَفٌ
auto *n* ألى	await *v* ينتظر
autograph *n* توقيع	awake *iv* يستيقظ
automatic *adj* أوتوماتيكي	awake *adj* يقظان
automobile *n* سيّارة	awakening *n* يقظة
autonomous *adj* استقلاليّ	award *v* يمنح
autonomy *n* الحكم الذاتيّ	award *n* جائزة
autopsy *n* تشريح الجثة	aware *adj* واع
autumn *n* الخريف	awareness *n* معرفة
auxiliary *adj* إضافيّ	away *adv* بعيدا جانبا
avail *v* يفيد	awe *n* رَوْع

awesome *adj* مُخيف

awful *adj* مُرعِب

awkward *adj* أخرق

awning *n* الظُلّة

ax *n* فأس

axiom *n* بديهية

axis *n* مِحْوَر

axle *n* محور العجلة

B

babble *v* يثرثر

baby *n* طفل

babysitter *n* جليسة أطفال

bachelor *n* حامل البكالوريا

back *n* ظَهْر

back *adv* خَلْفَ

back *v* يسند

back down *v* تنازل عن

back up *v* يَتَقَهْقَرُ

backbone *n* العمود الفقري

backdoor *n* بابٌ خلفيّ

background *n* خلفيّة

backing *n* عَوْن

backlash *n* الحركة الارتجاعية

backlog *n* ثأر

backpack *n* حقيبة ظهر

backup *n* دعم

backward *adj* ارتجاعيّ

backwards *adv* إلى الوراء

backyard *n* الفناء الخلفى

bacon *n* لحمُ خنزير مملّحٌ أ

bacteria *n* جراثيم

bad *adj* رديء

badge *n* شارَة

badly *adv* على نحو رديء

baffle *v* يحيّر , يُرْبك

bag *n* كيس

baggage *n* أمتعة

baggy *adj* فضفاض

baguette *n* عصا

bail *n* كفالة

bail out *v* يَكْفُل

bailiff *n* حاجب المحكمة

bait *n* طُعْم

bake *v* يَخْبِز

baker *n* الخبّاز

bakery *n* مَخْبَز

balance *v* يزن

balance *n* ميزان , باقي الحساب

balcony *n* شُرْقَة

bald *adj* أصلع

bale *n* رزمة ضخمة

ball *n* كرة , الكرة الأرضية	barbarian *n* الهمجيّ
balloon *n* مُنطاد	barbaric *adj* همجيّ
ballot *n* اقتراع	barbarism *n* همجيّة
ballroom *n* قاعة الرقص	barbecue *n* حفلة شواء,
balm *n* البَلسَم	barber *n* الحَلّاق
balmy *adj* بَلسَمِيّ	bare *adj* عارٍ
bamboo *n* خيزران	barefoot *adj* حافي القدمين
ban *n* حِرْم من الكنيسة	barely *adv* بالجهد
ban *v* يحظّر	bargain *n* صَفْقَة
banality *n* تفاهة	bargain *v* يساوم
banana *n* موز	bargaining *n* مساومة
band *n* قَيْد , حِزام	barge *n* البَرْج
bandage *n* عِصابة	bark *v* ينبح
bandage *v* يَعْصِب	bark *n* نُباح , لِحاء
bandit *n* لصّ	barley *n* شَعير
bang *v* يضرب بعنف	barmaid *n* الساقية في حانة
banish *v* ينفي	barman *n* الساقي في حانة
banishment *n* نفي,	barn *n* الهُرْي
bank *n* رُكام	barometer *n* البارومتر
bankrupt *v* يُفلّس	barracks *n* ثُكْنَة
bankrupt *adj* مفلِس	barrage *n* سد
bankruptcy *n* إفلاس	barrel *n* برميل
banner *n* راية,	barren *adj* عاقر
banquet *n* مأدبة	barricade *n* متراس
baptism *n* العماد,	barrier *n* حاجز
baptize *v* يُعمّد	barring *pre* باستثناء
bar *n* قضيب , رتاج	barter *v* يُقايض
bar *v* يُحكم إقفال باب	base *n* أساس

base v بنى على أساس	**bayonet** n حربة
baseball n البايسبول	**bazaar** n سوق خيرية
baseless adj لا أساس له	**be** iv كان
basement n دور سفلي,	**be born** v قدم للحياة
bashful adj خجول	**beach** n شاطئ
basic adj أساسيّ	**beacon** n منارة
basics n مبادئ	**beak** n مِنقار
basin n حوض, طشت	**beam** n عارضة
basis n أساس	**bean** n فاصوليا
bask v يتشمّس	**bear** n دُبّ
basket n سلّة	**bear** iv دعم , سند
basketball n رياضة كُرَةُ السَّلَّة	**bearable** adj مُحتَمَل
bastard n ابن زنا	**beard** n لحية
bat n النّبّوت	**bearded** adj مُلتَح
batch n خَبزَة , عَجْنَة	**bearer** n الحامل
bath n غَسْل	**beast** n بهيمة
bathe v يغسل	**beat** iv نبض , إنتصر عليه
bathrobe n بُرنُس	**beat** n ضربة , نبضة
bathroom n حمّام	**beaten** adj مَضرُوب
bathtub n حوض	**beating** n طرق
baton n هراوة	**beautiful** adj جميل
battalion n كتيب	**beautify** v يُجمّل
batter v مَخِيض	**beauty** n جمال
battery n ضَرب	**beaver** n القُنْدُس
battle n معركة	**because** c لأنّ
battle v يقاتل	**because of** pre بسبب
battleship n بارجة	**beckon** v يومئ
bay n فَرَس	**become** iv أصبح

bed n سرير , فراش	**belated** adj متأخر
bedding n شراشف	**belch** v يتجشّأ
bedroom n حُجرة النوم	**belch** n جشاء
bedspread n غطاء السرير	**belfry** n برج الحرس
bee n نَحْلة	**Belgian** adj بلجيكيّ
beef n لحم البقر	**Belgium** n دولة بلُجيكًا
beef up v قوى	**belief** n إيمان
beehive n خلية النحل	**believable** adj قابلٌ للتصديق
beer n جَعة	**believe** v يؤمن بـ
beet n شَمَنْدَر	**believer** n شخصية
beetle n خَنْفَساء	**belittle** v يصغّر
before adv قبلُ	**bell** n البل
before pre أمامَ ,	**bell pepper** n فُلفُل أسْوَد
beforehand adv مقدّماً	**belligerent** adj محارب
befriend v يصادق	**belly** n بطن
beg v يستعطي	**belly button** n السرة
beggar n شحّاذ	**belong** v يخصّ
begin iv بدأ,	**belongings** n أمتعة
beginner n مبتدئ	**beloved** adj محبوب
beginning n ابتداء	**below** adv اقل من
beguile v يضلّل	**below** pre مما لا يليق بـ
behalf (on) adv لأجل مصلحة	**belt** n حِزام
behave v يسلك	**bench** n مقعد
behavior n سلوك	**bend** iv وتر , ثنى
behead v يَقْطَع رأسَه	**bend down** v يَنْحَني
behind pre خلف	**beneath** pre دونَ
behold iv شاهد	**benediction** n مَنْح البَرَكَة
being n كينونة	**benefactor** n منعم

B

beneficial *adj* مفيد

beneficiary *n* المستفيد

benefit *n* فائدة

benefit *v* يُفيد

benevolence *n* الخيرية

benevolent *adj* خيِّر

benign *adj* لطيف

bequeath *v* يورّث بوصيّة

bereaved *adj* سالِب

bereavement *n* الثكل

beret *n* البيْريْه

berserk *adv* بسُعُر

berth *n* مَرْسَى

beseech *iv* توسل

beset *iv* ضايق

beside *pre* قرب

besides *pre* عدا

besiege *iv* حاصر

best *adj* أفضل

best man *n* وكيل العريس

bestial *adj* بهيميّ

bestiality *n* بهيمية

bestow *v* يمنح

bet *iv* راهن على

bet *n* رهان

betray *v* يضلّل

betrayal *n* خيانة,

better *adj* أعظم

between *pre* بين

beverage *n* شراب

beware *v* يحترس

bewilder *v* يُذْهِل

bewitch *v* يَسْحَر

beyond *adv* ابعد

bias *n* أثار

bible *n* الكتاب المقدّس

biblical *adj* كتابى

bibliography *n* بيبلوغرافيا

bicycle *n* دراجة هوائية

bid *n* أمْر

bid *iv* أصدر امرا الى

big *adj* كبير,

bigamy *n* المضارّة

bigot *adj* المتعصّب

bigotry *n* تعصّب أعمى

bike *n* دَرّاجَة

bile *n* مادة الصّفراء

bilingual *adj* ثنائيّ اللغة

bill *n* فاتورة, وثيقة

billiards *n* البليارد

billion *n* البليون

billionaire *n* المليونير

bimonthly *adj* نصف شهري

bin *n* صندوق للخزن

bind *iv* ربط

binding *adj* مُلْزِم

binoculars n مجهر	**blame** v يَلوم
biography n السِّيرة	**blameless** adj بريء
biological adj أحيائيّ	**bland** adj رقيق
biology n علم الأحياء	**blank** adj أبيض
bird n طَيْر	**blanket** n حِرام
birth n ولادة	**blaspheme** v يجدّف على الله
birthday n مولد	**blasphemy** n التجديف
biscuit n بَسْكويت	**blast** n هَبّة
bishop n أسْقُف	**blaze** v يلتهب
bison n البيسون	**bleach** v قصّر
bit n الحَكَمة , الشَكِيمة	**bleach** n تقصير مادة
bite iv يعض , يقضِم	**bleak** n السمك الابيض
bite n عضّ	**bleed** iv دمى
bitter adj مُرّ	**bleeding** n نَزْف
bitterly adv مرير	**blemish** n عَيب
bitterness n مرارة	**blemish** v يلطّخ
bizarre adj غريب	**blend** n مزيج
black adj أسْود ,	**blend** v يمزج
blackberry n ثمر العُلّيْق	**blender** n خَلّاطُ
blackboard n سَبّورة	**bless** v يكرّس
blackmail n ابتزاز المال	**blessed** adj مُبَارَك
blackmail v يبتزّ بالتهديد	**blessing** n مباركة
blackness n سواد	**blind** v أعمى
blackout n إلتعتيم	**blind** adj أعمى
blacksmith n الحدّاد	**blindfold** n عِصابة للعينين
bladder n مَثانة	**blindfold** v يَعْصِب العينين
blade n ورقة نبات	**blindly** adv عَشْوائِيّاً
blame n لوم	**blindness** n عمّى

B

blink v تَطْرَف العينُ	bluff v يخدع
bliss n منتهى السعادة	blunder n خطأ فاضح
blissful adj سعيد	blunt adj عديم الحس
blister n نَفْطَة	bluntness n استقامة
bloat v يَنفخ	blur v يلطّخ
bloated adj مُنْتَفِخ	blurred adj ضَبَابيّ
block n كتلة خشبية	blush v يحمرّ وجهُهُ
block v يسدّ	blush n نظرة
blockade v يحاصر	boar n خنزيرٌ
blockade n حِصار	board n لوح خشب
blockage n سدة,	boast v يَتَباهى
blond adj أشـقـر	boat n مركب
blood n دم	bodily adj ماديّ
bloodthirsty adj وحشيّ	body n جسد , جسم
bloody adj دمويّ	bog n مستنقَع
bloom v يُزْهر	bog down v يلتصق
blossom v يزهر	boil v يَغْلي
blot n لطخة	boil down to v يَتَلخَّص فِي
blot v يلطّخ	boil over v يَغْلِي
blouse n البُلُوزَة	boiler n غَلّاية
blow n عاصفة	boisterous adj شـديد
blow iv هب , صات	bold adj جريء , جَسُور
blow out iv انفجر	boldness n وقاحة
blow up iv يَنْفُخ	bolster v يسند
blowout n انفجار دولاب	bolt n سـهم قصير , صاعقة
bludgeon v يضرب	bolt v ينطلق
blue adj أزرق	bomb n قنبلة
blueprint n الطبعة الزرقاء	bomb v يقذف بالقنابل

bombing n قذف بالقنابل	boredom n ضَجَر
bombshell n قنبلة	boring adj مُمِلّ
bond n قَيْد , وثاق	born adj مولود
bondage n عبودية	borough n القَصَبَة
bone n عَظم	borrow v يستعير
bone marrow n مخ الغظم	bosom n حِضْن
bonfire n المَشْعَلَة	boss n رئيس
bonus n علاوة	boss around v يعنف
book n كتاب	bossy adj مُتَأمِّر
bookcase n خزانة كتب	botany n عالم النبات
bookkeeper n مسؤول الحسابات	botch v يخرّب
bookkeeping n إدارة حسابات	both adj كِلا
booklet n كُتيّب	bother v يُزعج
bookseller n الكُتبي	bothersome adj مُزعِج
bookstore n المكتبة	bottle n زجاجة
boom n ذراع التطويل	bottle v يعبئ في زجاجات
boom v يدوّي	bottleneck n مضيق
boost v يرفع	bottom n أدْنَى
boost n رفْع	bottomless adj عميق جدا
boot n جَزمَة	bough n غُصن
booth n سقيفة	boulder n صخب
booty n غنيمة	boulevard n جادة,
booze n شراب مسكر	bounce v يثب
border n حد, جانب	bounce n ضربة قوية
border on v يَحُدّ	bound adj قاصد إلى
borderline adj حُدُوديّ	bound for adj متوجه
bore v يَثقُب	boundary n تَخْم
bored adj مَحْفُور	boundless adj لانهائيّ

B

bounty n صدقة	**brand** n جَمْرَة
bourgeois adj بورجوازيّ	**brand-new** adj جديدٌ تماماً
bow n التواء , انحناء	**brandy** n البراندي
bow v يُذعن	**brat** adj طفلٌ مزعج
bow out v ودع بالانحناء	**brave** adj شجاع
bowels n أمعاء	**bravely** adv بشَجَاعَة
bowl n زُبْدية , سلطانية	**bravery** n شجاعة
box n صندوق	**brawl** n شجار
box office n شباك التذاكر	**breach** n خرق , نَقْض
boxer n الملاكم	**bread** n خبز
boxing n الصَّنْدَقة	**breadth** n عَرْض
boy n غُلام	**break** n كَسْر , ثُلْمة
boycott v مقاطعة	**break** iv كسر
boyfriend n رفيق	**break away** v انفصل
boyhood n الصِّبا	**break down** v يُعَطِّلُ
bra n صدار	**break free** v برز
brace for v استجمع قواه	**break in** v يقتحم بيتاً
bracelet n سوارٌ	**break off** v يَتَبَاعَد
bracket n رف	**break open** v يفتح قفلاً
brag v يتفاخر	**break out** v تندلع الحربُ
braid n جديلة	**break up** v يُكَسِّر
brain n دماغ	**breakable** adj قابل للكَسْر
brainwash v غسل دماغ	**breakdown** n تَعَطُّل
brake n فرملة	**breakfast** n الفَطور
brake v يكبح	**breakthrough** n اختراق
branch n غُصْن	**breast** n ثَدْي
branch office n مكتب فرعي	**breath** n نَفَس
branch out v يتَفَرَّع	**breathe** v يتنفّ

breathing n تنفس, لحظة

breathtaking adj مُثير,

breed iv فقس, ربى

breed n سلالة

breeze n نسيم

brethren n إخوة في الدين

brevity n قِصَر

brew v يخمّر

brewery n مصنع الجعة

bribe v يرشو

bribe n رشوة

bribery n ارتشاء

brick n آجرّة

bricklayer n بَنّاء

bridal adj زفافيّ

bride n العَروس

bridegroom n العريس

bridesmaid n إشْبينَةُ العَروس

bridge n جِسْر

bridle n لِجام

brief adj وجيز

brief v أرشد

briefcase n حَافظةُ أوْرَاق

briefing n بيان موجز

briefly adv باخْتِصار

briefs n سراويل

brigade n لواء,

bright adj نيّر

brighten v يسطع

brightness n إشراق

brilliant adj متألّق

brim n حافة

bring iv يجلب

bring back v يُعيدُ

bring down v يُسْقِط

bring up v يُربّي

brink n حَرْف

brisk adj رشيق

Britain n بريطانيا

British adj بريطانيّ

brittle adj قصيم

broad adj عريض

broadcast v ينثر الحَبّ

broadcast n برنامج إذاعي

broadcaster n مذيع

broaden v يتّسع

broadly adv باتساع

broadminded adj متحرر

brochure n كراسة

broil v يَشْوي

broiler n مِشْواة

broke adj مُفْلِس

broken adj مُهَشَّم

bronchitis n الالتهاب الشُعَبيّ

bronze n البرونز

broom n رتَمٌ

B

broth n مَرَقٌ

brothel n مَاخُور

brother n أخ

brotherhood n أُخُوَّة

brotherly adj أَخَوِيّ

brow n حاجب

brown adj أسمر

browse v يتصفّح

browser n متصفح

bruise n كدمة, رض

bruise v يَرُض

brunch n وجبة

brunette adj سمراء

brush n أجَمَة

brush v يفرك

brush aside v يَضَع جانبًا

brush up v يَصقُل

brusque adj فظّ ,

brutal adj وحشيّ

brutality n وحشيّة

brutalize v ,وحش

brute adj حَيَوانِيّ

bubble n فُقّاعة

bubble gum n العلكة

buck n الظبي

bucket n دلو

buckle n إبزيم

buckle up v إربط الحزام

bud n بُرْعم

buddy n رفيق

budge v يتزحزح

budget n كيس

buffalo n جاموس

bug n بَقّ

build iv بنى

builder n الباني

building n مَبْنى

buildup n إنشاء

built-in adj بني في

bulb n مصباح

bulge n انتفاخ ,

bulk n حَجْم , معظم الشيء

bull n ثور

bull fight n مصارعة الثيران

bull fighter n مصارع ثيران

bulldoze v أرهب

bullet n كرة صغيرة

bulletin n بلاغ

bully adj ممتاز

bulwark n حِصْن

bum n مستجد

bump n صدمة قوية

bump into v يَلْتَقِي به مُصَادَفَةً

bumper n كأس مترعة

bumpy adj متخبط

bun n كعكة محلّاة

bunch n عنقود	busily adv بِهمّة
bundle n حزمة	business n مهنة
bundle v يَحْزِم	businessman n رَجُل أعمال
bunk bed n سرير ذو طابقين	bust n تمثال نصفيّ
buoy n الطافية	bustling adj نَشيط
burden n حِمْل	busy adj مشغول
burden v يُثْقِل	but c لولا أنّ
burdensome adj ثقيل	butcher n الجزّار
bureau n منضدة	butchery n مَسْلَخ
bureaucracy n البيروقراطيّة	butler n الساقي
bureaucrat n الدواويني	butt n نَطْحَة , هدف
burger n شطيرة لحم	butter n زُبدة
burglar n لص	butterfly n فراشة
burglarize v سطا على	button n زرّ
burglary n السطو	buttonhole n عروة
burial n قَبْر	buy iv إشترى
burly adj ضخم الجسم	buy off v يَرْشُو
burn iv إحترق	buyer n المشتري
burn n حُرق	buzz n طنين
burp v تجشأ	buzz v يَطِنّ
burp n تجشؤ	buzzard n الصَّقر
burrow n جُحْر	buzzer n الطنان
burst iv إنفجر	by pre بجانب
burst into v يَقْتَحِم	bye e جانبيّ
bury v يطمر	bypass n طريق جانبي
bus n بَاص	bypass v تجنب
bus v يركب في الباص	by-product n حصيلة ثانية
bush n شُجَيْرَة	bystander n المتفرّج

B
C

C

cab n مركبة

cabbage n ملفوف

cabin n قمرة

cabinet n خزانة

cable n مرسة,

cafeteria n كافيتيريا

caffeine n كافيين, البنين

cage n قفَص

cake n كعكة

calamity n نكبة

calculate v يَحسُب رياضيّاً

calculation n حُسبان

calculator n آلة حاسبة

calendar n تقويم

calf n عجل

caliber n العِيار

calibrate v يُعايِر

call n صيحة , دعوة

call v يصيح , يصرخ

call off v يُلْغي

call on v يسأل

call out v نادى

calling n مناداة

callous adj صُلب

calm adj ساكن

calm n سكون

calm down v يَهْدَأ

calorie n سُعْر

calumny n افتراء

camel n جَمَل

camera n كاميرا

camouflage v يموّه

camouflage n تَمْويه

camp n مُخيّم

camp v يخيّم

campaign v يدير حملةً

campaign n حملة

campfire n نار

can iv يستطيع

can v يستطيع

can n صفيحة

can opener n مفتاح العلب

canal n قناة

cancel v يَشْطب

cancellation n شَطْب

cancer n سرطان

cancerous adj سَرَطانيّ

candid adj نزيه

candidacy n تَرَشُّح

candidate n مرشح

candle n شمعة

candlestick n شَمْعِدان

candor n صَرَاحَة

candy n حلوى	capture v يستولي على
cane n قَصَب , عصا	capture n أسْر
canister n علبة صغيرة	car n
canned adj معلّب	carat n القيراط
cannibal n آكل لحم البشر	caravan n قافلة
cannon n مِدْفَع	carburetor n المكربن
cance n زورق طويل	carcass n جثّة
canonize v طوب	card n مِمْشَطة للصوف
cantaloupe n البطيخ الأصفر	cardboard n كرتون
canteen n مَقْصِف	cardiac adj قلبيّ
canvas n قماش القنّب	cardiac arrest n سكتة قلبية
canvas v يغطي بالقما	cardiology n طب القلب
canyon n واد ضيق	care n همّ
cap n قَلَنْسُوَة	care v يهتم
capability n قدرة	care about v اعتنى
capable adj قابلٌ لِ	care for v رعى بإهتمام
capacity n سَعة	career n سرعة
cape n خليج, كاب	carefree adj سعيد
capital n رأس مال	careful adj حذِر
capital letter n أحرف كبير	careless adj خلوّ من الهموم
capitalism n الرأسماليّة	carelessness n لا مبالاة
capitulate v استسلم	caress n مُلاطَفة
capsize v ينقلب	caress v يلاطف
capsule n غشاء	caretaker n ناظر
captain n نقيب	cargo n حمولة السفينة
captivate v يفتن	caricature n فنّ الكاريكاتور
captive n أسير	caring adj لطيف
captivity n أسر	carnage n أشلاء

C

carnal adj جَسَدِيّ	**casual** adj عَرَضِيّ
carnation n لون البشرة	**casualty** n مصيبة
carol n أغنية مَرَحَة	**cat** n هِر
carpenter n النجّار	**cataclysm** n الجائحة
carpentry n النِّجارة	**catacomb** n سرداب الموتى
carpet n سجادة	**catalog** n بيان
carriage n حَمْل	**catalog** v يُفَهرِس
carrot n جَزَر	**cataract** n إعتام عدسة العين
carry v يَحْمِل	**catastrophe** n كارثة
carry on v يُتَابِع	**catch** iv أمسك بـ
carry out v يُنَفِّذ	**catch up** v أدركه
cart n كارّة	**catching** adj مُعْدِ
cart v نقل العربة	**catechism** n تعليم مسيحى
cartoon n كاريكاتور	**category** n طَبَقَة
cartridge n خرطوشة	**cater to** v بزوّد بالطعام
carve v ينحت , ينقش	**caterpillar** n اليُسْرُوع
cascade n شلال صغير	**cathedral** n كاتدرائية
case n حادثة , حالة	**catholic** adj كاثوليكى
cash n نَقْد	**Catholicism** n كثلكة
cashier n أمين الصندوق	**cattle** n الماشية
casino n الكازينو	**cauliflower** n قُنّبِيط
casket n تابوت	**cause** n سبب
casserole n كسرولة	**cause** v يسبّب
cassock n غفارة	**caution** n تحذير
cast iv ألقى , رمى	**cautious** adj حذِر
castaway n منبوذ	**cavalry** n الفُرسان
caste n طبقة إجتماعية	**cave** n كَهْف
castle n قلعة	**cave in** v يَهْبِط

C

cavern *n* كَهْف	cerebral *adj* مُخّي
cavity *n* فجوة	ceremony *n* مراسم
cease *v* يُوْقف	certain *adj* محدّد
cease-fire *n* وقف إطلاق النار	certainty *n* حقيقة
ceaselessly *adv* بإستمرار	certificate *n* تصديق
ceiling *n* سقف	certify *v* يصدّق على
celebrate *v* يحتفل ب	chagrin *n* غمّ
celebration *n* حفلة	chain *n* سلسلة
celebrity *n* شهرة	chain *v* يقيّد
celery *n* نبات الكَرَفْس	chainsaw *n* منشار ألي
celestial *adj* سماوي	chair *n* كرسيّ
celibacy *n* عُزوبة	chair *v* ترأس جلسة
celibate *adj* عَزَب	chairman *n* رئيسُ الجلسة
cellar *n* سرداب	chalet *n* الشاليه
cellphone *n* هاتف خلوي	chalice *n* كأس
cement *n* أسمنت	chalk *n* طباشير
cemetery *n* مقبرة	chalkboard *n* سبورة
censure *v* استنكر	challenge *v* يوقف
cent *n* سنت	challenge *n* اعتراض
centenary *n* عِيدٌ مئَويّ	challenging *adj* متحد
center *n* مركز	chamber *n* حجرة
center *v* يركّز	champ *n* يعضّ
centimeter *n* السّنتيمتر	champion *n* النّصير
central *adj* مركزيّ	champion *v* يناصر
centralize *v* يُمَرْكز	chance *n* مصادفة , حظّ
century *n* القرن	chancellor *n* مستشار
ceramic *n* الخِزافة	chandelier *n* ثُرَيّا
cereal *n* النبات الحبّي	change *v* يُغيّر

C

change n تغيير

channel n مجرى نهر

chant n أنشودة

chaos n اختلاط

chaotic adj مختلِط

chapel n معبد

chaplain n قَس

chapter n فَصْل من كتاب

char v يفحّم

character n رمز

characteristic adj مُميِّز

charade n التمثيلية التحزيرية

charbroil adj يشوي على الفحم

charcoal n الفحم

charge v يَشْحَن بطاريّة

charge n شِحنَة , حَشْوَة

charisma n قدرة خارقة

charismatic adj فاتن

charitable adj مُحسِن

charity n محبّة

charm v يعوّذ

charm n تعْويذة

charming adj ساحر

chart n خريطة

charter n صكّ , عقد

charter v يمنح براءة

chase n مطاردة

chase v يطارد

chase away v يَخْسَأ

chasm n هوّة

chaste adj عفيف

chastise v يؤدِّب

chastisement n معاقبة

chastity n طهارة

chat v يتكلّم

chauffeur n سائق السيّارة

cheap adj رَخيص

cheat v يخدع

cheater n مخادع

check n كَبْح , وَقْفٌ

check v يكبح

check in v نزل في الفندق

check up n يُراجِع

checkbook n دفتر شيكات

cheek n خدّ

cheekbone n العظم الوَجْنيّ

cheeky adj وقح

cheer v يشجّع

cheer up v يُفَرِّح

cheerful adj مرح

cheers n ابتهاج

cheese n جُبْن

chef n رئيس

chemical adj كيميائي

chemist n الكيميائي

chemistry n الكيمياء

C

cherish v يُعزّ	**choir** n الخُورَس
cherry n الكَرَز	**choke** v يخنق
chess n شِطرنج	**cholera** n الهَيْضَة
chest n صندوقٌ , خزانة	**cholesterol** n كولسترول
chestnut n كستناء	**choose** iv اختار
chew v مَضْغ	**choosy** adj مدقق في الاختيار
chick n كتكوت	**chop** v يقطع بفأس
chicken n دجاجة	**chop** n قطْع
chicken pox n مرض الجُديْري	**chopper** n مِفْرمة
chide v يوبِّخ	**chore** n عمل روتيني
chief n الرئيس	**chorus** n جوقة
chiefly adv خصوصاً	**christen** v يُعمِّد
child n طفل	**christening** n حفلة التعميد
childhood n الطفولة	**christian** adj مسيحي
childish adj صبيانيّ	**Christianity** n المسيحية
childless adj أبْتَر	**Christmas** n عيد الميلاد
children n طفل	**chronic** adj مُزْمِن
chill n قُشَعريرَة	**chronicle** n تاريخٌ
chill v فِعْل :	**chronology** n علم التاريخ
chill out v هدئ أعصابك	**chubby** adj رَيّان
chilly adj بارد	**chuckle** v يضحك ضحكاً خافتاً
chimney n المستوقد	**chunk** n قطعة
chimpanzee n البَعام	**church** n كنيسة
chin n ذَقْن	**chute** n شلال
chip n رُقاقة , الفيشة	**cider** n عصير التفاح
chisel n إزميل	**cigar** n سيْكار
chocolate n شوكولا	**cigarette** n سيجارة
choice n الاختيار	**cinder** n رماد , جمرة

C

cinema *n* سينما

cinnamon *n* قرفة

circle *n* حلقة

circle *v* يطوّق , يدور حول

circuit *n* محيط

circular *adj* مستدير

circulate *v* يدور

circulation *n* دَوَران

circumcise *v* يَخْتِن

circumcision *n* خِتان

circumstance *n* ظَرف

circumstancial *adj* ظرفى

circus *n* سِيْرْك

cistern *n* صِهْريج

citizen *n* مواطن

citizenship *n* مُواطَنَة

city *n* مدينة

city hall *n* بلدية

civic *adj* مَدينيّ

civil *adj* مَدَنيّ

civilization *n* الحضارة

civilize *v* يحضّر

claim *v* يطالب بـ , يدّعي

claim *n* مطالبةٌ بـ , ادعاء

clam *n* سمك صَدَفيّ

clamor *v* جعجع

clamp *n* مِلزم

clan *n* عَشيرة

clandestine *adj* سِرّي

clap *v* يصفع

clarification *n* توضيح

clarify *v* يصفّي

clarinet *n* شبّابة

clarity *n* وضوح

clash *v* يصطدم

clash *n* اصطدام

class *n* طبقة اجتماعية

classic *adj* كلاسيكيّ

classify *v* يصنّف

classmate *n* رفيق الصف

classroom *n* غرفة التدريس

clause *n* فقرة

claw *n* مِخْلَب

claw *v* يمزّق

clay *n* طَفَل

clean *adj* نظيف

clean *v* ينظف

cleanliness *n* نظافة

cleanse *v* ينظّف

cleanser *n* المنظفة

clear *adj* مشرق , صافٍ

clear *v* يجعله مشرقاً

clearance *n* التصفية

clear-cut *adj* حل

clearly *adv* بوضوح

clearness *n* وضوح

شِيّق cleft n	يُغْلِق close v
رحمة clemency n	مُغْلَق close adj
يثبِّت المسمارَ clench v	تحفظ close to pre
الإكليروس clergy n	مُغْلَق closed adj
كاهن clergyman n	بإحكام closely adv
كهنوتيّ clerical adj	مختَلى closet n
رَجُل دِين clerk n	إغلاق closure n
ذكيّ clever adj	كتلة clot n
يقرقع click v	قماش cloth n
الموكِّل client n	يُلبِس clothe v
زبائن clientele n	ملابس clothes n
الجُرُف cliff n	ملابس clothing n
مُناخ climate n	سحابة cloud n
مُناخي climatic adj	صافٍ cloudless adj
الذروة climax n	غائم cloudy adj
يرتفع climb v	الريفيّ clown n
التسلق climbing n	هراوة , مِضرب الكرة club n
احتضن clinch v	يضرب بهراوة club v
تماسك cling iv	الكِظامَة clue n
عيادة clinic n	ارتباك clumsiness n
يثبِّت بمشبك clip v	أخرق clumsy adj
قَصّ ,جَزّ clipping n	عنقود cluster n
عباءة cloak n	يَتَعَنقَد cluster v
ساعة كبيرة clock n	مخلب clutch n
يَعُوْق clog v	يعلِّم , يدرِّب coach v
دير cloister n	مركبة coach n
استنسخ clone v	تمرين coaching n
استنساخ cloning n	تخثر coagulate v

C

تخثر دمه n **coagulation**	يتعايش v **cohabit**
جَمرة n **coal**	ملتحم adj **coherent**
اندماج n **coalition**	التحام n **cohesion**
رديء , خشن adj **coarse**	عملة n **coin**
ساحل n **coast**	يحتلّ v **coincide**
ساحلي adj **coastal**	تطابُق n **coincidence**
خط ساحلى n **coastline**	متطابق adj **coincidental**
سترة , غطاء n **coat**	بارد adj **cold**
يلاطف v **coax**	جفاف n **coldness**
ذكر الإوزّ n **cob**	مَغْص n **colic**
حصاة كبيرة n **cobblestone**	يشترك في v **collaborate**
بَيْت العنكبوت n **cobweb**	تعاون n **collaboration**
الكوكايين n **cocaine**	متعاون n **collaborator**
ديك n **cock**	ينهار v **collapse**
مقصورة الطيار n **cockpit**	انهيار n **collapse**
الصُّرْصُور n **cockroach**	قَبَّةُ الثَّوْب n **collar**
الكوكتيل n **cocktail**	التَّرْقُوَة n **collarbone**
مغرور adj **cocky**	مُلازم adj **collateral**
كاكاو n **cocoa**	الزميل n **colleague**
جوزة الهند n **coconut**	يجمع v **collect**
القُدّ n **cod**	جَمْع n **collection**
رمز , مجموعة قوانين n **code**	الجابي n **collector**
المُعامِل n **coefficient**	كلية n **college**
يُكره v **coerce**	يتصادم v **collide**
إكراه n **coercion**	تصادُم n **collision**
يتواجد v **coexist**	كولونيا n **cologne**
بُنّ n **coffee**	القُولُون , النُّقْطَتان n **colon**
تابوت n **coffin**	كولونيل n **colonel**

colonial *adj* مُسْتَعْمَرِيّ	come in *v* يَدْخل
colonization *n* مستعمرة	come out *v* يَخْرُج
colonize *v* يستعمر	come over *v* يُصِيب
colony *n* مستعمرة	come up *v* طلع , نما
color *n* لون	comeback *n* جواب بارع
color *v* لون, صبغ	comedian *n* ممثّل هزليّ
colorful *adj* غنيّ بالألوان	comedy *n* الكوميديا
colossal *adj* ضخم	comet *n* المُذَنّب
colt *n* مسدس	comfort *n* تعزية
column *n* عمود	comfortable *adj* معزّ
coma *n* سبات	comforter *n* المعزي
comb *n* مُشْط	comical *adj* هزلي
comb *v* يمشّط	coming *n* مجيء
combat *n* قتال	coming *adj* قادم
combat *v* يقاتل	comma *n* الفاصِلَة
combatant *n* مُقاتِل	command *v* يأمر
combination *n* اتحاد	commander *n* الآمر
combine *v* دمج	commandment *n* أمر
combustible *n* قابل للاحتراق	commemorate *v* يحتفل بذكرى
combustion *n* إحراق	commence *v* يستهلّ
come *iv* جاء	commend *v* يُوْدِع
come about *v* يَحِدّ	commendation *n* توصية
come across *v* يلتقي به مُصادَفةً	comment *v* يعلّق على
come apart *v* تفكك	comment *n* تعليق
come back *v* يرجع	commerce *n* التِّجَارَة
come down *v* يَنْزل	commercial *adj* تجاريّ
come forward *v* قدم نفسه	commission *n* مهمةمأموري
come from *v* يَنْبَعِث مِنْ	commit *v* يُسْلِم إلى , يُوْدِع

C

committed *adj* حفظ	compelling *adj* قهري
committee *n* لجنة	compendium *n* خلاصة وافية
common *adj* عمومي	compensate *v* يُعوّض
commotion *n* اضطراب	compensation *n* تعويض
communicate *v* يُبلغ	compete *v* يتنافس مع
communication *n* إبلاغ	competence *n* دخل كافٍ
communion *n* تَشارُك	competent *adj* كافٍ
communism *n* الشيوعيّة	competition *n* منافسة
communist *adj* شيوعيّ	competitive *adj* تنافسيّ
community *n* مُجْتَمَع	competitor *n* المنافِس
commute *v* يستبدل , يغيّر	compile *v* يَجْمَع
compact *adj* مُدَمّج	complain *v* يشكو
compact *v* يُدَمّج	complaint *n* تذمّر
companion *n* رفيق	complement *n* تتمّة
companionship *n* رِفْقة	complete *adj* تامّ
company *n* شركة	complete *v* يتمّم
comparable *adj* قابلٌ للمقارنة بـ	completely *adv* تماماً
comparative *adj* مقارن	completion *n* إتمام
compare *v* يقارن بين	complex *adj* مُركّب
comparison *n* مقارَنة	complexion *n* لون البشرة
compartment *n* مقصورة	complexity *n* تعقيد
compass *n* حدّ	compliance *n* مطاوعة
compassion *n* إشفاق	compliant *adj* مطاوع
compassionate *adj* شَفُوق	complicate *v* يُعقّد
compatibility *n* انسجام	complication *n* تعقيد
compatible *adj* منسجم	complicity *n* تورط في جريمة
compatriot *n* مواطن المرء	compliment *n* مدْح
compel *v* بُكْره	complimentary *adj* مَدْحيّ , مُجامِل

comply v يطيع	concentrate v يركّز
component n عنصر	concentration n تركيز
compose v يركّب , يَنْظِم	concentric adj متراكز
composed adj هادئ	concept n فكرة
composer n المركّب	conception n فكرة
composition n تركيب , تنضيد	concern v يتعلّق بـ , يَهُمّ
compost n سماد	concern n شأن
composure n هدوء	concerning pre في ما يتعلق بـ
compound n كلمة مركّبة	concert n اتفاق
compound v يركّب	concession n منْح
comprehend v يفهم	conciliate v يَسْتَرْضِي
comprehensive adj شامل	conciliatory adj استرضائيّ
compress v يضغط	conciousness n شعور
compression n ضَغْط	concise adj إيجازي
comprise v يشمل	conclude v يُنْهِي , يعقد
compromise n تَسْوِيَة	conclusion n استنتاج , خاتمة
compromise v يسوّي نزاعاً	conclusive adj حاسم
compulsion n إكراه	concoct v يلفّق
compulsive adj مُكْرِه	concoction n طهو , إعداد
compulsory adj إلزاميّ	concrete n اسمنت
compute v يَحْسِب	concrete adj متماسك
computer n كومبيوتر	concur v يتزامن
comrade n رفيق	concurrent adj متفق عليه
con man n مشعوذ	concussion n هَزّة
conceal v يكْتُم	condemn v يَشْجُب
concede v يمنح	condemnation n شجب
conceited adj مغرور	condensation n تركيز
conceive v تصور	condense v ركز

C

condescend v يتنازل

condiment n تابل

condition n شَرْط

conditional adj مَشرُوْط

conditioner n منعم الشعر

condo n سيادة مشتركة

condolences n تعزية

condone v يَغْفِر

conducive adj مساعد

conduct n إدارة

conduct v يُرشد , يَهدي

conductor n الهادي

cone n كوز

confer v يَمنح , يتشاور

conference n تشاوُر

confess v يعترف

confession n اعتراف

confessional n كرسيّ الاعتراف

confessor n المعترف

confidant n كاتم السر

confide v يثق بـ

confidence n إيمان

confident adj واثق

confidential adj خصوصي

confine v يقيّد , يحجز

confinement n تَقْيِيْد

confirm v يقوّي

confirmation n تقوية

confiscate v يُصادر

confiscation n مصادرة

conflict n نزاع

conflict v يتضارب

conflicting adj متضارب

conform v يطابق

conformist adj ممتثل

conformity n مطابقة

confound v يُخْزي

confront v يتحدّى

confrontation n مواجهة

confuse v يُربك

confusing adj مُحَيِّر

confusion n إرباك

congenial adj متجانس

congested adj مزدحم

congestion n ازدحام

congratulate v يُهَنّئ

congregate v يجتمع

congregation n تجمع

congress n اجتماع

conjecture n حَدْس

conjugal adj زواجي

conjugate v يصرِّف الأفعال

conjunction n توحيد

conjure up v إستعاد

connect v يَربط

connection n رَبْط

connive v يتغاضى عن	console v يعزّي
connote v أشار	consolidate v يَدْمُج
conquer v بفتح بلداً	consonant n الحرف الساكن
conqueror n الفاتح	conspicuous adj واضح
conquest n فَتْح	conspiracy n تآمُرّ
conscience n الضمير	conspirator n المتآمر
conscious adj شاعرّ بـ	conspire v يتآمر
conscript n يجنّد	constancy n ثبات
consecrate v يَرْسم كاهناً	constant adj جَلد
consecration n تكريس	constellation n بُرْج
consecutive adj مُتعاقِب	consternation n رُعْب
consensus n إجماع	constipate v قبض الامعاء
consent v يوافق	constipated adj مقبوض الأمعاء
consent n موافقة	constipation n إمساك
consequence n نتيجة	constitute v يعيّن
consequent adj ناشئ عن	constitution n دستور
conservation n صيانة	constrain v يُكره , يقيِّد
conservative adj محافظ	constraint n إكراه , إجبار
conserve v يصون	construct v يبني
conserve n المربّى	construction n بناء
consider v يفكّر في	constructive adj بنائيّ
considerable adj هامّ	consul n قنصل
consideration n تفكير	consulate n قنصلية
consignment n إيداع	consult v يستشير
consist v يتألف من	consultation n استشارة
consistency n كثافة	consume v يستنفد
consistent adj متين , متماسك	consumer n مستهلك
consolation n تعزية	consumption n استهلاك

C

contact v يحتك بـ

contact n احتكاك

contagious adj مُعْدٍ

contain v يكبح

container n وعاء

contaminate v يلوّث

contamination n تلويث

contemplate v يتأمل

contemporary adj معاصر لـ

contempt n ازدراء

contend v يناضل

contender n المنافس

content adj مكتفٍ

content v يُرضي

contentious adj مشاكس

contents n فِهْرِسْت

contest n نضال

contestant n متبارٍ

context n القرينة

continent n قارّة

continental adj قارّي

contingency n احتمال

contingent adj مُحْتَمَل

continuation n استمرار

continue v يستمرّ

continuity n الاستمرارية

continuous adj متّصل

contour n الخط كفافي

contraband n تهريب

contract v يَعقد

contract n عَقْد

contraction n قَبْض

contradict v يُكذّب

contradiction n إنكار

contrary adj مضادّ

contrast v يتغاير

contrast n المغايرة

contribute v يتبرّع بـ , يقدّم

contribution n ضريبة , تبرّع

contributor n المتبرّع , المُسْهِم

contrition n ندَمّ

control n توجيه

control v يكبح

controversial adj خِلافي

controversy n جدل

convalescent adj ناقه

convene v يجتمع

convenience n وسائل الراحة

convenient adj مريح

convent n دير

convention n اتفاقية

conventional adj متمسّك بالعُرْف

conversation n محادثة

converse v يتحدّث مع

conversely adv بالعَكْس

conversion n تحويل

convert v يَهْدي	copier n آلة تصوير
convert n المهتدي	copper n نحاس
convey v ينقل	copy v يَنْسَخ
convict v يُدين	copy n نُسْخَة
conviction n إدانة , تجريم	copyright n حقّ النشر
convince v يُقنع بـ	cord n حبل
convincing adj مفحم	cordial adj حارّ
convoluted adj ملفوف	cordless adj بدو حبل
convoy n قوةٌ عسكرية	cordon n شريط زينيّ
convulse v يهزّ بعنف	cordon off v يحيط بحبل
convulsion n اضطراب عنيف	core n جوهر
cook v يطهو	cork n الفِلّين
cook n الطاهي	corn n حَبّة قمح
cookie n كعكة مُحلّاة	corner n زاوية
cooking n طَهْو	cornerstone n حجر الزاوية
cool adj بارد باعتدال	cornet n بوق
cool v يبرّد باعتدال	corollary n نتيجة مباشرة
cool down v أصبح باردا, أهدأ	coronary adj إكليلي
cooling adj بارد باعتدال	coronation n تتويج
coolness n رباطة جأش	corporal adj بدنيّ
cooperate v يتعاون	corporal n العريف
cooperation n تعاون	corporation n شركة
cooperative adj تعاونيّ	corpse n جُثّة
coordinate v يسوّي في الرتبة	corpulent adj سمين
coordination n تنسيق	corpuscle n جُسَيمة
coordinator n منسق	correct v يصحّح
cop n شرطي	correct adj صحيح
cope v يكافح بنجاح	correction n تصحيح

C

correlate v ترابط	countenance n سيماء
correspond v يتوافق	counter n معكوس
corresponding adj متطابق	counter v يقاوم , يعاكس
corridor n رواق	counteract v يضادّ
corroborate v يؤيِّد	counterfeit v يزيِّف
corrode v يتأكّل	counterfeit adj مزيَّف
corrupt v يرشو	counterpart n نسخة
corrupt adj مُرتَشٍ , فاسد	countess n زوجة الكونت
corruption n رشوة	countless adj لا يُعَدّ
cosmetic n تجميلي	country n بلد ريف
cosmic adj كَوْنيّ	countryman n وطني
cosmonaut n الفضائي	countryside n الريف
cost iv كلف	county n إقليم
cost n ثمن	coup n ضربة موفقة
costly adj غالٍ	couple n رابط, زوج اثنان
costume n زيّ	coupon n قسيمة
cottage n كوخ	courage n شجاعة
cotton n قطن	courageous adj شجاع
couch n مَضْجع	courier n ساعي
cough n سُعال	course n سَيْر , تقدّم
cough v يَسْعُل	court n تملق
council n مَجْلِس	court v يحاول اكتساب كذا
counsel v ينصح	courteous adj لطيف
counsel n نصيحة , مشورة	courtesy n لطف
counselor n الناصح	courthouse n دار العدل
count v يَعُدّ	courtship n تودُّد
count n عدّ , إحصاء	courtyard n فِنَاء
countdown n العد التنازلي	cove n جُوْن

covenant n عَهْد	crash n تحطُّم , تهشُّم
cover n مخبأ , غطاء	crash v يتحطّم , يُفلس
cover v يحمي , يصون	crass adj تامّ
cover up v حجب الحقائق	crater n فُوّهة البركان
coverage n تغطية	crave v يلتمس
covert adj سِرّيّ	craving n رغبة ملحّة
coverup n إسْتِتار	crawl v يَدِبّ
covet v يشتهي ما ليس له	crayon n قلم ملون
cow n بقرة	craziness n جنون
coward n الجبان	crazy adj مخبّل
cowardice n جُبْن , جَبانة	creak v يَصِرّ
cowardly adv بجُبْن	creak n صرير
cowboy n راعي البقر	cream n قِشْدَة
cozy adj دافئ	creamy adj قِشْدِيّ
crab n سرطان	crease n غَضَن , جَعْدَة
crack n طقطقة	crease v يغضّن
crack v يُطَقْطِق	create v يَخلق
cradle n مهد	creation n خَلْق
craft n براعة	creative adj مُبْدِع
craftsman n الحرَفيّ	creativity n إبْداع
cram v يَحْشُرُ	creator n الخالق
cramp n تشُّج	creature n مخلوق
cramped adj ضيق	credibility n مصداقية
crane n كُرْكيّ	credible adj معقول
crank n الكَرَنْك	creditor n الدائن
cranky adj معتوه	creed n عقيدة
crap n حماقة	creek n جُوْن
crappy adj قَذِر	creep v يَدِبّ

C

C

creepy adj داب	**cross** v شطب
cremate v يُحْرق جثَةَ مِيْت	**cross out** v يَحْذِفُ
crest n عُرْف الديك	**crossfire** n نيران متقاطعة
crevice n صَدْع	**crossing** n عبور
crew n طاقم	**crossroads** n مُفْتَرق الطُّرُق
crib n مَعْلَف	**crosswalk** n ممر مسمر
cricket n كريكيت	**crossword** n كَلِمَاتٌ مُتَقَاطِعَة
crime n جريمة	**crouch** v يربض
criminal adj جنائيّ	**crow** n غراب
cripple adj يصيبه بالعَرج	**crow** v يصيح الديك
cripple v يصيبه بالعَرج	**crowbar** n عَتَلة
crisis n أزمة حرجة	**crowd** n حَشْد من الناس
crisp adj منعش أو بار	**crowd** v يحتشد
crispy adj متموج	**crowded** adj مزدحم
criss-cross v متشابك	**crown** n تاج
criterion n معيار	**crown** v يتوّج
critical adj انتقاديّ , نقديّ	**crowning** n تتويج
criticism n انتقاد	**crucial** adj حاسم
criticize v ينتقد	**crucifix** n صَلْب
critique n نَقْد	**crucifixion** n صَلْب
crockery n آنية فخّاريّة	**crucify** v صلب
crocodile n التمساح	**crude** adj خام
crony n صديق حميم	**cruel** adj وحشيّ
crook n خُطّاف	**cruelty** n وحشيّة
crooked adj معقوف	**cruise** v يطوف في البحر
crop n محصول	**crumb** n كِسْرَة
cross n صلب	**crumble** v يفتّت
cross adj مسْتعرض	**crunchy** adj متفتت

C.

crusade n الصّليبيّة	**cumbersome** adj ثقيل
crusader n الصليبيّ	**cunning** adj بارع
crush v يَعْصر	**cup** n كوب
crushing adj ساحق	**cupboard** n صُوان
crust n قشرة الرغيف	**curable** adj قابل للشفاء
crusty adj قشري	**curator** n الوصيّ
crutch n عكاز	**curb** v يَشكُم
cry n صُراخ	**curb** n كابح
cry v يَصْرخ	**curdle** v يُخَثّر
cry out v يصرخ	**cure** v يشفي
crying n صياح	**cure** n الرعاية الروحيّة
crystal n بلّوْر	**curfew** n ناقوس الغروب
cub n جرو الثعلب أو الدبّ	**curiosity** n فضول
cube n المكعّب	**curious** adj فضوليّ
cubic adj مكعّب	**curl** v يَعْقِصُ الشّعْر
cubicle n مهجع	**curl** n عقصة
cucumber n خيار	**curly** adj جعد الشعر
cuddle v يعانق	**currency** n عملة
cuff n طرف الكم، صفعة	**current** adj جار
cuisine n مطبخ	**currently** adv بصورة عامة
culminate v يتكبّد	**curse** v يلعن
culpability n الملومية	**curtail** v يَبْتر
culprit n المُتّهم	**curtain** n ستارة
cult n عبادة	**curve** n مُنحَنى
cultivate v يفلح	**curve** v يَحْني
cultivation n حرائة	**cushion** n وسادة
cultural adj ثقافيّ	**cushion** v يوسّد
culture n ثقافة	**cuss** v يشتم

C
D

custard n كريم

custodian n القَيّم

custody n رعاية

custom n عادةٌ

customary adj معتاد

customer n زبون

custom-made adj موصى عليه

customs n جَمَارك

cut n قطعة لحم

cut iv يجرح

cut back v رجع

cut down v صرع,

cut off v توقف

cut out v توقف فجأة,

cute adj ذكيّ

cutlery n سكاكين

cutter n القاطع

cyanide n السيانيد

cycle n دَوْر

cyclist n الدَّرّاج

cyclone n زوبعة

cylinder n أسطوانة

cynic adj الكَلْبيّ

cynicism n تعبير ساخر

cypress n السّرو

cyst n كيس صغير

czar n القيصر

D

dad n أبٌ

dagger n خِنْجَر

daily adv يوميّ

dairy farm n مبقرة

daisy n زهرة اللؤلؤ

dam n سَدّ

damage n أذى

damage v تلف

damaging adj مؤذ

damn v يُدين

damnation n إدانة

damp adj رَطْبٌ

dampen v يرطّب , يندّي

dance n رَقْص

dance v يَرقُص

dancing n رَقْص

dandruff n نُخالة الرأس

danger n خَطَرٌ

dangerous adj خَطِرٌ

dangle v يتدلّى

dare v يَجرُؤ

dare n تحدّ

daring adj جَريء

dark adj مظلم

darken v يُظلم

D

darkness n ظُلمة	**deaf** adj أصم
darling adj حبيب	**deafen** v يُصِمّ
darn v يرفو	**deafening** adj يُصِمّ
dart n وثبة	**deafness** n صَمَم
dash v يقذف بعنف	**deal** iv يوزع
dashing adj مندفع	**deal** n مقدارٌ
data n مَعْلومَات	**dealer** n التاجر
database n قاعده بيانات	**dealings** n تعامل
date n تاريخ	**dean** n عميد كلية
date v يرقى إلى , يؤرّخ	**dear** adj عزيز
daughter n ابنة	**dearly** adv كثيراً
daughter-in-law n الكّنة	**death** n موت
daunt v يُرْهب	**death toll** n عدد الضحايا
daunting adj مرعب	**death trap** n مكان خطر
dawn n فجر	**deathbed** n فراش الموت
day n نهار	**debase** v أهان
daze v يدوّخ	**debatable** adj مُتَنازَعٌ عليه
dazed adj منبهر	**debate** v يناقش
dazzle v ينبهر	**debate** n مناقشة
dazzling adj لامع	**debit** n دين
de luxe adj فاخر	**debrief** v استخلص
deacon n الشمّاس	**debris** n حُطام
dead adj مَيْت	**debt** n إثم
dead end n طريق مسدود	**debtor** n المَدين
deaden v يُهْمد	**debunk** v سخر
deadline n الموعد الأخير	**debut** n الظّهور الأوّل
deadlock adj وَرْطَة	**decade** n عقد
deadly adj مُميت	**decadence** n تفسّخ

D

decapitate v يقطع الرأس

decay v يَفسُد

decay n فساد

deceased adj متوفى

deceit n خِداع

deceitful adj كذاب

deceive v يخدَع

December n ديسمبر

decency n احتشام

decent adj مُحْتَشِم

deception n خَدْع

deceptive adj خادِعٌ

decide v يقرِّر

deciding adj حاسم

decimal adj عَشْرِيّ

decimate v يأخذ

decipher v يفكّ المغالق

decision n قرار

decisive adj فاصِل

deck n ظَهْرُ المركب

declaration n إعلان

declare v صرح

declension n تصريف الأسماء

decline v ينحرف

decline n ذبول

décor n زخرفة

decorate v يزخرف

decorative adj زخرفي

decorum n لياقة

decrease v يَنْقُص

decrease n نَقْص

decree n مرسوم

decree v يرسم بـ

decrepit adj عاجز

dedicate v يكرِّس

dedication n تكريس

deduce v يستنتج

deduct v بقتطع

deductible adj قابل للحسم

deduction n حَسْم

deed n عَمَل

deem v يَعْتَبر

deep adj عميق

deepen v يُعمِّق

deer n ظبي

deface v يُشوِّه

defame v يفتري على

defeat v يُبْطِل

defeat n إحباط

defect n خَلَلٌ

defect v إرتد

defection n رِدَّة

defective adj ناقص

defend v يحمي

defendant n المُدَّعَى عليه

defender n مُدَافِع

D

defense n حماية	**degree** n دَرَجَة
defenseless adj بدون حماية	**dehydrate** v أزال الماء
defer v يؤجّل	**deign** v يتلطّف
defiance n تحدّ	**deity** n وهية
defiant adj متحدِ	**dejected** adj يُكئب
deficiency n نقص	**delay** v يؤجّل
deficient adj ناقص	**delay** n تأخير
deficit n عجز بشكل عام	**delegate** v ينتدب
defile v يلوّث	**delegate** n مندوب
define v يحدّد	**delegation** n تفويض
definite adj محدّد	**delete** v شطب
definition n تحديد	**deliberate** v يدرس
definitive adj حاسم	**deliberate** adj مدروس
deflate v فرغ الهواء	**delicacy** n طعام شهيّ
deform v يُشوّه	**delicate** adj شهيّ
deformity n تشوُّه	**delicious** adj مُبهج
defraud v يخدع	**delight** n بهجة
defray v يدفع	**delight** v بهجة
defrost v أزال الصقيع	**delightful** adj مُبهج
deft adj رشيق	**delinquency** n تقصير
defuse v ينزع الفتيل	**delinquent** n المقصّر
defy v يَتَحَدّى	**deliver** v يُحرّر، يحوّل
degenerate v ينحلّ	**delivery** n تحرير، إطلاق سراح
degenerate adj مُنْحَلّ	**delude** v يُضلّل
degeneration n انحلال	**deluge** n طوفان
degradation n تنزيل رتبة	**delusion** n تضليل
degrade v يُنزل رتبتهُ	**demand** v يَطْلب
degrading adj مذل	**demand** n طلبّ

demanding adj كثير المطالب

demean v يسلك

demeaning adj تحقير

demeanor n سلوك

demented adj مُخبّل

democracy n الديموقراطيّة

democratic adj ديموقراطيّ

demolish v يدمّر

demolition n هدم

demon n شيطان

demonstrate v يُظهِر بوضوح

demoralize v يُفسِد الأخلاق

demote v يُنزل درجته

den n عرين

denial n رَفْض

denigrate v سوّد

Denmak n الدنمارك

denominator n المقام

denote v يدلّ على

denounce v يَشْجُب

dense adj كثيف , أبله

density n كثافة

dent v يَبْعَج

dent n بَعْجَة

dental adj سِنّي

dentist n طبيب الأسنان

dentures n أسنان إصطناعية

deny v يُنكر

depart v يَرْحل

department n قِسْم

departure n رحيل

depend v يثق بـ

dependable adj موثوق

dependence n توقُّف على

dependent adj متوقُّف على

depict v يرسم

deplete v يَفْصِد

deplorable adj بائس

deplore v يرثي لـ

deploy v يَنْشُر

deployment n إنتشار الجند

deport v يتصرّف

deportation n طرد ,

depose v يخلع

deposit n وديعة

depot n مستودع , مخزن

deprave adj يُفسِد الأخلاق

depravity n فساد

depreciate v إلغاء قيمته

depreciation n انخفاض

depress v يضغط على

depressing adj كئيب

depression n خَفْض

deprivation n حرمان

deprive v يَحْرِم

deprived adj مجرد

depth n موضع عميق	**desist** v كف عن
derail v خرج عن الخط	**desk** n مكتب, استقبال
derailment n خروج عن الخط	**desolate** adj مهجور
deranged adj مختل	**desolation** n خراب
derelict adj مهجور	**despair** n يأسّ
deride v يسخر من	**desperate** adj يائس
derivative adj مشتقّ	**despicable** adj حقير
derive v يشتقّ , ينشأ عن	**despise** v يحتقر
derogatory adj ازدرائيّ	**despite** c برغم
descend v يهبط	**despondent** adj قانط
descendant n سليل	**despot** n الطاغية
descent n هبوط , نزول	**despotic** adj طغيانيّ
describe v يصف	**destination** n غرض
description n وَصْف	**destiny** n القِسْمَة
descriptive adj وَصْفيّ	**destitute** adj محروم من
desecrate v يدنّس	**destroy** v يَهْدِم
desegregate v أزال	**destroyer** n الهادم
desert n صحراء	**destruction** n هَدْم
desert v يهجر , يَخْذل	**destructive** adj مُهْلِك
deserted adj مهجور	**detach** v يَفْصِل
deserter n هارب من الجندية	**detachable** adj ممكن فصلها
deserve v يستحقّ	**detail** n تفصيل
deserving adj مستجقّ	**detail** v يروي بتفصيل
design n خِطّة , تصميم	**detain** v يحتجز
designate v يعيّن	**detect** v يكتشف
desirable adj جذاب	**detective** n بوليس سرى
desire n رغبة	**detector** n مكشاف
desire v يرغب في	**detention** n احتجاز

D

deter v يَثْني

detergent n مطهر

deteriorate v يُفسِد

deterioration n تلف

determination n الفصل في نزاع

determine v يحدِّد

deterrence n جيش ردع

detest v يَمْقُت

detestable adj مُقيت

detonate v يفجِّر

detonation n تفجير

detonator n المفجِّر

detour n انعطاف

detriment n علي حساب

detrimental adj مؤذٍ

devalue v يخفض قيمة العملة

devastate v يدمِّر

devastating adj مخرب

devastation n تدمير

develop v يوسِّع

development n توسيع

deviation n انحراف

device n مكيدة

devil n ابليس

devious adj ناءٍ

devise v يخترع

devoid adj خِلوٌ من

devote v يكرِّس

devotion n تقوى

devour v يلتهم

devout adj وَرِع

dew n نَدىً

diabetes n الديابيتس

diabolical adj شيطانيّ

diagnose v يُشخِّص حالةً أو داءً

diagnosis n التشخيص

diagonal adj قُطْريّ

diagram n رسم بيانيّ

dial n قرص الساعة

dial v يتلفن إلى

dial tone n إشارة صونية

dialect n لهجة

dialogue n محادثة

diameter n القُطْر

diamond n ماسٌّ

diaper n حفاظ الطفل

diarrhea n الإسهال

diary n اليوميّات

dice n النَّرد

dictate v يُمْلي

dictator n الطاغية

dictatorial adj ديكتاتوريّ

dictatorship n الديكتاتوريّة

dictionary n مُعْجَم

die v يموت

die out v اختفى

diet n غِذاء	diner n متناول الغَداء
differ v يختلف	dining room n حجرة الطعام
difference n اختلاف	dinner n غَداء
different adj مختلف	dinosaur n الديناصُور
difficult adj صعب	diocese n الأبَرَشيّة
difficulty n صعوبة	diphthong n إدغام
diffuse v يصبّ	diploma n دبلوم
dig iv يحفر,	diplomacy n الديبلوماسيّة
digest v ينظّم	diplomat n دبلوماسي
digestion n تصنيف	diplomatic adj ديبلوماسيّ
digestive adj هضميّ	dire adj رهيب
digit n رقم تحت العشرة	direct adj مستقيم
dignify v يُبجّل	direct v يُعَنْون
dignitary n صاحب مقام رفيع	direction n إدارة
dignity n كرامة	director n المدير
digress v يستطرد	directory n مدير
dike n خندق	dirt n قذر
dilapidated adj خَرِب	dirty adj قذر
dilemma n مأزق	disability n عجز
diligence n كدّ	disabled adj معاق
diligent adj كادّ	disadvantage n عائق
dilute v يُشعْشِع	disagree v تعارض
dim adj مُعتم	disagreeable adj مزعج
dim v بهت	disagreement n مخالفة
dime n الدّائم	disappear v اختفى
dimension n بُعْد	disappearance n اختفاء
diminish v يقلّل	disappoint v خيب الأمل
dine v يتغدّى	disappointing adj مخيب للأمل

D

disappointment n خيبة أمل	**discover** v اكتشف
disapproval n استنكار	**discovery** n اكتشاف
disapprove v استهجن	**discredit** v لوث
disarm v نزع السلاح	**discreet** adj حذر
disarmament n نزع السلاح	**discrepancy** n تعارض
disaster n مصيبة	**discretion** n حذر
disastrous adj مشؤوم	**discriminate** v ميز
disband v حل جمعية	**discrimination** n تمييز
disbelief n جحود	**discuss** v ناقش
disburse v أنفق	**discussion** n مناقشة
discard v رمى	**disdain** n ازدراء
discern v تبين	**disease** n مرض
discharge v أطلق سراح	**disembark** v نزل من السفينة
discharge n تسديد	**disentangle** v حل
disciple n تابع	**disfigure** v شوه شيئا
discipline n انضباط	**disgrace** n خزي
disclaim v عدم معرفة	**disgrace** v أخزى
disclose v كشف عن	**disgraceful** adj شائن
discomfort n مكروه	**disgruntled** adj ساخط
disconnect v فصل	**disguise** v تنكر
discontent adj ساخط	**disguise** n قناع
discontinue v (قطع) عن	**disgust** n غثيان
discord n تضارب	**disgusting** adj شائن
discount n خصم	**dish** n طبق
discount v حسم	**dishearten** v ثبط العزيمة
discourage v ثبط العزيمة	**dishonest** adj خادع
discouraging adj معوق عن	**dishonesty** n تضليل
discourtesy n فظاظة	**dishonor** n خزي

dishonorable adj مخز

dishwasher n غسالة الأواني

disillusion n تحرير من الوهم

disinfect v طهر

disinfectant v يطهر

disinherit v حرم من الوراثة

disintegrate v فسد

disintegration n تفسخ

disinterested adj نزيه

disk n أسطوانة

dislike v كره

dislike n قرصي الشكل

dislocate v شوش

dislodge v أزاح

disloyal adj خائن

disloyalty n خيانة

dismal adj كئيب

dismantle v أزال

dismay n رعب

dismay v أرعب

dismiss v صرف النظر

dismissal n إقالة

dismount v ترجل

disobedience n تمرد

disobedient adj رافض

disobey v تمرد

disorder n فوضى

disorganized adj مشوش

disown v تبرأ من

disparity n تفاوت

dispatch v بعث

dispel v أزال

dispensation n إدارة

dispense v ركب الادوية

dispersal n تشتيت

disperse v شتت

displace v حل محل

display n عرض

display v عرض

displease v غضب

displeasing adj غضب

displeasure n استياء

disposal n تخلص من

dispose v نظم

disprove v فند

dispute n مناظرة

dispute v تجادل

disqualify v جرد

disregard v تجاهل

disrepair n في حالة سيئة

disrespect n ازدراء

disrupt v أزعج

dissatisfied adj مستاء

disseminate v نثر

dissent v خالف

dissident adj مختلف

D

dissimilar adj مختلف	**distrust** v ارتاب
dissipate v بذر	**distrustful** adj ظنان
dissolute adj متهتك	**disturb** v ضايق
dissolution n فض البرلمان	**disturbance** n إزعاج, شغب
dissolve v ذاب	**disturbing** adj متعب
dissonant adj نشاز	**disunity** n شقاق
dissuade v نصح بالعدول	**disuse** n هجر
distance n مسافة	**ditch** n خندق
distant adj بعيد	**dive** v انغمس
distaste n نفور	**diver** n غطاس
distasteful adj كريه	**diverse** adj مختلف
distill v يتقطر	**diversify** v أنتج محاصيل
distinct adj متميز	**diversion** n تحويل
distinction n تميز	**diversity** n تنوع
distinctive adj مميز	**divert** v انحرف
distinguish v ميز	**divide** v قسم
distort v حرف	**dividend** n حصة
distortion n تحريف	**divine** adj رائي
distract v لهى	**diving** n غوص
distraction n إلهاء	**divinity** n الهوية
distraught adj ذاهل	**divisible** adj قابل للقسمة
distress n عسر	**division** n تقسيم
distress v وجع	**divorce** n طلاق
distressing adj مؤلم	**divorce** v أطلق
distribute v وزع	**divorcee** n مطلق
distribution n توزيع	**divulge** v أفشى سرا
district n منطقة	**dizziness** n دوار
distrust n ارتياب	**dizzy** adj دواري

D

do iv ينفذ يفعل	**door** n باب
docile adj قابل للتعليم	**doorbell** n جَرَسُ الباب
docility n طاعة	**doorstep** n درجة الباب
dock n قتل	**doorway** n مدخل
dock v بتر ذيلا	**dope** n مخدرات
doctor n طبيب	**dope** v تناول مخدرات
doctrine n مذهب	**dormitory** n المهجع
document n وثيقة	**dosage** n جرعة
documentary n كتابي	**dossier** n إضبارة
dodge v راوغ	**dot** n نقطة
dog n كلب	**double** adj مزدوج
dogmatic adj عقائدي	**double** v ضاعف
dole out v تصدق	**double-check** v فحص مجدد
doll n دمية	**double-cross** v خيانة
dollar n دولار	**doubt** n شك
dolphin n دلفين	**doubt** v شك
dome n قبة	**doubtful** adl مشكوك فيه
domestic adj منزلي	**dough** n عجين
domesticate v دجن	**dove** n حمامة
dominate v سيطر	**down** adv تحت
domination n سيطرة	**downcast** adj مسدل
domineering adj مستبد	**downfall** n سقوط
dominion n سيادة	**downhill** adv نحو وضع أدنى
donate v منح	**downpour** n انهمار
donation n هبة	**downsize** v خفض العمالة
donkey n حمار	**downstairs** adv سفلى
donor n منعم	**down-to-earth** adj بسيط
doom n قدر غاشم	**downtown** n قلب المدينة

downtrodden adj مدوس بالاقدام	**dresser** n خزانة مطبخ
downturn adj مهبر	**dressing** n مرق التوابل
dowry n مهر	**dried** adj جافة
doze n نوم خفيف	**drift** v انجرف
doze v نعس	**drifter** n شخص غير مستقر
dozen n إثنا عشر	**drill** ll ثقب, حفر
draft v جند	**drill** n دريل نسيج
draftsman n مصمم	**drink** iv يشرب
drag v جر	**drink** n مشروب
dragon n تنين	**drinkable** adj صالح للشرب
drain v جف	**drinker** n شارب
drainage n مصرف	**drip** v قطر
dramatic adj مسرحى مفاجئ	**drip** n تقطر
dramatize v مسرح	**drive** n قيادة, رحلة
drape n ستارة	**drive** iv يدفع الى الامام
drastic adj عنيف	**drive at** v رمىى إلى
draw n تعادل	**drive away** v قصا
draw iv	**driver** n سائق
drawback n أخرج	**driveway** n طريق خاصة
drawer n جارور	**drizzle** v تمطر رذاذا
drawing n تخطيط	**drizzle** n رذاذ
dread v أرهب	**drop** n ترجل, قطرة
dreaded adj مَخُوف	**drop** v ترك, سقوط
dreadful adj مفزع	**drop in** v طفيلية
dream iv يحلم	**drop off** v غلبه النعاس
dream n حلم	**drop out** v خرج
dress n ثوب	**drought** n قحط
dress v لبس	**drown** v غرق

drowsy adj نعسان	**dungeon** n زنزانة
drug n عقار	**dupe** v خدع
drug v خدر	**duplicate** v كرر
drugstore n صيدلية	**duplication** n تكرار
drum n طبلة, طبل	**durable** adj متين
drunk adj الثمل	**duration** n دوام
drunkenness n السكر	**during** pre طوال
dry v جفف	**dusk** n الغسق
dry adj جاف	**dust** n تربة
dryer n مجفف	**dusty** adj مغبر
dual adj ثنائي	**Dutch** adj هولندي
dubious adj ملتبس	**duty** n خدمة
duchess n دوقة	**dwarf** n قزم
duck n بط	**dwell** iv يقطن
duck v انحنى, تجنب	**dwelling** n دار
duct n أنبوب	**dwindle** v تضاءل
due adj كاف	**dye** v صبغ , انصبغ
duel n مبارزة	**dye** n دهان , صبغ
dues n استحقاقات	**dying** adj فناء
duke n دوق	**dynamic** adj ديناميكي
dull adj كليل	**dynamite** n ناسف
duly adv كما ينبغي	**dynasty** n سلالة حاكمة
dumb adj أبكم, أخرس	
dummy n دمية , طاولة بريدج	
dummy adj زائف	
dump v غمر الاسواق	
dump n مزبلة	
dung n روث	

E

each adj كل
each other adj آخر
eager adj شخص متحمس
eagerness n لهفة
eagle n نسر
ear n إذن
earache n ألم الأذن
eardrum n طبلة الأذن
early adv مبكرا
earmark v خصص
earn v جنى
earnestly adv جديا
earnings n أرباح
earphones n المسماع
earring n حلق
earth n اليابسة
earthquake n زلزال
ease v سهل
ease n راحة
easily adv بسهولة
east n شرق
Easter n عيد الفصح
eastern adj الجانب الشرقي
easterner n شرقى
eastward adv شرقي

easy adj سهل
eat iv يأكل
eat away v يزيل التراب
eavesdrop v استرق
eccentric adj شاذ
echo n صدى
eclipse n كسوف
ecology n علم البيئة
economical adj مقتصد
economize v اقتصد
economy n توفير
ecstasy n نشوة
ecstatic adj وجد
edge n حاشية
edgy adj متوتر
edible adj صالح للأكل
edifice n صرح
edit v حرر كتب
edition n نشر
educate v ثقف
educational adj ثقافي
eerie adj غريب
effect n انطباع
effective adj ناجح
effectiveness n فاعلية
efficiency n فعالية
efficient adj فعال
effigy n شخصية مكروهة

effort *n* جهد	elegant *adj* كيس
effusive *adj* منفتح القلب	element *n* عامل
egg *n* بيضة	elementary *adj* ابتدائي
egg white *n* بَياض البَيض	elephant *n* فيل
egoism *n* أنانية	elevate *v* رفع
egoist *n* أناني	elevation *n* ارتفاع
eight *adj* الثامن	elevator *n* مصعد
eighteen *adj* ثماني عشر	eleven *adj* أحد عشر
eighth *adj* ثامن	eleventh *adj* الحادي عشر
eighty *adj* الثمانون	eligible *adj* مؤهل
either *adj* كل	eliminate *v* أزال
either *adv* احد الامرين	elm *n* دردار
eject *v* قذف	eloquence *n* فصاحة
elapse *v* انقضى	else *adv* بطريقة أخرى
elastic *adj* قابل للتمدد	elsewhere *adv* في مكان آخر
elated *adj* مبتهج	elude *v* تملص
elbow *n* مرفق	elusive *adj* متهرب
elder *n* زعيم	emaciated *adj* مهزول
elderly *adj* عجوز	emanate *v* انبعث
elect *v* انتخب	emancipate *v* أعتق
election *n* انتخاب	embalm *v* عطر
electric *adj* مكهرب	embark *v* صعد
electrician *n* كهربائي	embarrass *v* أربك
electricity *n* كهرباء	embassy *n* سفارة
electrify *v* كهرب	embellish *v* جمل
electrocute *v* أعدم بالكهرباء	embers *n* جمرة
electronic *adj* إلكتروني	embezzle *v* اختلس
elegance *n* كياسة	embitter *v* زاده مرارة

E

emblem n شعار	**empty** adj أجرد
embody v جسد	**empty** v فرغ
emboss v نتأ	**enable** v مكن
embrace v إعتنق دينا	**enchant** v فتن
embrace n إعتناق	**enchanting** adj فاتن
embroider v طرز	**encircle** v طوق
embroidery n تطريز	**enclave** n مقاطعة
embroil v شوش	**enclose** v طوق
embryo n جنين	**enclosure** n تطويق
emerald n زمرد	**encompass** v طوق
emerge v انبثق	**encounter** v نجز
emergency n طارئ	**encounter** n مقابلة
emigrant n مهاجر	**encourage** v شجع
emigrate v اغترب	**encroach** v تجاوز
emission n إصدار	**encyclopedia** n دائرة المعارف
emit v لفظ	**end** n نهاية
emotion n عاطفة	**end** v فرغ
emotional adj مهتاج	**end up** v أنهى
emperor n إمبراطور	**endanger** v عرض للخطر
emphasis n تشديد	**endeavor** v حاول
emphasize v شدد	**endeavor** n محاولة
empire n إمبراطورية	**ending** n نهاية
employ v استخدم	**endless** adj أبدي
employee n المستخدم	**endorse** v حول شيك, أقر
employer n صاحب العمل	**endorsement** n تحويل
employment n عمل	**endure** v تحمل
empress n إمبراطورة	**enemy** n عدو
emptiness n فراغ	**energetic** adj نشيط

energy *n* حيوية

enforce *v* طبق

engage *v* استخدم

engaged *adj* نازل

engagement *n* خطوبة, تعهد

engine *n* محرك

engineer *n* مهندس

England *n* إنجلترا

English *adj* إنكليزي

engrave *v* نقش

engraving *n* نقش

engrossed *adj* منهمك

engulf *v* نسخ, ابتلع

enhance *v* عزز

enjoy *v* فرض

enjoyable *adj* ممتع

enjoyment *n* متعة

enlarge *v* كبر

enlargement *n* تكبير

enlighten *v* أضاء

enlist *v* جند

enormous *adj* تجنيد

enough *adv* إلى حد كاف

enrage *v* غضب

enrich *v* زخرف

enroll *v* جند

enrollment *n* تسجيل

ensure *v* ضمن

entail *v* استلزم

entangle *v* عقد

enter *v* دخل

enterprise *n* مشروع

entertain *v* استضاف

entertaining *adj* مسلي

entertainment *n* متعة

enthrall *v* شد

enthralling *adj* آسر

enthuse *v* تحمس

enthusiasm *n* حماسة

entice *v* أغرى

enticement *n* إغواء

enticing *adj* مغو

entire *adj* كامل

entirely *adv* تماما

entrance *n* تماما

entreat *v* توسل

entree *n* دخول

entrenched *adj* إثْباتِيّ

entrepreneur *n* مقاول

entrust *v* فوض

entry *n* دخول

enumerate *v* عدد

envelop *v* يغلّف

envelope *n* ظرف مغلف

envious *adj* حسود

environment *n* بيئة

envisage v تخيل

envoy n مبعوث

envy n حسد

envy v حسد

epidemic n وباء

epilepsy n داء الصرع

episode n حدث

epistle n رسالة

epitaph n نقش على ضريح

epitomize v لخص

epoch n عصر

equal adj متواز

equality n مساواة

equate v سوى

equation n توازن

equator n خط الاستواء

equilibrium n توازن

equip v زود

equipment n التجهيزات

equivalent adj معادل

era n عصر

eradicate v استأصل

erase v محا

eraser n ممحاة

erect v أقام

erect adj مستقيم

err v أثم

errand n مهمة

erroneous adj خاطئ

error n خطأ

erupt v ثور البركان , انفجر

eruption n ثوران, هيجان

escalate v صعد

escalator n درج متحرك

escapade n مغامرة

escape v تخلص من

escort n مرافق

esophagus n المريء

especially adv خاصة

espionage n تجسس

essay n محاولة

essence n قلب

essential adj جوهري

establish v أسس

estate n مقاطعة

esteem v ثمن

estimate v حزر

estimation n تثمين

estranged adj مُتَبَاعِد

estuary n مصب النهر

eternity n خلود

ethical adj أخلاقي

ethics n علم الأخلاق

Europe n أوروبا

European adj أوروبي

evacuate v بول

evade v تجنب	exalt v أثار
evaluate v خمن	examination n فحص
evaporate v تبخر	examine v اختبر
evasion n مراوغة	example n نموذج
evasive adj متهرب	exasperate v غضب
eve n مباشر	excavate v حفر
even adj منتظم	exceed v تجاوز
even if c حتى لو	exceedingly adv بإفراط
evening n غروب	excel v بز
event n حادثة	excellence n بز
eventuality n احتمال	excellent adj فاخر
eventually adv أخيرا	except pre إلا
ever adv دائما	exception n استثناء
everlasting adj مؤبد	exceptional adj نادر
every adj كل	excerpt n مقتطفات
everybody pro الجميع	excess n فرط
everyday adj كل يوم	excessive adj مفرط
everyone pro كل شخص	exchange v بدل
everything pro كل شيء	excite v أثار
evict v نزع ملكية	excitement n انفعال
evidence n بينة	exciting adj مثير
evil n شر	exclaim v أعلن بقوة
evil adj ملعون	exclude v استبعد
evoke v أثار	excruciating adj موجع
evolution n تقدم	excursion n انحراف
evolve v طور	excuse v غفر
exact adj متقن	excuse n حجة
exaggerate v بالغ	execute v قضى

إدارة n **executive**
تمثيلي adj **exemplary**
مثل v **exemplify**
معفى adj **exempt**
إعفاء n **exemption**
حفلة n **exercise**
رياضة v **exercise**
بذل v **exert**
كد n **exertion**
أرهق v **exhaust**
منهك adj **exhausting**
إعياء n **exhaustion**
رسم v **exhibit**
معرض n **exhibition**
منعش adj **exhilarating**
حذر v **exhort**
اغترب v **exile**
إبعاد n **exile**
إحتفظ ببقائه v **exist**
كيان n **existence**
مخرج n **exit**
هجرة جماعية n **exodus**
أبرئ v **exonerate**
باهظ adj **exorbitant**
شاذ adj **exotic**
امتد v **expand**
تضخم n **expansion**
توقع، ترقب v **expect**

توقع n **expectancy**
احتمال n **expectation**
ملاءمة n **expediency**
نفعي adj **expedient**
سرعة n **expedition**
طرد v **expel**
إنفاق n **expenditure**
نفقة n **expense**
غالي السعر adj **expensive**
تجربة n **experience**
تجربة n **experiment**
خبير adj **expert**
كفر عن v **expiate**
كفارة n **expiation**
زفير n **expiration**
مات v **expire**
فسر v **explain**
بين adj **explicit**
تفجر v **explode**
استغل v **exploit**
مأثرة n **exploit**
بحث v **explore**
مستكشف n **explorer**
انفجار, n **explosion**
انفجاري adj **explosive**
استغلال n **explotation**
يصدّر الى الخارج v **export**
عرض v **expose**

exposed adj مكشوف	**extricate** v خلص
express n شحن السريع	**extroverted** adj اِنْيسَاطِيّ
expression n إبانة	**exude** v تفصد
expressly adv بشكل معبر	**exult** v جذل
expropriate v صادر	**eye** n عين
expulsion n طرد	**eyebrow** n حاجب العين
exquisite adj فاتن	**eye-catching** adj جداب
extend v نشر , حسن	**eyeglasses** n نظارة طبية
extension n وصلة تلفون	**eyelash** n هدب الجفن
extent n مدى	**eyelid** n جفن
extenuating adj مُخَفِّف	**eyesight** n بصر
exterior adj خارجي	**eyewitness** n شاهد عيان
exterminate v فني	
external adj سطحي	
extinct adj منقرض	
extinguish v أطفأ	
extort v ابتز	**F**
extortion n ابتزاز	
extra adv نحو خاص	
extract v اقتلع	**fable** n أسطورة
extradite n تسلم	**fabric** n نسيج القماش
extradition n تسليم مجرم	**fabricate** v ركب
extraneous adj خارجي	**fabulous** adj رائع
extravagance n تبذير	**face** n وجه
extravagant adj مسرف	**face up to** v يتقبل الأمر
extreme adj متطرف	**facet** n السطيح , وجيه
extremist adj متطرف	**facilitate** v سهل
extremities n أطراف الجسم	**facing** pre مواجهة
	fact n حقيقة

E
F

factor n عامل	falsehood n كذبة
factory n مصنع	falsify v شوه
factual adj حقيقي	falter v عى في الكلام
faculty n قابلية	fame n سمعة
fad n زي	familiar adj مألوف
fade v ذبل	family n عائلة
faded adj باهت	famine n مجاعة
fail v سقط	famous adj مشهور
failure n إخفاق	fan n هاو, معجب
faint v اغمى عليه	fanatic adj متعصب
faint n إغماء	fancy adj مزخرف
faint adj باهت	fang n ناب
fair n وسط	fantastic adj خيالي
fair adj وسيم , مقبول	fantasy n خيال
fairness n عدل	far adv بعيد
fairy n جن	faraway adj حالم
faith n معتقد , دين	farce n تمثيلية
faithful adj مخلص	fare n ثمن التذكرة
fake v لفق	farewell n وداع
fake adj مستعار	farm n مزرعة
fall n خريف	farmer n مزارع
fall iv يسقط	farming n العمل بالزراعة
fall back v تراجع	farmyard n فناء المزرعة
fall behind v تخلف عن	farther adv إلى مكان
fall down v أهمل مهمة	fascinate v فتن
fall through v خفق في التفاوض	fashion n زي
fallacy n مغالطة	fashionable adj أنيق
fallout n نتيجة	fast adj سريع

F

fasten v ثبت	federal adj فدرالي
fat n دهن	fee n رسم دخول
fat adj سمين	feeble adj واهن
fatal adj مصيري	feed iv يطعم
fate n قضاء	feel iv يلمس
fateful adj مصيري	feeling n شعور
father n أب	feelings n عاطفة
fatherhood n الأبوة	feet n قدم
father-in-law n الحمو	feign v تظاهر
fatherly adj أبوي	fellow n زميل
fatigue n ملل	fellowship n منحة جامعية
fatten v سمن	felon n مجرم
fatty adj بدين	felony n جريمة
faucet n حنفية	female n نثى
fault n خلل	feminine adj المؤنث
faulty adj ناقص	fence n مبارزة بالسيف
favor n فضل	fencing n مبارزة بالسيف
favorable adj واعد	fend v تصرف
favorite adj محبوب	fend off v صد
fear n خوف	fender n وقاء
fearful adj خائف	ferment v خمر
feasible adj ملائم	ferment n خميرة
feast n موسم	ferocious adj ضار
feat n عمل بطولي	ferocity n ضراوة
feather n ريشة	ferry n معدية
feature n ميزة	fertile adj خصيب
February n شباط	fertility n خصب
fed up adj ضجر	fertilize v أخصب

F

fervent _adj_ حماسي	fighter _n_ المقاتل
fester _v_ تقيح	figure _n_ قد قوام
festive _adj_ احتفالي	figure out _v_ عرف
festivity _n_ مراسيم إحتفالية	file _v_ نقح, هذب
fetid _adj_ نتن	file _n_ إضبارة, ملف
fetus _n_ جنين	fill _v_ حشا السن
feud _n_ عداء	filling _n_ حشوة السن
fever _n_ حمى	film _n_ طبقة رقيقة
feverish _adj_ حمي	filter _n_ مصفاة
few _adj_ بعض	filter _v_ صفى
fewer _adj_ بسيط	filth _n_ نتانة
fiancé _n_ خطيب	filthy _adj_ قذر
fiber _n_ خيط	fin _n_ زعنفة السمك
fickle _adj_ متقلب	final _adj_ نهائي
fiction _n_ قصة	finalize _v_ جمل
fictitious _adj_ خرافي	finance _v_ مول
fiddle _n_ كمان	financial _adj_ مالي
fidelity _n_ إخلاص	find _iv_ يلاقى
field _n_ ملعب	find out _v_ اكتشف
fierce _adj_ ضار	fine _n_ نهاية
fiery _adj_ ناري	fine _v_ غرم
fifteen _adj_ خمسة عشر	fine _adv_ في أحسن حال
fifth _adj_ خمس	fine _adj_ لطيف
fifty _adj_	finger _n_ إصبع
fifty-fifty _adv_ تساوى	fingernail _n_ ظفر
fig _n_ تين	fingerprint _n_ بصمة
fight _iv_ يتقاتل	fingertip _n_ البنانة
fight _n_ مقاومة	finish _v_ فرغ

Finland *n* فنلندا	flamboyant *adj* صارخ
Finnish *adj* فنلندي	flame *n* متوهج
fire *v* أطلق , أشعل	flammable *adj* سريع الأشتعال
fire *n* نار	flank *n* خاصرة
firearm *n* قطعة سلاح	flare *n* نار
firecracker *n* مفرقعة نارية	flare-up *v* إستشاط غضبا
firefighter *n* إطْفائيّ	flash *n* وميض
fireman *n* إطفائي	flashlight *n* الضوء الومضي
fireplace *n* مدفأة	flashy *adj* مبهرج
firewood *n* حطب	flat *n* إطار ضارب
fireworks *n* الألعاب نارية	flat *adj* انبطاحا
firm *adj* قاس	flatten *v* سطح
firm *n* شركة تجارية	flatter *v* طرى
firmness *n* تحمل	flattery *n* إطراء
first *adj* أولي	flaunt *v* تبرج
fish *n* سمك	flavor *n* توابل
fisherman *n* صياد سمك	flaw *n* نقص
fishy *adj* مشبوه	flawless *adj* بلا عيب
fist *n* قبضة	flea *n* برغوث
fit *n* نوبة	flee *iv* يتلاشى
fit *v* ناسب	fleece *n* جزة صوف
fitness *n* ملاءمة	fleet *n* أسطول
fitting *adj* مناسب	fleeting *adj* عابر
five *adj* الخامس من	flesh *n* لحم
fix *v* حدد	flex *v* ثنى
fjord *n* زقاق بحري	flexible *adj* لدن
flag *n* راية	flicker *v* اضطرب
flagpole *n* سارِيَةُ العَلَمِ	flier *n* نشرة إعلانية

fly iv يطير	**flight** n رحلة جوية , طيران
fly n ذبابة	**flimsy** adj رقيق
foam n رغوة	**flip** v (نقر (بطرف الإصبع
focus n بؤرة	**flirt** v غازل
focus on v يركز على	**float** v عوم
foe n عدو	**flock** n قطيع
fog n ضباب	**flog** v جلد
foggy adj ضبابي	**flood** v طوفان
foil v هزم	**floodgate** n سد
fold v طوى	**flooding** n فيض
folder n ملف	**floodlight** n إضاءة
folks n أنسباء المرء	**floor** n قعر
folksy adj شَعْبِيّ	**flop** n فشل
follow v تبع	**floss** n لفة حرير
follower n المريد	**flour** n دقيق
folly n حماقة	**flourish** v ازدهر
fond adj مغرم, محب	**flow** v جرى
fondle v لاطف	**flow** n تيار
fondness n إعزاز	**flower** n زهرة
food n طعام	**flowerpot** n أصيص ورود
foodstuff n مادة غذائية	**flu** n الإنفلونزا
fool v خادع	**fluctuate** v تموج
fool adj مجنون	**fluently** adv بتدفق
foolproof adj غير خطر	**fluid** n مائع
foot n قدم	**flunk** v خفق
football n كرة القدم	**flush** v تورد
footnote n هامش	**flute** n الفلوت
footprint n أثر القدم	**flutter** v رفرف

F

footstep n خطوة	forget v نسى
footwear n حذاء	forgivable adj مَعْذُور
for pre لأجل	forgive v سامح
forbid iv يحظر	forgiveness n مغفرة
force n ضغط	fork n مفرق طرق
force v تجبر	form n هيئة,
forceful adj قوي	formal adj أشكلي
forcibly adv بنشاط	formality n شكلانية
forecast iv يتكهن	formalize v جعله رسميا
forefront n صدارة	formally adv رسميا
foreground n أمام	format n بنية
forehead n جبهة	formation n تنشكيل
foreign adj أجنبي, غريب	former adj سالف
foreigner n أجنبي	formerly adv سابقا
foreman n كبير العمال	formidable adj هائل
foremost adj رئيسي	formula n صيغة
foresee iv يتنبأ بـ	forsake iv يتخلى عن
foreshadow v أذن ب	fort n حصن
foresight n بصيرة	forthcoming adj قادم
forest n غابة	forthright adj مباشر
foretaste n دلالة منذرة	fortify v قوى
foretell v تكهن	fortitude n صرامة
forever adv إلى الأبد	fortress n معقل
forewarn v حظر	fortunate adj سعيد
foreword n تصدير	fortune n حظ
forfeit v فقد	forty adj الأربعون
forge v طرق الحديد	forward adv أمامي
forgery n تزوير	fossil n الأحفور

foster v تبنى, شجع

foul adj رطب

foundation n مؤسسة

founder n منشئ

foundry n مسبك

fountain n ينبوع

four adj الرابع

fourteen adj الرابع عشر

fourth adj رابع

fox n ثعلب

foxy adj ماكر

fraction n كسر

fracture n كسر العظم

fragile adj هش

fragment n شظية

fragrance n شذا

fragrant adj أرج

frail adj سهل الإنقياد

frailty n ضعف

frame n هيكل, إطار

frame v أطر, ضبط

framework n الإطار, هيكل

France n فرنسا

franchise n حق الانتخاب

frank adj صريح

frankly adv بصراحة حقا

frankness n صرامة

frantic adj مسعور

fraternal adj أخوي

fraternity n نادي رجال

fraud n خداع,

fraudulent adj مخادع

freckle n نمش

freckled adj ذو نمش

free v حرر, تخلص من

free adj مطلق الحرية

freedom n تحرر

freeway n شارع المرور السريع

freeze iv يتجمد

freezer n المجمد

freezing adj التجليد,

freight n اجرة الشحن

French adj فرنسي

frenetic adj مسعور

frenzied adj مسعور

frenzy n سعر

frequency n التكرر

frequent adj متكرر الحدوث

frequent v تردد الى مكان

fresh adj جديد

freshen v تعيش

freshness n طراوة

friar n راهب

friction n حك, احتكاك

Friday n الجمعة

fried adj محمر

friend n صديق
friendship n صداقة
fries n قلا
frigate n بارجة
fright n رعب
frighten v خوف
frightening adj مفزع
frigid adj فاتر
fringe n الحدود , حافة
frivolous adj طائش
frog n ضفدع
from pre من
front n جبهة
front adj أمامي
frontage n واجهة مبنى
frontier n حد
frost n صقيع
frostbite n سفح الجليد
frostbitten adj يؤذي بالصقيع
frosty adj بارد جدا
frown v قطب
frozen adj مجمد
frugal adj مقتصد
frugality n اقتصاد
fruit n محصول
fruitful adj مثمر
fruity adj فاكهي
frustrate v ثبط

frustration n إحباط
fry v قلا
frying pan n مقلي
fuel n وقود
fuel v زود بالوقود
fugitive n هارب
fulfill v نجز
fulfillment n تحقيق
full adj مطلق
fully adv تماما
fumes n بخار
fumigate v دخن
fun n مزاح
function n وظيفة
fund n رأسمال
fund v رصد مبلغا
fundamental adj أصلي
funds n أموال
funeral n دفن
fungus n فطر
funny adj مسل
fur n فرو
furious adj غاضب
furiously adv بغضب
furnace n فرن
furnish v جهز
furnishings n تأثيث
furniture n فرش

F

furor n فضيحة

furrow n أخدود

furry adj فروي

further adv من ناحية أخرى

furthermore adv علاوة على ذلك

fury n حنق

fuse n قاطع تيار

fusion n صهر

fuss n اهتياج

fussy adj سريع الإهتياج

futile adj عقيم

futility n عقم

future n مستقبل

fuzzy adj غامض

G

gadget n آلة صغيرة

gag n نكتة

gag v نكت

gage v راهن

gain v نجز,

gain n ثمرة

gal n القالون

galaxy n مجرة فضائية

gale n عاصفة,

gall bladder n كيس المرارة

gallant adj مؤدب

gallery n معرض

gallon n غالون

gallop v عدا بسرعة

gallows n مشنقة

galvanize v كلفن

gamble v قامر

game n لعبة

gang n عصابة

gangrene n غرغرينا

gangster n قاطع طريق

gap n ممر ضيق , فجوة

garage n ورشة عمل

garbage n نفاية

garden n حديقة

gardener n بستاني

gargle v تغرغر بالماء

garland n تاج

garlic n ثوم

garment n ملابس

garnish v زخرف

garnish n زينة

garrison n موقع عسكري

garrulous adj ثرثار

gas n بنزين

gash n جرح بليغ

gasoline n الغازولين	gentleness n لطافة
gasp v لهث,	genuflect v حنى الركبة تعبدا
gastric adj معدي	genuine adj حقيقي
gate n ممر ضيق	geography n جغرافية
gather v تجمع	geology n عالم بطبقات الأرض
gathering n جلسة,	geometry n علم الهندسة
gauge v تبأر	germ n جرثومة
gauze n ضمادة خفيفة	German adj ألماني
gaze v تفرس	Germany n ألمانيا
gear n ملابس	germinate v برعم
geese n أوز	gerund n صيغة الفعل
gem n جوهرة	gestation n مرحلة الحمل
gender n جنس	gesticulate v وما أ
gene n جينة	gesture n إشارة
general n جنرال	get iv ينال
generalize v عمم	get along v تقدم
generate v ولد	get away v انطلق
generation n تكاثر	get back v استرد
generator n مرجل	get by v تدبر
generic adj شامل	get down v نزل
generosity n سخاء	get down to v يبدي إهتمام
genetic adj وراثي	get in v دخل
genial adj ودي	get off v فر
genius n موهبة	get out v انصرف
genocide n إبادة جماعية	get over v تغلب
genteel adj متميز	get together v كدس
gentle adj دمث	get up v تسلق
gentleman n مؤدب	geyser n مرجل تسخين

G

ghastly *adj* مروع	**glasses** *n* نظارات
ghost *n* شبح	**glassware** *n* آنية زجاجية
giant *n* المارد,	**gleam** *n* ضوء ضعيف
gift *n* موهبة	**gleam** *v* أضاء بضعف
gifted *adj* موهوب	**glide** *v* نزل
gigantic *adj* عظيم	**glimmer** *n* وميض
giggle *v* ضحك	**glimpse** *n* لمحة
gimmick *n* وسيلة للتحايل	**glimpse** *v* لمح
ginger *n* زنجبيل	**glitter** *v* تألق
gingerly *adv* رقيق	**globe** *n* الكرة الارضية
giraffe *n* زرافة	**globule** *n* كرية دم
girl *n* فتاة	**gloom** *n* غم
girlfriend *n* صديقة	**gloomy** *adj* متجهم
give *iv* يعطى	**glorify** *v* أجل
give away *v* تخلص منه	**glorious** *adj* مجيد
give back *v* دعم	**glory** *n* كبرياء
give in *v* أعطى	**gloss** *n* لمعان
give out *v* خرج,	**glossary** *n* قائمة كلمات
give up *v* استسلم	**glossy** لامع
glacier *n* نهر الجليد	**glove** *n* قفاز
glad *adj* سعيد	**glow** *v* توهج
gladiator *n* مجالد	**glucose** *n* جلوكوز
glamorous *adj* باهر	**glue** *n* غراء
glance *v* أومض	**glue** *v* غرا
glance *n* لمحة	**glut** *n* وفرة
gland *n* غدة	**glutton** *n* نهمة
glare *n* حملقة	**gnaw** *v* قرض
glass *n* كوب	**go** *iv* يذهب

G

go ahead v تقدم

go away v ذهب

go back v دعم

go down v ,خسر

go in v دخل

go on v واصل

go out v خرج

go over v خرق القانونة

go through v فتش

go under v انهار

go up v صعد

goad v همز

goal n سجل هدف , مرمى

goalkeeper n حارس المرمى

goat n عنزة

gobble v التهم

God n الخالق

goddess n ربة الاهة

godless adj ملحد

goggles n نظارات للوقاية

gold n الذهب

golden adj ذهبي

good adj كريم

good-looking adj أنيق

goodness n طيب القلب

goods n بضاعة

goodwill n رغبة حسنة

goof v أخطأ

goof n الأبله

goose n أوز

gorge n حلق

gorgeous adj رائع

gorilla n سفاح

gory adj تفرج

gospel n إنجيل

gossip v ثرثر

gossip n نمام

gout n نقرس

govern v حكم

government n حكومة

governor n حاكم

gown n لباس

grab v اختطف

grace n سمو

graceful adj كيس

gracious adj كريم

grade n منزلة

gradual adj متدرج

graduate v تدرج

graduation n حفل التخرج

graft v إبتز المال

graft n تطعيم النبات

grain n بذرة

gram n غرام

grammar n (قواعد (اللغة

grand adj فخم

G

grandchild n	حفيد
granddad n	جد
grandfather n	جد
grandmother n	جدة
grandparents n	أجداد
grandson n	حفيد
granite n	غرانيت
granny n	جدة
grant v	اعترف
grant n	هبة
grape n	عنب
grapefruit n	ليمون الجنة
grapevine n	كرمة اشاعة
graphic adj	نابض
grasp n	مقبض
grasp v	قبض على, فهم
grass n	عشب
grassroots adj	أساسي
grateful adj	مقر بالجميل
gratify v	أستمتع
gratifying adj	ممتع
gratitude n	عرفان بالفضل
gratuity n	عطية
grave adj	متزن
grave n	قبر
gravel n	حصى
gravely adv	بجدية
gravestone n	الشاهد

graveyard n	مقبرة
gravitate v	انجذب
gravity n	جاذبية الارض
gravy n	صلصة اللحم
gray adj	أشيب
graze v	رعى الماشية
graze n	يسيم
grease v	أزال الشحم
grease n	شحم
greasy adj	مدهن
great adj	عظيم
greatness n	عظمة
Greece n	يونان
greed n	شره
greedy adj	أناني
Greek adj	يوناني
green adj	قليل الخبرة
green bean n	فاصوليا خضراء
greenhouse n	دفيئة
Greenland n	الجزيرة الخضراء
greet v	حيا
greetings n	ترحيبات
gregarious adj	اجتماعي
grenade n	قذيفة
greyhound n	السلوقي
grief n	كآبة
grievance n	شكوى
grieve v	أكمد

grill v شوى

grill n مشواة

grim adj متجهم

grimace n كشرة

grime n سخام

grind iv يطحن

grip v قبض على

grip n قبضة

gripe n مظلمة

grisly adj مخيف

groan v أن

groan n أنين

groceries n سلع

groin n أربية

groom n عريس

groove n أخدود

gross adj جاف, فادح

grossly adv على نحو فادح

grotesque adj غريب

grotto n غار

grouch v تذمر,

grouchy adj متذمر

ground n أرض

ground floor n طابق أرضي

groundless adj لا أساس له

groundwork n العمل التحضيري

group n قطيع

grow iv ينمو

grow up v زرع,

growl v هدر

grown-up n البالغ

growth n نماء

grudge n حقد

grudgingly adv بمرارة

gruelling adj إشْكالِيّ

gruesome adj مروع

grumble v دمدم

grumpy adj غاضب

guarantee v كفل

guarantee n كفالة, ضمان

guarantor n الكفيل, ضامن

guard n حارس

guardian n قيم

guerrilla n حرب العصابات

guess v خمن

guess n تخمين

guest n ضيف

guidance n إرشاد

guide v أرشد,

guide n مرشد

guidebook n دليل

guidelines n الدليل الموجز

guild n نقابة

guile n مكر

guillotine n مقصلة

guilt n إثم

guilty adj مذنب
guise n هيئة
guitar n قيثارة
gulf n هاوية,
gull n نورس
gullible adj ساذج
gulp v ارتشف
gulp n بلعة
gulp down v ابتلع
gum n صمغ, لثة
gun n مدفع,
gun down v يجرح بطلقة نارية
gunfire n اطلاق المدافع
gunman n المسلح ببندقية
gunpowder n بارود
gunshot n إطلاق نار
gust n عاصفة
gusto n ميل
gusty adj صاخب
gut n وعاء جلدي
guts n جرأة
gutter n مزراب
guy n سخر
guzzle v التهم
gymnasium n قاعة رياضية
gynecology n طب النساء
gypsy n غجر

H

habit n بذلة ركوب الخيل
habitable adj صالح للسكن
habitual adj اعتيادي
hack v ولع ب
haggle v ساوم
hail n برد
hail v حيا
hair n شعر
hairbrush n فرشاة للشعر
haircut n الحلا قة
hairdo n تسريحة
hairdresser n المزين
hairpiece n شعر مستعار
hairy adj زغبي
half n نصف
half adj نصفى
hall n بيت ريفي
hallucinate v هلوس
hallway n رواق
halt v ترنح
halve v شطر
ham n للحم خنزير مدخن
hamburger n شطيرة لحم
hamlet n قرية صغيرة
hammer n مدقة

hand n إشراف	**happening** n حادثة
hand down v انتقل	**happiness** n السعادة السماوية
hand in v يدا بيد	**happy** adj مسرور
hand out v وزع	**harass** v أرهق
hand over v تخلى	**harassment** n إزعاج
handbag n حقيبة	**harbor** n ميناء
handbook n كتيب	**hard** adj قاس
handcuff n قيد	**harden** v تحمل المشاق
handcuffs n أصفاد	**hardly** adv بالجهد
handful n حفنة	**hardness** n قسوة
handgun n طَبَنْجَة	**hardship** n أذى
handicap n إعاقة	**hardware** n أدوات منزلية
handle v عالج موضوعا	**hardwood** n خشب قاس
handle n مقبض الة	**hardy** adj جريء
handmade adj صناعة يدوية	**hare** n أرنب الوحشية
handout n حسنة	**harm** v آذى
handrail n درابزون	**harm** n أذى
handshake n مصافحة	**harmful** adj مؤذ
handsome adj حسن	**harmless** adj بريئ
handwritting n كتابة	**harmonize** v أتلف
handy adj بارع	**harmony** n الانسجام
hang iv أدلى	**harp** n قيثار
hang around v تسكع	**harpoon** n حربون
hang on v انتظر	**harrowing** adj مؤلم
hang up v شنق	**harsh** adj لاذع
hanger n الجلاد	**harshly** adv بخشونة
hangup n استحواذ	**harshness** n فظاظة
happen v حدث	**harvest** n ثمرة الجهد

H

harvest v كسب	**head** n أعلى الشئ
hashish n حشيش مخدر	**head for** v اتجه
hassle v تشاجر	**headache** n صداع
hassle n صراع	**heading** n رأسية
haste n تسرع	**head-on** adv رئيسي
hasten v استعجل	**headphones** n سماعة الرأس
hastily adv بسرعة	**headquarters** n القيادة العامة
hasty adj سريع الغضب	**headway** n تقدم
hat n قبعة	**heal** v برىء
hatchet n البليطة	**healer** n المعالج
hate v أبغض	**health** n الصحة
hateful adj بغيض	**healthy** adj في تمام الصحة
hatred n حزازة	**heap** n تل
haughty adj مغرور	**heap** v كدس
haul v جذب	**hearing** n إدلاء بشهادة
haunt v تردد على	**hearsay** n إشاعة
have iv تضمن	**hearse** n عربة الموتى
have to v وجب	**heart** n لب
haven n حمى	**heartbeat** n نبض القلب
havoc n خراب	**heartburn** n حرقة في المعدة
hawk n صقر	**hearten** v شجع
haystack n كومة قش	**heartfelt** adj الإخلاص
hazard n تصادف	**hearth** n بيت
hazardous adj خطير	**heartless** adj جبان
haze n سديم	**hearty** adj قلبي
hazelnut n بندق	**heat** v ثور
hazy adj ضبابي	**heat** n احترار
he pro هو من	**heater** n مدفأة

heathen n الوثني	**hemorrhage** n نزيف دم
heating n عنف	**hen** n أنثى الطير
heatstroke n ضربة الحر	**hence** adv سنتين من الآن
heaven n الجنة	**henchman** n تابع أمين
heavenly adj رائع	**her** adj خاص بالمفردة الغائبة
heaviness n ارتفاع	**herald** v أذيع
heavy adj بطيء	**herald** n الرائد
heckle v قاطع بالكلام	**herb** n عشب
hectic adj عصيبي	**here** adv الآن
heed v اهتم	**hereafter** adv بعد
heel n كعب	**hereby** adv بموجب هذا القانون
height n أرض مرتفعة	**hereditary** adj ذو لقب
heighten v برز	**heresy** n إلحاد
heinous adj شائن	**heretic** adj زنديق
heir n وارث	**heritage** n إرث
heiress n وريثة	**hermetic** adj سحري
heist n صه	**hermit** n الناسك
helicopter n طائرة عامودية	**hernia** n فتاق مرض
hell n جحيم	**hero** n الشخصية الرئيسية
hello e أهلا	**heroic** adj بطل
helm n إدارة	**heroin** n الهيرويين مخدر
help v عاون	**heroism** n بطولة
help n معاون	**hers** pro خاصتها
helper n المساعد	**herself** pro نفسها حالتها السوية
helpful adj مساعد	**hesitant** adj ترددي
helpless adj بائس	**hesitate** v تثنى
hem n تنحنح	**hesitation** n تردد
hemisphere n عالم, نصف كرة	**heyday** n عمر الشباب

hiccup *n* حازوقة	hire *v* ثنى
hidden *adj* خفي	his *adj* ضمير الغائب المتصل
hide *iv* أخفى	his *pro* خاصته
hideaway *n* ملاذ	Hispanic *adj* إسبانى
hideous *adj* فظيع	hiss *v* إستهجن بالوسهسة
hierarchy *n* رتب	historian *n* مؤرخ
high *adj* ثمل	history *n* تاريخ
highlight *n* العناوين الرئيسية	hit *n* إصابة, ارتطام
highly *adv* بإرتفاع مبالغ	hit *iv* أصاب
Highness *n* سمو	hit back *v* صد
highway *n* طريق سريع	hitch *n* تأخير
hijack *v* خطف	hitch up *v* توقف
hijack *n* إختطاف طائرة	hitchhike *n* سافر متطفلا
hijacker *n* خاطف	hitherto *adv* حتى هنا
hike *v* تنزه	hive *n* قفير خلية نحل
hilarious *adj* جذل	hoard *v* خزن
hill *n* تل	hoarse *adj* أجش
hillside *n* جانب التل	hoax *n* خدعة
hilly *adj* جبلي	hobby *n* صقر
hilt *n* عكاز	hog *n* خنزير
hinder *v* عاق	hoist *v* رفع
hindrance *n* مانع	hoist *n* رافعة
hindsight *n* الإدراك المتأخر	hold *iv* يملك
hinge *v* توقف	hold back *v* تأخر
hinge *n* مفصلة	hold on to *v* أمسك بقوة
hint *n* أثر	hold out *v* قاوم
hint *v* لمح	hold up *v* عطل
hip *n* ثمر الورد البرى	holdup *n* هجوم مفاجئ

hole n ثقب	**hooligan** n سفاح
holiday n عيد	**hop** v غادر
holiness n قداسة	**hope** n أمل
Holland n هولندة	**hopeful** adj مفعم بالأمل
hollow adj غائر	**hopefully** adv بأمل
holocaust n محرقة يهود أوروبا	**hopeless** adj يائس
holy adj تقي	**horizon** n الأ فق
homage n احترام	**horizontal** adj أفقي
home n بيت	**hormone** n هورمون
homeland n وطن	**horn** n بوقة
homeless adj مشرد	**horrendous** adj رهيب
homely adj بيتي	**horrible** adj فظيع
homemade adj صناعة البيت	**horrify** v أرعب
homesick adj حنين للوطن	**horror** n رعب
hometown n مسقط رأس	**horse** n حصان
homework n الواجب المنزلي	**hose** n جورب
homicide n القاتل، قتل	**hospital** n مستشفى
homily n عظة دينية	**hospitality** n كرم
honest adj برئ،	**host** n مضيف
honesty n براءة	**hostage** n رهينة
honey n حلو،	**hostess** n مضيفة طيران
honeymoon n شهر العسل	**hostile** adj معاد
honk v بوق	**hostility** n خصومة
honor n احترام	**hot** adj متحمس
hood n قلنسوة،	**hotel** n الفندق
hoodlum n سفاح	**hound** n كلب صيد
hoof n حافر	**hour** n ساعة
hook n عقاف	**hourly** adv أي لحظة

H

house n بيت
household n سكان البيت
housekeeper n مدبرة المنزل
housewife n ربة المنزل,
housework n عمل البيت
hover v رفرف
how adv بكم
however c لكن
howl v عوى
howl n ولولة
hub n محور
huddle v احتشد
hug v تشبث
hug n عناق
huge adj بكل ضخامة
hull n هيكل السفينة
hum v همهم
human adj آدمي
human being n إنسان
humanities n العلوم الأدبية
humankind n الجنس البشرى
humble adj وضيع,
humbly adv باحتشام
humid adj رطب
humidity n رطوبة
humiliate v ذل
humility n تواضع
humor n دعابة

humorous adj فكه
hump n سنام
hunch n سنام
hunchback n الأحدب
hunched adj مُحْدَوْدِب
hundred adj المائة
hundredth adj بالغ جزءا من المئة
hunger n جوع
hungry adj جائع
hunt v اصطاد
hunter n صياد
hunting n مطاردة
hurdle n عقبة
hurl v رشق
hurricane n إعصار مداري إ
hurriedly adv على نحو سريع
hurry v أسرع
hurry up v سرع
hurt iv يجرح
hurt adj مجروح
hurtful adj مضر
husband n زوج قرين
hush n سكوت
hush up v كتم
husky adj أجش
hustle n كوخ
hut n كوخ
hydraulic adj هيدروليكي

hydrogen n هيدروجين	**ideal** adj خيالي
hyena n ضبع	**identical** adj مماثل
hygiene n علم الصحة,	**identify** v تماثل
hymn n ترنيمة	**identity** n مطابقة
hyphen n واصلة	**ideology** n أيديولوجية
hypnosis n مغناطيسي	**idiom** n مصطلح
hypnotize v نوم مغناطيسيا	**idiot** n الأبله
hypocrisy n نفاق	**idiotic** adj أبلة
hypocrite adj منافق	**idle** adj كسول
hypothesis n افتراض	**idol** n معبود
hysteria n هستيريا	**idolatry** n الوثنية
hysterical adj هستيري	**if** c لو
	ignite v أشعل
	ignorance n جهل
	ignorant adj جاهل

I

	ignore v تجاهل
	ill adj مريض
	illegal adj غير شرعي
ice n جليد	**illegible** adj مستغلق
ice cream n دندرمة	**illegitimate** adj غير شرعي
ice cube n مكعب ثلجى	**illicit** adj محرم
ice skate v تزلج على الجليد	**illiterate** adj أمي
iceberg n جبل جليد	**illness** n مرض
icebox n ثلاجة	**illogical** adj غير منطقي
ice-cold adj مثلج	**illuminate** v أضاء
icon n أيقونة	**illusion** n وهم
icy adj جليدي	**illustrate** v وضح
idea n فكرة	**illustration** n توضيح

illustrious *adj* شهير	immutable *adj* ثابت
image *n* صورة	impact *n* تأثير
imagination *n* خيال	impact *v* اصطدم
imagine *v* تخيل	impair *v* أضعف
imbalance *n* لاتوازن	impartial *adj* نزيه
imitate *v* قلد	impatience *n* برم
imitation *n* تقليد	impatient *adj* نفاذ صبر
immaculate *adj* نقي	impeccable *adj* معصوم
immature *adj* فج	impediment *n* إعاقة
immaturity *n* عدم نضوج	impending *adj* قريب
immediately *adv* فورا	imperfection *n* نقص
immense *adj* ضخم	imperial *adj* إمبراطوري
immensity *n* اتساع	imperialism *n* استعمار
immerse *v* غمر	impersonal *adj* مجهول
immersion *n* انغمار	impertinence *n* وقاحة
immigrant *n* مهاجر	impertinent *adj* وقح
immigrate *v* هاجر	impetuous *adj* متهور
immigration *n* اغتراب	implacable *adj* عنيد
imminent *adj* وشيك	implant *v* غرس
immobile *adj* ثابت	implement *v* حقق
immobilize *v* جمد	implicate *v* ورط
immoral *adj* فاسق	implication *n* توريط
immorality *n* فسوق	implicit *adj* ضمني
immortal *adj* خالد	implore *v* توسل
immortality *n* خلود	imply *v* لمح
immune *adj* منيع	impolite *adj* فظ
immunity *n* مناعة	import *v* استورد
immunize *v* حصن	importance *n* خطر

importation n استيراد	inaccurate adj خاطئ
impose v فرض	inadequate adj غير ملائم
imposing adj فخم	inadmissible adj مرفوض
imposition n التوجب	inappropriate adj غير ملائم
impossibility n استحالة	inasmuch as c نظرا لأن
impossible adj مستحيل	inaugurate v دشن
impotent adj ضعيف	inauguration n تدشين
impound v حجز	incalculable n متقلب
impoverished adj أفقر	incapable adj عاجز
impractical adj غير عملي	incapacitate v أضعف
imprecise adj غير دقيق	incarcerate v سجن
impress v أثر	incense n بخور
impressive adj مثير للإعجاب	incentive n مكافأة
imprison v سجن	inception n بداية
improbable adj غير محتمل	incessant adj متواصل
impromptu adv مرتجل	inch n بوصة
improper adj بذيء	incident n حادث
improve v حسن	incidentally adv عرضا
improvement n تحسين	incision n شق
improvise v ارتجل	incite v حرض
impulse n اندفاع	incitement n تحريض
impulsive adj مندفع	inclination n انحناءة
impunity n حصانة	incline v إنحنى
impure adj قذر	include v تضمن
in pre في	inclusive adv ضمنا
in depth adv بعمق	incoherent adj متنافر
inability n عجز	income n دخل
inaccessible adj متعذر بلوغه	incoming adj الوارد

incompatible *adj* متضارب

incompetence *n* عجز

incompetent *adj* عاجز

incomplete *adj* ناقص

inconsistent *adj* متضارب

inconvenient *adj* مضايق

incorporate *v* اندمج

incorrect *adj* خاطئ

incorrigible *adj* عنيد

increase *v* تزايد

increase *n* زيادة

increasing *adj* متزايد

incredible *adj* لا يصدق

increment *n* زيادة

incriminate *v* جرم

incur *v* تحمل

incurable *adj* المعضول

indecency *n* قلة إحتشام

indecision *n* تردد

indecisive *adj* متردد

indeed *adv* حقا

indefinite *adj* مجهول

indemnify *v* عوض

indemnity *n* تعويض

independence *n* استقلال

independent *adj* مستقل

index *n* دليل

indicate *v* أشار

indication *n* دلالة

indict *v* إتهم

indifference *n* لا مبالاه

indifferent *adj* لامبال

indigent *adj* فقير

indigestion *n* عسر الهضم

indirect *adj* غير مباشر

indiscreet *adj* طائش

indiscretion *n* طيش

indispensable *adj* ضروري

indisposed *adj* متوعك

indisputable *adj* لايقبل الجدل

indivisible *adj* لا يتجزأ

indoctrinate *v* لقن

indoor *adv* داخلي

induce *v* أقنع

indulge *v* تساهل

indulgent *adj* متساهل

industrious *adj* كادح

industry *n* صناعة

ineffective *adj* باطل

inefficient *adj* غير كفؤ

inept *adj* أحمق

inequality *n* تفاوت

inevitable *adj* محتوم

inexcusable *adj* متعذر

inexpensive *adj* رخيص

inexperienced *adj* غير خبير

inexplicable *adj* متعذر تفسيره

infallible *adj* معصوم

infamous *adj* شائن

infancy *n* طفولة

infant *n* طفل

infantry *n* المشاه

infect *v* عدى

infection *n* عدوى

infectious *adj* معد

infer *v* استنتج

inferior *adj* ثانوي

infertile *adj* قاحل

infested *adj* أزعج

infidelity *n* كفر

infiltrate *v* رشح

infiltration *n* ارتشاح

infinite *adj* مطلق

infirmary *n* مستشفى

inflammation *n* اشتعال

inflate *v* نفخ

inflation *n* تضخم

inflexible *adj* قاس

inflict *v* أصاب

influence *n* أثر

influential *adj* مؤثر

influenza *n* إنفلونزا

influx *n* تيار

inform *v* خبر

informal *adj* غير رسمي

informality *n* العامية

informant *n* راوية

information *n* معلومات

informer *n* مخبر

infraction *n* مخالفة

infrequent *adj* نادر

infuriate *v* غضب

infusion *n* سكب

ingenuity *n* إبداع

ingest *v* ابتلع

ingot *n* سكيبة

ingrained *adj* متأصل

ingratiate *v* تودد

ingratitude *n* كفران

ingredient *n* عنصر

inhabit *v* سكن

inhabitable *adj* صالح للسكن

inhabitant *n* مقيم

inhale *v* استنشق

inherit *v* ورث

inheritance *n* إرث

inhibit *v* منع

inhuman *adj* وحشي

initial *adj* ابتدائي

initially *adv* بداية

initials *n* استهلالي

initiate *v* بادر

initiative n مبادرة	**insanity** n جنون
inject v حقن	**insatiable** adj نهم
injection n حقنة	**inscription** n كتابة
injure v جرح	**insect** n حشرة
injurious adj ضار	**insecurity** n عدم الأمان
injury n جرح	**insensitive** adj غير حساس
injustice n ظالم	**inseparable** adj متلازم
ink n حبر	**insert** v أدخل
inkling n شك	**insertion** n إدخال
inlaid adj مرصع	**inside** adj باطن
inland adv في الداخل	**inside** pre داخل
inland adj داخلي	**inside out** adv بالمقلوب
in-laws n أصهار	**insignificant** adj ضئيل
inmate n نزيل	**insincere** adj منافق
inn n نزل	**insincerity** n نفاق
innate adj فطري	**insinuate** v دس
inner adj داخلي	**insinuation** v تلميح
innocence n براءة	**insipid** adj لا طعم له
innocent adj بريئ	**insist** v ألح
innovation n ابتكار	**insistence** n إصرار
innuendo n تلميح	**insolent** adj متغطرس
innumerable adj لايعد	**insoluble** adj لايذوب
input n مساهمة	**insomnia** n ارق
inquest n استنطاق	**inspect** v فحص
inquire v سأل	**inspection** n فحص
inquiry n استعلام	**inspector** n مفتش
inquisition n تحقيق	**inspiration** n إيحاء
insane adj مخبول	**inspire** v ألهم

instability n عدم استقرار	integrity n سلامة
install v ينصب	intelligent adj ذكي
installation n تنصيب,	intend v قصد
installment n قسط	intense adj حاد
instance n مثل	intensify v قوى
instant n فوري	intensity n قوة
instantly adv فورا	intensive adj كثيف
instead adv بدلا من	intention n قصد
instigate v بادر	intercede v تشفع
instil v غرس	intercept v اعترض
instinct n غريزة	intercession n تسوية
institute v معهد	interchange v بادل
institution n مؤسسة	interchange n تبادل
instruct v علم	interest n اهتمام
instructor n معلم	interested adj مهتم
insufficient adj ناقص	interesting adj ممتع
insulate v عزل	interfere v تدخل
insulation n عزل	interference n تدخل
insult v أهان	interior adj داخلي
insult n إهانة	interlude n فترة فاصلة
insurance n تأمين	intermediary n واسطة
insure v أمن	intern v سجن
insurgency n عصيان	interpret v فسر
insurrection n انتفاضة	interpretation n ترجمة
intact adj سليم	interpreter n مترجم
intake n استيعاب	interrogate v استجوب
integrate v دمج	interrupt v اعترض
integration n توحيد	interruption n إعاقة

intersect v تتقاطع

intertwine v جدل

interval n فاصل

intervene v تدخل

intervention n تدخل

interview n مقابلة

intestine n أمعاء مفرد

intimacy n مودة

intimate adj حميم

intimidate v أرعب

intolerable adj لا يحتمل

intolerance n تعصب

intoxicated adj سكران

intravenous adj وريدي

intrepid adj جريء

intricate adj معقد

intrigue n كيْد

intriguing adj شاذ

intrinsic adj جوهري

introduce v يُدخل

introduction n مقدّمة

introvert adj انطوائي

intrude v يتطفّل

intruder n المتطفل

intrusion n تطفُّل

intuition n حَدْس

inundate v يَغْمر

invade v يغزو

invader n غاز

invalid n باطل

invalidate v يُلْغِي

invaluable adj نَفِيس

invasion n غزو

invent v يلفّق

invention n تلفيق

inventory n جرد

invest v استثمر

investigate v يحقّق

investigation n تحقيق

investment n استثمار

investor n الممول

invincible adj منيع

invisible adj خفيّ

invitation n دعوة

invite v يدعو

invoice n فاتورة

invoke v يتوسّل

involve v يورّط

involved v متورّط

involvement n تورط

inward adj داخليّ

inwards adv داخلا

iodine n اليُود

irate adj غاضب

Ireland n إيرلندا

Irish adj إيرلندي

iron *n* حديد

iron *v* يكوي

ironic *adj* تهكّمي

irony *n* سخرية

irrational *adj* لا عقلاني

irrefutable *adj* لا يُدْحَض

irregular *adj* شاذّ

irrelevant *adj* غير متصل

irreparable *adj* متعذر إصلاحه

irresistible *adj* لا يُقاوَم

irrespective *adj* غير منتبه

irreversible *adj* لا يقلب

irrevocable *adj* نهائي

irrigate *v* يروي

irrigation *n* ريّ

irritate *v* يُغْضِب

irritating *adj* مضايق

Islamic *adj* إسلامي

island *n* جزيرة

isle *n* جزيرة

isolate *v* يَعْزِل

isolation *n* عَزْل

issue *n* قضية

Italian *adj* إيطالي

Italy *n* إيطاليا

itch *v* حك

itchiness *n* مكر

item *n* بند

itemize *v* حدد

itinerary *n* مسار الرحلة

ivory *n* عاجّ

J

jackal *n* ابن آوى

jacket *n* سترة , جاكيت

jail *n* سِجْن

jail *v* سِجْن

jailer *n* السّجّان

jam *n* ازدحام

janitor *n* الحاجب , البوّاب

January *n* يناير

Japan *n* اليابان

Japanese *adj* ياباني

jar *n* صرير , صريف

jasmine *n* ياسمين

jaw *n* فَكّ , حَنَك

jealous *adj* غَيور , حَسود

jealousy *n* غَيْرَة , حسد

jeans *n* بنطلون الجينز

jeopardize *v* يعرّض للخطر

jerk *n* نَخْعة , رجّة

Jew *n* اليهودي

jewel n حِلْية

jeweler n الجوهريّ

jewelry store n محل مجوهرات

Jewish adj يهوديّ , عِبْريّ

job n عمل , مهمّة

jobless adj بدون عمل

join v يربط , يضمّ

joint n وُصْلَة

jointly adv معًا

joke n نكتة

joke v يَمْزَح

jokingly adv بمزاح

jolly adj مبتهج

jolt v يَنْخَع

jolt n نخعة

journal n صحيفة, مجلة

journalist n الصحافيّ

journey n رحلة

jovial adj مَرِح

joy n ابتهاج

joyful adj مبتهج

joyfully adv باْبتهاج

jubilant adj متهلّل

Judaism n اليهوديّة

judge n قاضٍ

judgment n حكم

judicious adj حكيم

jug n إبريق

juggler n المحتال

juice n عصير

juicy adj كثير العُصارة

July n يوليو

jump v يقفز

jump n قفزّ

jumpy adj عصبي

junction n وصلة

June n يونيو

jungle n أدغال

junior adj أصغر

junk n خردة

jury n هيئة المحلّفين

just adj صحيح

justice n عدالة

justify v يُبرّر

justly adv بتبرير

juvenile n الحَدَث

juvenile adj حَدَث

K

kangaroo n كنغر
karate n رياضة الكَارَاتِيه
keep iv صان
keep on v استمر
keep up v واظب
keg n برميل صغير
kennel n وجار الكلب
kettle n غلّاية
key n مفتاح , مفتاح الرموز
key ring n ماسك المفاتيح
keyboard n لوحة المفاتيح
kick v يرفس
kickback n رشوة
kickoff n ضربة الإفتتاح
kid n جَدْي , طِفل
kidnap v خطف
kidnapper n خاطف
kidnapping n اختطاف
kidney n كُلْيَة
kidney bean n لوبياء
kill v يقتل
killer n القاتل
killing n قتل
kilogram n الكِيلُوغْرام
kilometer n الكيلومتر

kilowatt n الكيلووات
kind adj حنون
kindle v أشعَل
kindly adv بعطف
kindness n فَضْل
king n مِلِك
kingdom n مملكة
kinship n قرابة
kiosk n كشك
kiss v يقبِّل
kiss n قُبلة
kitchen n مطبخ
kite n الحَدَأة
kitten n هُرَيْرَة
knee n الرُّكبة
kneecap n الرَّضفة
kneel iv ركع
knife n سكّين
knight n فارس
knit v يَرْبط
knob n عُقْدَة
knock n ضربة عنيفة
knock v يقرع. يخبِّط
knot n عُقْدة
know iv علم
know-how n مهارة
knowingly adv بدراية
knowledge n معرفة

L

lab n مختبر

label n رُقعة

labor n عمل

laborer n العامل

labyrinth n متاهة

lace n تخريم

lack v معوز

lack n فقدان

lad n ولد

ladder n سلم

laden adj مُحَمَّل

lady n سيدة

ladylike adj مُخَنَّث

lagoon n الهَوْر

lake n بحيرة

lamb n حَمَل

lame adj مُقعَد . كسيح

lament v يُعْول

lament n عويل

lamp n مصباح

lamppost n عمود الإنارة

lampshade n خيال اللمبة

land n اليابسة

land v يُنْزل إلى اليابسة

landfill n ظهور اليابسة

landing n هُبوط

landlady n مالكة الأرض

landlocked adj محاط بالأرض

landlord n مالك الأرض

landscape n مناظر الطبيعة

lane n زُقاق

language n لُغَة

languish v أضعف

lantern n المِشْكاة

lap n حُجْر . حِضْن

lapse n زلّة . هَفوَة

lapse v غلط

larceny n سرقة

lard n شحم الخنزير

large adj واسع

larynx n الحَنْجَرَة

laser n اللازر

lash n جَلْدَة . ضربة

lash v يجلد

lash out v أنفق ماله بطيش

last v يدوم

last adj أخير

last name n اسم العائلة

last night adv أمس

lasting adj دائم

lastly adv أخيراً

latch n مِزلاج

late adv متأخّرا

lately adv حديثاً	**lay** iv وضع, طرح
later adv فيما بعد	**lay off** v إقالة
later adj لاحِق	**layer** n طبقة
lateral adj جانبيّ	**layman** n علماني
latest adj أخير	**lay-out** n خطط
lather n زَبَد	**laziness** n كسل
latitude n خطّ العرض	**lazy** adj كسول
latter adj ثانٍ	**lead** iv قاد
laugh v يضحك	**lead** n مبادرة , قيادة
laugh n ضَحكة	**leaded** adj مرصص
laughable adj مضحِك	**leader** n قائد
laughter n ضَحِكٌ	**leadership** n قيادة
launch n اللّنْش	**leading** adj موجّه , هادٍ
launch v يُطلِق	**leaf** n ورقة
laundry n مغسلة	**leaflet** n وُرَيْقة
lavatory n مغسلة	**league** n حِلْف
lavish adj مُسْرِفٌ	**leak** v يتسرّب
lavish v يبدّد	**leak** n تسرُّب
law n قانون	**leakage** n تسرُّب
law-abiding adj مُطيع للقانون	**lean** adj هزيل , نحيل
lawful adj قانونيّ , شرعيّ	**lean** iv انحنى
lawmaker n الشارع	**lean back** v ينحني
lawn n شاشٌ	**lean on** v استند
lawsuit n قضيّة	**leaning** n مَيْل
lawyer n المحامي	**leap** iv وثب
lax adj مُنحَلّ	**leap** n وثبة
laxative adj مُسهِّلٌ	**leap year** n سنةٌ كبيسةٌ
lay n علمانيّ	**learn** iv تعلم

L

learned adj عالِم

learner n المتعلّم

learning n تعلُّم

lease v يؤجِّر

lease n عقد الإيجار

leash n رَسَن

least adj الأدنى

leather n جلدٌ مدبوغ

leave iv ترك

leave out v أهمل

lectern n المِقرأ

lecture n محاضرة

ledger n دفتر الحسابات

leech n عَلَقَة

leftovers n بقايا

leg n رجل

legacy n ميراث

legal adj قانونيّ

legality n قانونيّة

legalize v قنن

legend n أسطورة

legible adj واضح

legion n فَيْلَق

legislate v شرع

legislation n تشريع

legitimate adj شرعيّ

leisure n فراغ

lemon n ليمون

lemonade n ليمُونادَة

lend iv أقرض

length n طول

lengthen v يُطِيْل

lengthy adj طويل

leniency n تساهل

lenient adj متساهل

lense n عدسة

Lent n الصوم الكبير

lentil n عَدَس

leopard n نَمِر

leper n المجذوم

leprosy n جذام

less adj أقلّ

lessee n المستأجِر

lessen v يَقِلّ

lesser adj أقلّ

lesson n درس

lessor n مؤجر

let iv خلى

let down v أسقط

let go v يَتْرُك

let in v أدخل

let out v مكنه من الفرار

lethal adj مُميت

letter n حرف . رسالة

lettuce n الخس

leukemia n اللوكيميا

level v سوّى	**lifestyle** n أسلوب الحياة
level n ميزان البناء	**lifetime** adj العُمْر
lever n رافعة	**lift** v حَمْل
leverage n نُفُوذ	**lift off** v ارتفع
levy v يَفْرض	**lift-off** n على بعد
lewd adj فاسق	**ligament** n رباط
liability n مسئولية	**light** iv أشرق
liable adj مسؤول	**light** adj خفيف
liaison n ارتباط	**light** n ضوء
liar adj كذاب	**lighter** n ولاعة
libel n قذف	**lighthouse** n منارة
liberate v يحرّر	**lighting** n ضوء
liberation n تحرير	**lightly** adv بِرفْق
liberty n حريّة	**lightning** n بَرْق
librarian n أمين المكتبة	**lightweight** n وزن خفيف
library n مكتبة	**likable** adj محبوب
lice n قمل	**like** pre مثل
licence n ترخيص	**like** v يودّ
license v يجيز	**likelihood** n احتمال
lick v يلعق	**likely** adv على الأرجح
lid n غطاء	**likeness** n تشابه
lie iv تمدد	**likewise** adv بطريقة مماثلة
lie v يتمدّد	**liking** n ولوع
lie n كَذِبٌ	**limb** n عُضو
lieu n مكان	**lime** n كلس
lieutenant n ملازم أول	**limestone** n حجر الكلس
life n حياة	**limit** n حَدّ . قيْد
lifeless adj مَيْت	**limit** v يَحْصر

L

limitation *n* تحديد	literate *adj* غير أمّي
limp *v* يَعْرج	literature *n* آداب اللغة
limp *n* عَرَج	litigate *v* يقاضي
linchpin *n* جزء حيوي	litigation *n* دعوى
line *n* خيط	litre *n* لتر
line up *v* إنتظم في صف	litter *n* نفايات
linen *n* كتّان	little *adj* صغير
linger *v* يتوانى	little bit *n* قليل
lingering *adj* طويل	little by little *adv* شَيْئًا فَشَيْئًا
lining *n* تبطين	liturgy *n* طقوس دينيّة
link *v* وصل	live *adj* حيّ , نابض بالحياة
link *n* صِلة	live *v* يعيش
lion *n* أسَد	live off *v* يكتفي
lioness *n* لُبوءة	live up *v* يتعايش
lip *n* شَفَة	livelihood *n* الرّزق
liqueur *n* ليكيور	lively *adj* نشيط
liquid *n* السائل	liver *n* العائش
liquidate *v* صفى	livestock *n* مواش
liquidation *n* تصفية	livid *adj* شاحب
liquor *n* شراب كحوليّ	living room *n* حجرة الجلوس
list *v* يعدّد	lizard *n* العظاءة
list *n* قائمة	load *v* يُرهق
listen *v* يصغي	load *n* حُمُولة
listener *n* مستمع	loaded *adj* مُحمّل , مَحْشُوّ
litany *n* ابتهال	loaf *n* رغيف
liter *n* وحدة مكابيل مترية	loan *v* يُقرض
literal *adj* حَرْفيًّا	loan *n* قرْض
literally *adv* حَرْفيًّا	loathe *v* يعاف

loathing n اشمئزاز	lonesome adj منعزل
lobby n رواق , رَدْهَة	long adj طويل
lobby v ضغط	long for v اشتاق
lobster n سرطان البحر	longing n تَوْق
local adj موضعيّ	longitude n خطّ الطول
localize v يُمَرْكِز	long-standing adj إنتظار طويل
locate v علم	long-term adj طويل الأجل
located adj كائن	look n نَظَرٌ . نظرة
location n موقع	look v ينظر . يبدو
lock v يُقْفِل	look after v يَعْتَني بـ
lock n قفل	look at v يَنْظُرُ إلى
lock up v اعتقل	look down v ازدرى
locksmith n القَفّال	look for v يَبْحَثُ عَنْ
locust n جَراد	look forward v تشوق
lodge v يُؤوي	look into v تصفح
lodging n منزل	look out v حذر
lofty adj متغطرس	look over v تصفح
log n سجل طائرة	look through v تطلع الى
log v سجل	looking glass n مرآة
log in v يسجل اسم الدخول	looks n نظرة
log off v ينهي	loom n نَوْل
logic n منطق	loom v ظهر. ارتسم
logical adj منطقيّ	loophole n شق
loin n خاصرة	loose v يَفكّ
loiter v يتوانى	loose adj فضفاض
loneliness n عزلة	loosen v يحلّ
lonely adv بانفراد	loot v يَنْهَب
loner adj متوحد	loot n غنيمة

L

lord n لورد

lordship n سيادة

lose iv أضاع

loser n الخاسر

loss n خُسران

lot adv مقدار

lotion n الغَسُول

lots adj يُساهِم

lottery n يانصيب

loud adj مرتفع

loudly adv بصَوْت عالٍ

loudspeaker n مكبّر الصوت

lounge n صالون

louse n قملة

lousy adj مُقمِّل

lovable adj مُحبّب

love v يُحِبّ

love n محبّة

lovely adj جميل

lover n المُحِبّ

loving adj محبّ

low adj منخفض

lower adj أدنى

lowkey adj مكبوح

lowly adj وضيع

loyal adj مخلص

loyalty n وفاء

lubricate v شحم

lubrication n تشحيم

lucid adj صافٍ

luck n حظّ

lucky adj مَحْظوظ

lucrative adj رابح

ludicrous adj مضحك

luggage n أمتعة

lukewarm adj فاتر

lull n هدوء

lumber n خشب

luminous adj نيّر , مضيء

lump n قطعة . كتلة

lump sum n دفعة واحدة

lunacy n جنون

lunatic adj مجنون

lunch n غداء

lung n رئة

lure v يُغري

lurid adj رهيب

lurk v يترصّد

lush adj خصب

lust v يشتهي

lust n شهوة

lustful adj شَهوانيّ

luxurious adj فاخر

luxury n رفاهية

lynx n حيوان الوَشَق

lyrics n منشود

M

machine n آلة

machine gun n الرّشاش

mad adj مجنون

madam n سيّدة

madden v يُجَنّ

madly adv بجنون

madman n المجنون

madness n جنون

magazine n مستودع

magic n سِحر

magical adj ساحر

magician n السّاحر

magistrate n الحاكم

magnet n مغناطيس

magnetic adj مغنطيسيّ

magnetism n المغنطيسيّة

magnificent adj عظيم

magnify v يكبّر

magnitude n عِظَمٌ

mahagony n الماهوغانية

maid n البِكر

maiden n العذراء

mail v أرسل بالبريد

mail n بريد

mailbox n صُنْدُوقُ بَريد

mailman n ساعي البريد

maim v يشوّه

main adj رئيسيّ

mainland n يابسة

mainly adv على الغالب

maintain v حافظ

maintenance n صيانة

majestic adj ملوكيّ

majesty n جلالة

major n الراشد

major adj راشد

major in v يتخصّص في

majority n الأكثرية

make n صنع

make iv أحدث

make up v تجمل

make up for v عوض

maker n الله

makeup n تركيب

malaria n ملاريا

male n ذَكَر

malevolent adj حاقد

malfunction v قَصَرَ عَنْ

malfunction n اختلال

malice n حِقْد

malign v يعيب

malignancy n خبث

malignant adj حقود

M

mall n رصيف للمشاة

malnutrition n سوء التغذية

malpractice v إهمال

mammal n الثَّدْييّ

man n إنسان

manage v يُدير

manageable adj طيِّع

management n إدارة

manager n المدير

mandate n تفويض

mandatory adj إلزاميّ

maneuver n مناورة

manger n معلف

mangle v يشوِّه

manhandle v حرك باليد

manhunt n حملة البحث

maniac adj مهووس

manifest v يُظهر

manipulate v تلاعب

mankind n الجنس البشري

manliness n رجولة

manly adj قويّ

manner n أسلوب

mannerism n تصنع

manners n سُلوك

manpower n طاقة البشرية

mansion n قصر

manslaughter n قتل غير متعمد

manual n كتيّب

manual adj يدويّ

manufacture v يصنع

manure n سَماد

manuscript n مخطوطة

many adj كثير

map n خريطة

marble n رُخام

march v يزحف

march n شهر مارس

March n مسيرة

mare n الفَرَس

margin n هامش

marginal adj هامشيّ

marinate v نقع بالخل

marine adj بحريّ

marital adj زوجي

mark n علامة

mark v حدد

mark down v سجل

marker n المسجل

market n سُوق

marksman n الرامي

marmalade n المَرْمَلاد

marriage n زواج

married adj متزوّج

marrow n لب

marry v يزوّج

Mars n اَلْمِرّيخ

marshal n المشير , المارشال

martyr n شهيد

martyrdom n استشهاد

marvel n أعجوبة

marvelous adj مُدْهِش

marxist adj مصدق الماركسية

masculine adj مذكر

mash v يَهْرس

mask n قناع

masochism n الماسوشية

mason n البنّاء

masquerade v يتنكّر

mass n كتلة , حجم

massacre n مذبحة

massage n تدليك

massage v يدلّك

masseur n المدلّك

masseuse n المدلّكة

massive adj ضخم

mast n سارية

master n المدرس

master v يبرع في

mastermind n العقل الموجه

mastermind v قاد

masterpiece n التحفة

mastery n سيادة

mat n حصير

match n نظير, ند

match v كافأ, لاءمر

mate n الرفيق

material n مادة, أدوات

materialism n الماديّة

maternal adj أمومية

maternity n أمومة

math n الرياضيات

matriculate v سجل للجامعة

matrimony n زواج

matter n مسألة , أمر

mattress n فِراش

mature adj ناضج

maturity n نُضْج

maul v يدقّ

maxim n حكمة

maximum adj أعلى

May n شهر مايو

may iv يستطيع

may-be adv ربما

mayhem n تَشْويه

mayor n المحافظ

maze n حيرة

meadow n مَرْج

meager adj هزيل

meal n وَجْبَة

mean iv نوى

mean adj حقير

meaning n معنى

meaningful adj ذو معنى

meaningless adj لا معنى له

meanness n حقارة

means n الوَسَط

meantime adv في غضون

meanwhile adv خلال ذلك

measles n مرض الحَصْبة

measure v يقيس

measurement n قياس

meat n لحم

meatball n لحم مكور

mechanic n الميكانيكيّ

mechanism n الآليّة

mechanize v يُمَكّن

medal n مَدالية

medallion n مَدالية كبيرة

meddle v يتطفّل

mediate v يتوسّط

mediator n الوسيط

medication n تطبيب

medicinal adj شفائيّ

medicine n الطبّ

medieval adj قروسطي

mediocre adj متوسّط

mediocrity n توسط

meditate v يعتزم

meditation n تأمل

medium adj متوسّط

meek adj حَليم

meekness n تواضع

meet iv قابل

meeting n اجتماع

melancholy n كآبة

mellow adj يانع

mellow v جعله يانعا

melodic adj لحني

melody n لحن

melon n بطيخ

melt v يَذُوب

member n عضو

membership n عُضويّة

membrane n غشاء

memento n تَذْكِرة

memo n مذكرة

memoirs n مذكّرات

memorable adj بارز

memorize v حفظ

memory n ذاكرة

men n الرجال

menace n تهديد

mend v يُصْلِح

meningitis n التهاب سحايا

menopause n سِنّ اليأس

mental adj عقليّ

mentality n عقلية

mentally adv عقليا	metaphor n المجاز
mention v يَذْكر	meteor n شهاب
mention n ذِكُر	meter n وحدة لقياس
menu n لائحة الطعام	method n منهج
merchandise n بضائع	methodical adj منهجيّ
merchant n تاجر	meticulous adj مُوَسْوَس
merciful adj رحيم	metric adj مِتْريّ
merciless adj قاس	metropolis n العاصمة
mercury n زئبق	Mexican adj المكسيكيّ
mercy n رحمة	mice n فأرة
merely adv فحسب	microbe n ميكروب
merge v يُدْمِج	microphone n الميكروفون
merger n اتحاد، الاندماج	microscope n الميكروسكوب
merit n استحقاق	microwave n موجة الصغرى
merit v يستحقّ	midair n البكر
mermaid n إمرأة فاتنة	midday n لظُهْر
merry adj مَرحٌ	middle n مُنتصف
mesh n شبكية العين	middleman n الوسيط
mesmerize v يُمَسْمِر	midget n قزَم
mess n فوضى	midnight n منتصف الليل
mess around v تسكع	midsummer n منتصف الصّيف
mess up v عبث	midwife n القابلة
message n رسالة	mighty adj جبار
messenger n الرسول	migraine n صداع نصفي
Messiah n المسيح	migrant n المهاجر
messy adj مشوش	migrate v يهاجر
metal n مَعْدِن	mild adj لطيف
metallic adj مَعْدِنيّ	mildew n العَفَن الفُطْريّ

M

mile *n* وحدة لقياس	minimum *n* الحدّ الأدنى
mileage *n* الرسم بالميل	miniskirt *n*
milestone *n* مَعْلَم	minister *n* وزير, كاهن
militant *adj* مقاتل	minister *v* يخدم
milk *n* حليب	ministry *n* وزارة كهنوت
milky *adj* لبني	minor *adj* ثانوي
mill *n* مِطحنة	minority *n* سنّ القصور
millennium *n* ألف عام	mint *n* نعناع
milligram *n* مليغرام	mint *v* سك العملة
millimeter *n* المِليمتر	minus *adj* ناقص
million *n* المليون	minute *n* دقيقة
millionaire *adj* المليونير	miracle *n* مُعجزة
mime *v* قلد	miraculous *adj* أعجوبي
mince *v* يَفْرم	mirage *n* سراب
mincemeat *n* لحم مفروم	mirror *n* مِرآة
mind *v* يُذَكِّر . يتذكّر	misbehave *v* يسيء السلوك
mind *n* ذاكرة	miscalculate *v* يخطئ التقدير
mindful *adj* منتبه	miscarriage *n* إجهاض
mindless *adj* غبي	miscarry *v* تُجْهِض
mine *n* مَنْجم	mischief *n* أذى
mine *v* يقوّض	mischievous *adj* مؤذٍ
mine *pro* مِلكي	misconduct *n* فاحشة
minefield *n* حقل ألغام	misconstrue *v* يسيء الفهم
miner *n* المعدّن	misdemeanor *n* جُنْحة
mineral *n* مَعْدِن	miser *n* الشحيح
mingle *v* يخلط	miserable *adj* بائس
miniature *n* مصغر	misery *n* بُؤس
minimize *v* خفض	misfit *adj* غير كفؤ

M

misfortune *n* بليّة	mitigate *v* يسكّن
misgiving *n* هاجس	mix *v* يمزج
misguided *adj* مضلل	mixed-up *adj* يمزج
misinterpret *v* أساء التفسير	mixer *n* خلاطة
misjudge *v* يفتقد	mixture *n* مَزْج
mislead *v* يَخدع	mix-up *n* شوش
misleading *adj* مخادع	moan *v* يُعْول
mismanage *v* يُسيء الادارة	moan *n* عويل
misprint *n* خطأ مطبعيّ	mob *v* تجمهر
miss *v* يُخفق	mob *n* الغَوْغاء
miss *n* إخفاق	mobile *adj* نَقّال
missile *n* قذيفة	mobilize *v* يحرّك
missing *adj* ضائع	mobster *n* قاطع طريق
mission *n* مهمّة	mock *v* هزأ
missionary *n* المبشّر	mockery *n* سخرية
mist *n* غشاوة	mode *n* صيغة
mistake *iv* أخطئ	model *n* نموذج
mistake *n* خطأ	moderate *adj* معتدل
mistaken *adj* مخطئ	moderation *n* الاعتدال
mister *n* سيّد	modern *adj* عصريّ
mistreat *v* يسيء المعاملة	modernize *v* يُعصّر
mistreatment *n* معاملة سيئة	modest *adj* متواضع
mistress *n* سيّدة	modesty *n* تواضع
mistrust *n* ارتياب	modify *v* يحوّر
mistrust *v* يرتاب	module *n* وحدة
misty *adj* ضبابيّ	moisten *v* يُرطّب
misunderstand *v* يسيء الفهم	moisture *n* رطوبة
misuse *n* استعمال خاطئ	molar *n* ضِرْس

M

mold v يصوغ	month n الشَّهر
mold n قالب	monthly adv شـهريًّا
moldy adj عتيق	monument n نُصُب
mole n شامة	monumental adj نُصُبيّ
molecule n الجُزَيئ	mood n مزاج
molest v يضايق	moody adj كئيب
mom n أُمّ	moon n القمر
moment n لحظة	moor v يُوثق
momentarily adv لِلَحْظَة	mop v ينظِّف
momentous adj هامّ جدًّا	moral adj أخلاقيّ
monarch n الملكية	moral n أخلاق
monarchy n ملكية مطلقة	morality n الأخلاقيّة
monastery n دَيْر	more adj أكثر
monastic adj رهْبانيّ	moreover adv علاوةً على ذلك
Monday n الاثنين	morning n الصباح
money n نقد	moron adj الأبله
money order n حوالة بريديّة	morphine n المُورفين
monitor v راقب	morsel n لقمة
monk n راهب	mortal adj مُميت
monkey n النَّسناس	mortality n الفَنَائيّة
monogamy n زواج أحادي	mortar n هاوَن
monologue n المُونُولُوج	mortgage n رَهنٌ
monopolize v يحتكر	mortification n إماتة الجسد
monopoly n احتكار	mortify v أمات
monotonous adj رتيب	mortuary n مُستَودَع الجُثَث
monotony n رَتابة	mosaic n فُسَيْفُساء
monster n الهُوْلَة	mosque n المسجد
monstrous adj هُوليّ	mosquito n بَعُوضَة

M

moss n طُحْلُب	move out v خرج
most adj معظم	move up v يرتفع
mostly adv في الأغلب	movement n حركة
motel n الموتيل	movie n فيلم
moth n قمل	mow v يحصد
mother n أمّ	much adv بكثير
motherhood n الأمومة	mucus n مخاط
mother-in-law n الحماة	mud n وَحْل
motion n اقتراح	muddle n تشوُّش ذهني
motionless adj ساكن	muddy adj مشوّش
motivate v يحثّ	muffle v يُخمد
motive n الحافز	muffler n خمار
motor n المحرِّك	mug n إبريق
motorcycle n دراجة نارية	mug v كشر
motto n شِعار	mugging n الإبلاغ عن سطو
mouldy adj متعفن	mule n بَغْل
mount n مطيّة	multiple adj متعدّد
mount v يرتفع	multiplication n مضاعفة
mountain n جبل	multiply v يضاعف
mountainous adj جبليّ	multitude n تعدّد
mourn v يندب	mumble v يُتمتم
mourning n حِداد	mummy n مومياء
mouse n فأر	mumps n النُّكاف
mouth n فم	munch v قضم
move n حركة	munitions n ذخائر
move v يحرِّك	murder n قتل
move back v تراجع	murderer n القاتل
move forward v تقدم	murky adj مظلم

M

murmur v يتذمّر

murmur n تذمُّر

muscle n عَضَلة

museum n مُتحَف

mushroom n الفُطر

music n موسيقى

musician n الموسيقيّ

Muslim adj مُسْلِم

must iv يجب

mustache n الشارب

mustard n خَرْدَل

muster v يحشد

mutate v تحول

mute adj صامت

mutilate v بتر

mutiny n تمرُّد

mutually adv متبادل

muzzle v يكمّم

muzzle n كِمامة . فُوّهة

my adj لي

myopic adj أحسر

myself pro أنا

mysterious adj غامض

mystery n غموض

mystic adj خفيّ

mystify v يُلغز

myth n خرافة

N

nag v تذمر

nagging adj متذمر

nail n مسمار

naive adj ساذج

naked adj عارٍ

name n اسم

namely adv أعني

nanny n مربية

nap n قيلولة

napkin n منديل

narcotic n مخدّر

narrate v يروي

narrow adj ضيّق

narrowly adv بدقّة

nasty adj مُقْرف

nation n شعب

national adj وطنيّ

nationality n الجنسيّة

nationalize v يجنّس

native adj وطنيّ

natural adj طبيعيّ

naturally adv طَبْعًا

nature n طبيعة

naughty adj بذيء

nausea n غَثَيان

nave n محور الدولاب	negotiate v يفاوض
navel n السُّرَّة	negotiation n تفاوض
navigate v يُبْحِر	neighbor n جارٌ
navigation n إبحار	neighborhood n جِوار
navy n أسطول	neither adj و لا واحد من
navy blue adj الأزرق البحري	neither adv أيضاً
near pre عند	nephew n ابن الأخ
nearby adj مجاور	nerve n عَصَب
nearly adv تقريباً	nervous adj عصَبيّ
nearsighted adj حسير	nest n عشّ
neat adj أنيق	net n شبكة
neatly adv بإتقان	Netherlands n هُولَنْدَا
necessary adj ضروريّ	network n شبكة
necessitate v يحتّم	neurotic adj عُصابيّ
necessity n ضرورة	neutral adj محايد
neck n عنق	neutralize v يُبْطِل
necklace n عِقد	never adv أبداً
necktie n ربطة عنق	nevertheless adv ومع ذلك
need v احتاج	new adj جديد
need n ضرورة	newborn n مولود حديثا
needle n إبرة	newcomer n الوافد
needless adj غير ضروري	newly adv حديثاً
needy adj فقير	newlywed adj لمتزوج حديثا
negative adj سلبيّ	news n خبر
neglect v يُهْمِل	newscast n نشرة الأخبار
neglect n إهْمال	newsletter n الرسالة الاخبارية
negligence n إهمال	newspaper n جريدة
negligent adj مهمِل	newsstand n كُشْك الصحف

N

next adj تالٍ	**noise** n ضَجيج
next door adj البيت المجاور	**noisily** adv بضجّة
nibble v يأكل بتأنٍ	**noisy** adj ضاجّ
nice adj متأنّق	**nominate** v يعيّن
nicely adv بِدِقّة	**none** pre لا أحد
nickel n معدن النيكل	**nonetheless** c مَعَ ذَلِكَ
nickname n لقب	**nonsense** n هراء
nicotine n النيكوتين	**nonsmoker** n غير مدخن
niece n ابنة الأخ	**nonstop** adv بلا توقف
night n لَيْل	**noon** n الظُّهر
nightfall n الغروب	**noose** n شَرَكٌ
nightgown n المنامَة	**no one** pro لا احد
nightingale n العندليب	**nor** c ولا
nightmare n كابوس	**norm** n معيار
nine adj بالغ عدده تسعة	**normal** adj عادِيّ
ninety adj تسعون	**normalize** v طبع
ninth adj التاسع	**normally** adv عَادَةً
nip n برد قارس	**north** n الشمال
nip v يَقْرص	**northeast** n شَمَالٌ شَرْقيٌّ
nipple n الحلمة	**northern** adj شَمالِيّ
nitpicking adj عائب	**northerner** adj الشَّمالِيّ
nitrogen n النتروجين	**Norway** n النرويج
nobility n نبالة	**Norwegian** adj نرويجي
noble adj شهير	**nose** n أنف
nobleman adj النبيل	**nosedive** adv يهبط على الأنف
nobody pro لا أحد	**nostalgia** n حنين
nocturnal adj ليليّ	**nostril** n المَنْخِر
nod v ومأ، حرك	**nosy** adj فضولي

not adv لم

notable adj وجيه

notably adv على نحو وجيه

notary n الكاتب العدل

notation n التّنويت

note v يلاحظ

notebook n مذكّرة

noteworthy adj ملحوظ

nothing n لا شيء

notice v يلاحظ . يرى

notice n إنذار . إشعار

noticeable adj لافتٌ للنظر

notification n إعلام

notify v يُبلغ

notion n فكرة

notorious adj مُشَهّر

noun n الإسم

nourish v يغذّي

nourishment n تغذية

novel n رواية

novelist n الرّوائيّ

novelty n البدْع

November n نوفمبر

novice n مبتدئ

now adv الآن

nowadays adv فى هذه الايام

nowhere adv لا مكان

noxious adj مؤْذٍ

nozzle n صنبور

nuance n فارق بسيط

nuclear adj نَوَويّ

nude adj عار

nudism n مذهب العُرْي

nudist n العُرْيّي

nudity n عري

nuisance n إزعاج

null adj باطل

nullify v يُبّطِل

numb adj خَدِر

number n رقم

numbness n تخدير

numerous adj عديد

nun n راهبة

nurse n مُمرضة

nurse v يربّي

nursery n غرفة أطفال , حضانة

nurture v يغذي

nut n جوزة , بندقة

nutrition n تغذية

nutritious adj مُغَذٍ

nut-shell adv باختصار

nutty adj كثير الجوز

O

oak *n* البلّوط

oar *n* مِجذاف

oasis *n* واحة

oath *n* قَسَم

oatmeal *n* دقيق

obedience *n* إجلال

obedient *adj* ممتثل

obese *adj* بدين

obey *v* يمتثل

object *v* يعترض

object *n* هدف

objection *n* اعتراض

objective *n* غرض

obligate *v* يُلزم

obligation *n* واجب

obligatory *adj* إجباريّ

oblige *v* يُلزم

obliged *adj* مجبر

oblique *adj* منحرف

obliterate *v* يطمس

oblivion *n* نسيان

oblivious *adj* غافل

oblong *adj* مستطيل

obnoxious *adj* بغيض

obscene *adj* فاحش

obscenity *n* فُحْش

obscure *adj* مظلم

obscurity *n* ظلمة

observation *n* ملاحظة

observatory *n* مَرْصَد

observe *v* يلاحظ

obsess *v* أقلق

obsession *n* هاجس

obsolete *adj* مهجور

obstacle *n* عائق

obstinacy *n* عناد

obstinate *adj* عنيد

obstruct *v* يسدّ

obstruction *n* سدّ

obtain *v* يُحْرز

obvious *adj* واضحٌ

obviously *adv* بوضوح

occasion *n* فرصة

occasionally *adv* أحياناً

occult *adj* خفيّ

occupant *n* الشاغل

occupation *n* شُغْل

occupy *v* يَشْغَل

occur *v* يَحْدُث

ocean *n* محيط

October *n* تشرين الأول

octopus *n* أخطبوط

ocurrence *n* بروز

odd *adj* مُفْرَد

oddity *n* شذوذ

odds *n* تحيز

odious *adj* بغيض

odometer *n* عداد المسافات

odor *n* رائحة

odyssey *n* ملحمة الأوديسة

of *pre* مِنْ

off *adv* بعيداً

offend *v* يزعج

offense *n* هجوم

offensive *adj* هجوميّ

offer *v* يَعْرِض

offer *n* عَرْض

offering *n* عَرْض

office *n* منصِب

officer *n* موظّف

official *adj* رسميّ

officiate *v* تولى منصب

offset *v* وازن

offspring *n* نِتاج

off-the-record *adj* ليس للنشر

often *adv* كثيراً ما

oil *n* زيت

ointment *n* مَرْهَم

okay *adv* حسنا

old *adj* عتيق

old age *n* شَيْخُوخَة

old-fashioned *adj* عتيق الطراز

olive *n* زيتون

olympics *n* الأُولمْبِيَاد

omelette *n* عُجَّةُ بَيْض

omen *n* فألٌ

ominous *adj* مشؤومٌ

omission *n* حذف

omit *v* يحذف

on *pre* على

once *adv* مرّة

once *c* حالَما

one *adj* واحد

oneself *pre* نفسه

ongoing *adj* جارية

onion *n* البَصَل

onlooker *n* المشاهد

only *adv* فحسب

onset *n* هجوم

onslaught *n* انقضاض

onwards *adv* إلى الأمام

opaque *adj* غير شفاف

open *v* يفتَح

open *adj* مفتوح

open up *v* شنّ هجوما

opening *n* تفتُّح

open-minded *adj* متحرّر

openness *n* انفتاح

opera *n* أوبرا

O

operate v يُعْمِل , يُدير	orbit n مَدار
operation n عمل	orchard n بستان
opinion n اعتقاد	orchestra n الأوركسترا
opinionated adj متعنت	ordain v نسق
opium n مخدّر	ordeal n مِحنَة
opponent n خصْم	order n ترتيب
opportune adj ملائم	ordinarily adv عادةً
opportunity n مناسَبة	ordinary adj عاديّ
oppose v يعارض	ordination n رسامة الكاهن
opposite adj متضادّ	ore n خامة
opposite adv معاكس	organ n عضو
opposite n النّقيض	organism n المتعضي
opposition n معارضة	organist n الأرغني
oppress v يضطهد	organization n تنظيم
oppression n اضطهاد	organize v ينظّم
opt for v اختار	orient n المَشرق
optical adj بَصَريّ	oriental adj مَشْرقيّ
optician n النظّاراتيّ	orientation n توجيه
optimism n التفاؤل	oriented adj موجه
optimistic adj متفائل	origin n مصدر
option n اختيار	original adj أصليّ
optional adj اختياريّ	originally adv أصلاً
opulence n ثروة	originate v ينشئ
or c أو	ornament n زينة
oracle n المَوْحى	ornamental adj زينيّ
orally adv شِفَاهًا	orphan n يَتيم
orange n برتقالة	orphanage n مَيْتَم
orangutan n من القرَدة	orthodox adj أرثوذكسيّ

O

ostentatious adj متفاخر	**outlet** n مَخْرَج , مَنْفَذ
ostrich n نعامة	**outline** n مختصر , موجَز
other adj آخَر	**outline** v اختصر
otherwise adv وإلاّ	**outlive** v يعمّر
otter n القُضاعَة	**outlook** n مَشْرَف
ought to iv سوف	**outmoded** adj عتيق الزي
ounce n أونصة	**outnumber** v فاقه عددا
our adj خاصّتنا	**outpatient** n المريض الخارجي
ours pro مِلكنا	**outperform** v تفوق
ourselves pro نفسُنا	**outpouring** n انهمار
oust v يطرد	**output** n مردود
out adv خارجاً	**outrage** n اعتداء
outbreak n اندلاع	**outrageous** adj شنيع
outburst n انفجار	**outright** adj تامّ
outcast adj منبوذ	**outrun** v يسبق
outcome n حصيلة	**outset** n بداية
outcry n احتجاج	**outshine** v تألق
outdated adj مهجور	**outside** adv خارجاً
outdo v تغلب	**outsider** n الدَّخيل
outdoor adv في الهواء الطلق	**outskirts** n ضاحية
outdoors adv في الخلاء	**outspoken** adj صريح
outer adj خارجيّ	**outstanding** adj معلّق
outfit n تجهيزات	**outstretched** adj ممدود
outgoing adj منسحبٌ	**outward** adj ظاهري
outgrow v نما بسرعة	**outweigh** v رجح
outing n نزهة	**oval** adj بَيْضَوِيّ
outlaw v يحرّم	**ovary** n المَبيض
outlast v صمد	**ovation** n احتفاء

O

oven n فُرن

over pre خلال

overall adv عُمومًا

overbearing adj متعجرف

overcast adj معتم

overcharge v طلب ثمنا أعلى

overcoat n مِعْطَف

overcome v يقهر

overcrowded adj مكتظ

overdo v يبالِغ

overdone adj مغال

overdose n جرعة مفرطة

overdue adj متأخر

overestimate v بالغ في التقدير

overflow v يَغمر

overhaul v يُصْلِح

overlap v تداخل

overlook v يطلّ

overnight adv طوالَ الليل

overpower v يغلب

overrate v بالغ في التقدير

override v تجاوز

overrule v يتحكّم

overrun v يكتسح

overseas adv عَبْر البحار

oversee v راقب

overshadow v ظلل

oversight n مراقبة

overstate v بالغ

overstep v يتجاوز

overtake v أدرك

overthrow v يهزم

overthrow n هزيمة

overtime adv إضافيًّا

overturn v ينقلب

overview n ملخص

overweight adj بدين

overwhelm v قهر

owe v كن له

owing to adv بداعي

owl n بومة

own v يَملِك

own adj خاصّتُهُ

owner n مالك

ownership n ملكية

ox n ثَوْر

oxen n ثيران

oxygen n الأكسـجين

oyster n المَحار

O

P

pace v ركض

pace n العَدْو

pacify v هدأ

pack v يعلّب

package n صُرّة

pact n معاهدة

pad v يُبطّن

padding n حَشْوَة

paddle v يجذّف

padlock n قُفْل

pagan adj وثنيّ

page n الوصيف , صفحة

pail n دَلْوٌ

pain n ألم

painful adj مؤلم

painkiller n مخدر

painless adj غير مؤلم

paint v يصبغ

paint n دهان

paintbrush n فرشاة الدهن

painter n الرسّام

painting n صورة زيتيّة , دَهْن

pair n زوج

pajamas n مَنامَة

pal n صديق

palace n بَلاط

palate n الحَنَك

pale adj شاحب

paleness n شحوب

palm n نخلة

palpable adj محسوس

paltry adj تافه

pamper v يُدلّل

pamphlet n كُرّاسَة

pan n مِقْلاة

pancreas n البنكرياس

pander v عمل قوادا

pang n وخز

panic n رُعْب

panorama n البانوراما

panther n نَمِر

pantry n حجرة المؤن

pants n بنطلون

pantyhose n جوارب طويلة

papacy n البابويّة

paper n ورق

paperclip n مشبك

paperwork n عمل ورقي

parable n مَثَل

parachute n مظلّة هبوط

parade n عَرْض

paradise n الجَنّة

paradox n مُفارَقة

paragraph n فِقْرَة

parakeet n ببغاء صغير

parallel n متوازٍ

paralysis n شَلَل

paralyze v شل

parameters n عامل متغير

paramount adj أسمى

paranoid adj مجنون بالشك

parasite n الطُفَيْليّ

paratrooper n مظلي

parcel n قطعة

parcel post n بَريدُ الطُّرود

parch v يحمّص

parchment n ورق نفيس

pardon v غفر

pardon n عَفو

parenthesis n جُمَلةٌ مُعْتَرَضَة

parents n الوالدان

parish n أبرشية

parishioner n الابرشى

parity n تكافؤ

park v أوقف السيارة

park n الموقف

parking n موقف سيارات

parliament n البرلمان

parochial adj أبرشيّ

parrot n بَبْغاء

parsley n البَقْدُونس

parsnip n الجزر الأبيض

part v يفترق

part n جزء

partial adj جزئيّ

partially adv جُزْئيًّا

participate v يشترك

participation n اشتراك

participle n اسم الفاعل

particle n جُسَيْم

particular adj استثنائيّ

particularly adv خصوصاً

parting n مُفْتَرَق

partisan n مُوالٍ

partition n تقسيم

partly adv جزئيًّا

partner n شريك

partnership n شراكة

partridge n الحَجَل

party n حفلة أنس وسَمَر

pass n طريق

pass v مر

pass around v نشر

pass away v زال

pass out v يُغْمَى عَلَيه

passage n ممرّ

passenger n المسافر

passer-by n عابر سبيل

passion n انفعال

passionate *adj* انفعاليّ	patrol *n* خَفْر
passive *adj* منفعل	patron *n* النصير , الراعي
passport *n* جواز سفر	patronage *n* رعاية
password *n* كلمة المرور	patronize *v* يَرْعَى
past *adj* سابق	pattern *n* نموذج
paste *v* يُلصق	pavement *n* رصيف
paste *n* لَصُوق	pavilion *n* جناح
pasteurize *v* يُعَقّم	paw *n* كف الحيوان
pastime *n* تسلية	pawn *v* يَرْهن
pastor *n* قسيس	pawnbroker *n* المسترهِن
pastoral *adj* رعوي	pay *n* راتب
pastry *n* فطائر	pay *iv* يدفع
pasture *n* عشب	pay back *v* سدد الدين
pat *n* تربيتة	pay off *v* سد دينه
patch *v* يُصْلِح	payable *adj* واجب دفعه
patch *n* بقعة	paycheck *n* شيك أجر العمل
patent *n* رخصة	payee *n* مدفوع له
patent *adj* مُسجّل	payment *n* دفعة
paternity *n* أبوّة	payroll *n* كشف الأجور
path *n* طريق	payslip *n* كشف الراتب
pathetic *adj* مُحْزِن	pea *n* بازلّاً
patience *n* صَبْرٌ	peace *n* سلام
patient *adj* صبور	peaceful *adj* سلمي
patio *n* فِناء	peach *n* خَوْخ
patriarch *n* بطريرك	peacock *n* الطاووس
patrimony *n* ميراثٌ	peak *n* ذروة
patriot *n* الوطنيّ	peanut *n* الفول السوداني
patriotic *adj* وطنيّ	pear *n* الإجّاص

P

pearl *n* لؤلؤة	peninsula *n* شِبْه جزيرة
peasant *n* الفَلّاح	penitent *n* نادم
pebble *n* حصاة	penniless *adj* معدم
peck *v* يَنقُر	penny *n* البنس
peck *n* نقر	pension *n* منحة
peculiar *adj* خصوصيّ	pentagon *n* البنتاغون
pedagogy *n* بيداغوجيا	pent-up *adj* مكبوت
pedal *n* دوّاسَة	people *n* الناس
pedantic *adj* حذلقي	pepper *n* فُلفُل
pedestrian *n* الماشي	per *pre* بواسطة
peel *v* يَقْشُرُ	perceive *v* يدرك
peel *n* قشرة	percent *adv* في المائة
peep *v* يزقو	percentage *n* نسبة مئوية
peer *n* النّظير	perception *n* إدراك
pelican *n* البَجَع	perennial *adj* خالد
pellet *n* حبة صغيرة	perfect *adj* كامل
pen *n* قلم	perfection *n* إتقان
penalize *v* يعاقب	perforate *v* يثقّب
penalty *n* عِقاب , غرامة	perforation *n* تثقيب
penance *n* كفّارة	perform *v* يُنجز , يصنع
penchant *n* وَلُوعٌ	performance *n* عمل , إنجاز
pencil *n* قلم رصاص	perfume *n* عِطر
pendant *n* قلادة	perhaps *adv* ربما
pending *adj* معلّق	peril *n* خَطَرٌ
pendulum *n* البندول	perilous *adj* خطِر
penetrate *v* يخترق	perimeter *n* محيط
penguin *n* البطْريق	period *n* فترة
penicillin *n* البنيسيلين	perish *v* يَهْلك

P

perishable adj هالك	**pervert** v شوه
perjury n حنث باليمين	**pervert** adj منحرف
permanent adj دائم	**pessimism** n تشاؤم
permeate v اخترق	**pessimistic** adj متشائم
permission n رُخْصة	**pest** n طاعون
permit v يرخّص	**pester** v يزعج
pernicious adj ضارّ	**pesticide** n مبيد الحشرات
perpetrate v ارتكب	**pet** n حيوان مدلل
persecute v يضطهد	**petal** n البَتَلة
persevere v يثابر	**petite** adj أنيق
persist v يُصِرّ	**petition** n عريضة
persistence n إصرار	**petrified** adj حول لمادة صلبة
persistent adj مُثابر	**petroleum** n البترول
person n شخص	**pettiness** n تفاهة
personal adj شخصيّ	**petty** adj صغير , تافه
personality n شخصيّة	**pew** n مَقعد
personify v يُشَخّص	**phantom** n شَبَح
personnel n الموظفين	**pharmacist** n الصيدليّ
perspective n منظور	**pharmacy** n صيدليّة
perspiration n تعرُّق	**phase** n طَوْر
perspire v يَعْرَق	**pheasant** n التدرج
persuade v يُقْنِع	**phenomenon** n ظاهرة
persuasion n إقناع	**philosopher** n الفيلسوف
persuasive adj مُقْنِع	**philosophy** n فلسفة
pertain v يَخُصّ	**phobia** n فُوبِيَا
pertinent adj وثيق الصلة	**phone** n تلفون
perturb v يُقلق	**phone** v هاتف
perverse adj منحرف	**phoney** adj زائف

P

phosphorus n الفُوسفُور	pile v دعم
photo n صورة فوتوغرافية	pile n دعامة
photocopy n نسخة صورة	pile up v كدس
photograph v يصوّر	pilfer v اختلس
photographer n المصوّر	pilgrim n الحاجّ
photography n الفوترغرافي	pilgrimage n حِجّة
phrase n عبارة	pill n حبة دواء
physically adj طبيعيًّا	pillage v يسلب
physician n حكيم	pillar n ركيزة
physics n الفيزياء	pillow n وسادة
pianist n عازف البيانو	pillowcase n غطاء الوسادة
piano n بيانو	pilot n رُبّان الطائرة
pick v يلتقط , يقطف	pimple n بَثَرة
pick up v يَلْتَقِطُ	pin n وَتد
pickpocket n النّشّال	pincers n كُمّاشة
pickup n انتعاش	pinch v قرص
picture n صورة	pinch n لَذْع
picture v يصوّر	pine n صنوبرة
picturesque adj تصويري	pineapple n الأناناس
pie n فطيرة	pink adj قرنفليّ
piece n قطعة	pinpoint v حدد
piecemeal adv تدريجيًّا	pint n الباينت
pier n دعامة	pioneer n الرائد
pierce v يطعن	pious adj تقيّ
piercing n نقب	pipe n مِزمار
piety n تقوى	pipeline n خط أنابيب
pig n خنزير	piracy n قرصنة
pigeon n حمامة	pirate n قُرصان

P

pistol n مُسَدّس	**platinum** n البلاتين
pit n حفرة	**platoon** n فصيلة
pitch-black adj فاحم	**plausible** adj معقول
pitchfork n مِذراة	**play** v يلعب , يعبث
pitfall n وجرة, مأزق	**play** n لعب , لهو
pitiful adj حقير	**player** n اللاعب
pity n شفقة	**playful** adj لَعُوب
placard n إعلان	**playground** n مَلعَب
placate v يهدئ	**plea** n ذريعة
place n مكان	**plead** v يدافع
placid adj هادئ	**pleasant** adj مسلي
plague n بلاء	**please** v يشاء
plain n مستو	**pleasing** adj ممتع
plain adj سهل	**pleasure** n مشيئة
plainly adv بوُضُوح	**pleat** n طيّة
plaintiff n المدّعي	**pleated** adj مَطوِيّ
plan v يخطّط	**pledge** v تعهد
plan n تصميم	**pledge** n عَهد
plane n طائرة	**plentiful** adj وافر
planet n الكوكب	**plenty** n وفرة
plant v يغرس	**pliable** adj مَرِن
plant n شجيرة	**pliers** n زَرَديّة
plaster n اللّصوق	**plot** v يتآمر
plaster v يجصّص	**plot** n مؤامرة
plastic n البلاستيك	**plow** v يحرُثُ
plate n صفيحة	**ploy** n دهاء
plateau n هضبة	**pluck** v يقتلع
platform n رصيف	**plug** v يسُدّ , يضرب

P

plug n سِدادة , المأخذ	**Poland** n بُولَنْدَا
plum n برقوق	**polar** adj قُطْبيّ
plumber n الرّصّاص	**pole** n قُطْب
plumbing n سمكرية	**police** n الشرطة
plummet v انهار	**policeman** n شُرْطِيّ
plump adj ملحم	**policy** n سياسة
plunder v سلب	**Polish** adj بولندي
plunge v يُغَطّس	**polish** n البولندية
plunge n غَطْس	**polish** v صقل
plural n جَمْع	**polite** adj لطيف
plus adv فائض	**politeness** n لطف
plush adj بلشي	**politician** n السياسي
plutonium n بلوتونيوم	**politics** n السياسة
pneumonia n الْتِهَاب رِئَويّ	**poll** n اقتراع
pocket n جَيْب	**pollen** n لَقَاح
poem n قصيدة	**pollute** v يلوّث
poet n الشاعر	**pollution** n تلويث
poetry n الشِّعْر	**polygamy** n تعدُّد الزوجات
poignant adj حادّ	**pomegranate** n الرُّمّان
point n نقطة , ميزة	**pomposity** n تباهي
point v يحدّد	**pond** n مُسْتَنْقَع
pointed adj محدّد	**ponder** v يتأمل
pointless adj تافه	**pontiff** n الأسقف
poise n توازن	**pool** n حَوْض
poison v يُسَمّم	**pool** v أسهم
poison n سُمّ	**poor** n فقير
poisoning n تسميم	**poorly** adv فَقيرًا
poisonous adj سامّ	**popcorn** n الفُشار

P

Pope n البابا	**possibility** n إمكانيّة
poppy n الخَشْخاش	**possible** adj ممكن
popular adj شعبيّ	**post** n بريد , سارية
popularize v أشاع	**post office** n مكتب البريد
populate v سكن	**postage** n أجرة البريد
population n السّكّان	**postcard** n بطاقة بريدية
porcelain n فخار	**poster** n الملصق
porch n رواق	**posterity** n الذّرّية
porcupine n الشَّيْهم	**postman** n ساعي البريد
pore n سُمّ	**postmark** n ساعي البريد
pork n لحم الخنزير	**postpone** v يؤجّل
porous adj مسامّيّ	**postponement** n تأجيل
port n ميناء	**pot** n قِدْر , أصيص
portable adj المحمول	**potato** n البطاطا
portent n نذير	**potent** adj قحل
porter n البوّاب	**potential** adj كامن
portion n قسمة	**pothole** n أخدود
portrait n صورة	**poultry** n دواجن
portray v يصوّر	**pound** v يسحق
Portugal n البُرتُغَال	**pound** n الباوند
Portuguese adj برتغاليّ	**pour** v ينهمر
pose v يستوضع , تكلف	**poverty** n فَقْر
pose n الوضْعَة	**powder** n مسحوق
posh adj أنيق	**power** n قوة
position n موضع	**powerful** adj قويّ
positive adj إيجابيّ	**powerless** adj ضعيف
possess v حاز	**practical** adj عمليّ
possession n حيازة	**practice** v يمارس

P

practice v يزاول

practising adj ممارسة

pragmatist adj ذرائعي

prairie n مَرْج

praise v يُطْري

praise n إطْراء

praiseworthy adj جديرٌ بالإطراء

prank n مَزْحَةٌ

prawn n القُرَيْدِس

pray v يصلي

prayer n صلاة

preach v يعظ

preacher n الواعظ

preaching n وَعْظٌ

preamble n تمهيد

precarious adj متقلقل

precaution n حَذَرٌ

precede v يسبق

precedent n سابقة

preceding adj سابق

precept n مبدأ

precious adj نفيس

precipice n جُرُفٌ

precipitate v ترسب

precise adj دقيق

precision n دقّة

precocious adj مبكر

precursor n البشير

predecessor n سَلَفٌ

predicament n مأزق

predict v يتنبّأ

prediction n تنبُّؤ

predilection n مَيْل

predisposed adj حساس

predominate v يسود

preempt v يحتلّ

prefabricate v صنع مقدما

preface n مقدّمة

prefer v يُفضّل

preference n تفضيل

prefix n بادئة

pregnancy n حَمْل

pregnant adj حامل

prehistoric adj قَبْتاريخي

prejudice n إجْحاف

preliminary adj تمهيديّ

prelude n مقدمة

premature adj سابق لأوانه

premeditate v يتعمّد

premeditation n التعمُّد

premier adj أوّل

premise n فَرْض

premises n إفتراض

premonition n هاجسٌ

preoccupation n انهماك

preoccupy v شغل

preparation n استعداد	**prevail** v ساد
prepare v يستعد	**prevalent** adj سائد
preposition n حرف جرّ	**prevent** v يعوق
prerequisite n شرطٌ	**prevention** n وقاية
prerogative n امتياز	**preventive** adj وقائيّ
prescribe v يصف	**preview** n عرض مسبّق
prescription n وصفة طبّية	**previous** adj سابق
presence n حضور	**previously** adv سابقاً
present adj حاضر	**prey** n فريسة
present v حضر	**price** n سِعْر
presentation n عرض	**pricey** adj غال
preserve v يحفظ	**prick** v يثقب
preside v يترأس	**pride** n غرور
presidency n الرئاسة	**priest** n قِسّيس
president n رئيس	**priestess** n قسّيسة
press n طباعة , الصحافة	**priesthood** n جماعة الكَهَنة
press v يُصرّ على , يحثّ	**primacy** n الأوّلية
pressing adj ضاغط	**primarily** adv أولاً
pressure v ضغط	**prime** adj أوليّ
pressure n ضَغْط	**primitive** adj بدائيّ
prestige n هيبة	**prince** n أمير
presume v يفترض	**princess** n أميرة
presumption n افتراض	**principal** adj رئيسيّ
presuppose v إفترض مسبقا	**principle** n قاعدة
pretend v تظاهر	**print** v يطبع
pretense n دعوى	**print** n طبعة
pretension n ذريعة	**printer** n طابع
pretty adj ظريف	**printing** n طباعة

P

prior adj سابق

priority n الأسبقية

prism n مَوْشـور

prison n سِجْن

prisoner n السجين

privacy n عزلة

private adj خصوصيّ

privilege n امتياز

prize n جائزة

probability n احتمال

probable adj مُحْتَمَل

probe v سبر

probing n مِسْبَر

problem n مشكلة

problematic adj مُشْكِل

procedure n إجراءات

proceed v ينبثق

proceedings n محضر

proceeds n رِبْح

process v يُعامل

process n عملية

procession n موكب

proclaim v يعلن

proclamation n إعلان

procrastinate v يماطل

procreate v يُنْجِب

procure v يدبّر

prod v يَنْخَس

prodigious adj مذهل

prodigy n معجزة

produce v يُخْرج

produce n نِتاج

product n مُنْتَج

production n نِتاج

productive adj منتج

profane adj دنيويّ

profess v درس

profession n مهنة

professional adj مِهْنيّ

professor n الأستاذ

proficiency n براعة

proficient adj بارع

profile n صُورَةٌ جانِبيّة

profit v يستفيد

profit n فائدة

profitable adj مُفيد

profound adj عميق

program n برنامج

programmer n مبرمج

progress v يتقدّم

progress n تقدّم

progressive adj تقدمي

prohibit v يحرّم

prohibition n تحريم

project v خطط

project n مشروع

projectile n قذيفة	**prosecute** v قاضى
prologue n مقدمة	**prosecutor** n المدّعي
prolong v يَمُدّ	**prospect** n أفاق
promenade n نزهة	**prosper** v يزدهر
prominent adj ناتئ	**prosperity** n ازدهار
promiscuous adj لاأخلاقي	**prosperous** adj مزدهر
promise n وعْدٌ	**prostate** n البروستات
promote v رقى	**prostrate** adj ساجد
promotion n ترقية	**protect** v يحمي
prompt adj يَقِظ	**protection** n حماية
prone adj مَيّال إلى	**protein** n البروتين
pronoun n ضمير	**protest** v يحتجّ
pronounce v أعلن	**protest** n احتجاج
proof n برهان	**protocol** n البروتوكول
propaganda n دعاية	**prototype** n النموذج
propagate v انتشر	**protract** v خطط
propel v يدفع	**protracted** adj يخطّط
propensity n مَيْل	**protrude** v نتأ
proper adj مناسب	**proud** adj متكبّر
properly adv بضبط	**proudly** adv بغَطرَسَة
property n خاصيّة	**prove** v يختبر
prophecy n نُبوّة	**proven** adj مُثْبَت
prophet n نبيّ	**proverb** n مَثَلٌ
proportion n نسبة	**provide** v يزوّد
proposal n اقتراح	**providence** n العناية الإلهية
propose v اقترح	**providing that** c بشرط
proposition n مُقْتَرَحٌ	**province** n إقليم
prose n النَثْر	**provision** n احتياط

P

provisional *adj* مؤقّت	**puff** *n* نفخة
provocation *n* تحريض	**puffy** *adj* منتفخ
provoke *v* حرض	**pull** *v* يقتلع
prow *n* مقدمة المركب	**pull ahead** *v* تقدم
prowl *v* يَجُوْس	**pull down** *v* نزل
prowler *n* متسكع	**pull out** *v* رحل
proximity *n* جوار	**pulley** *n* بَكَرة
proxy *n* وكالة	**pulp** *n* لُبّ
prudence *n* حذَر	**pulpit** *n* مِنْبر
prudent *adj* حذِر	**pulsate** *v* ينبض
prune *v* يقلّم	**pulse** *n* الحبوب
prune *n* برقوق	**pulverize** *v* يسحق
prurient *adj* شَهواني	**pump** *v* يضّخ
pseudonym *n* الاسم المستعار	**pump** *n* مِضَخّة
psychiatrist *n* طبيب نفساني	**pumpkin** *n* قَرْعَة
psychiatry *n* طبّ النفس	**punch** *v* لكم , نخس
psychic *adj* نفسيّ	**punch** *n* لكمة
psychology *n* السيكولوجيا	**punctual** *adj* دقيق
psychopath *n* السيكوباتي	**puncture** *n* ثُقْب
puberty *n* البلوغ	**punish** *v* يُعَاقِب
public *adj* عامّ	**punishable** *adj* مستحق للعقاب
publication *n* إذاعة	**punishment** *n* عقاب
publicity *n* دعاية	**pupil** *n* تلميذ
publicly *adv* جهاراً	**puppet** *n* دمية
publish *v* يُذيع	**puppy** *n* جَرْو
publisher *n* الناشر	**purchase** *v* اشترى
pudding *n* البودنْغ	**purchase** *n* شراء
puerile *adj* صِبْياني	**pure** *adj* خالص

P

puree n هريس	
purgatory n الأعْراف	# Q
purge n تطهير	
purge v يطهّر	**quagmire** n مستنقع
purification n تَطْهير	**quail** n السَّلْوَى
purify v يُطهّر	**quake** v يهتز
purity n طهارة	**qualify** v يؤهّل
purple adj أرجواني	**quality** n نوعيّة
purpose n غاية	**qualm** n غثيان
purposely adv عمداً	**quandery** n مأزق
purse n مَحْفَظَةُ	**quantity** n كميّة
pursue v تعقب , طارد	**quarrel** v يتنازع
pursuit n مطاردة , ملاحقة	**quarrel** n نزاع
pus n قَيْح	**quarrelsome** adj مشاكس
push v يَدْفع	**quarry** n طريدة
pushy adj انتهازي	**quarter** n رُبْع
put iv رمية	**quarterly** adj فصْليّ
put aside v يدّخر	**quarters** n رُبْع
put away v يطّرح	**quash** v يسحق , يقمع
put off v يتخلّص من	**queen** n مَلِكة
put out v يَمُدّ	**queer** adj غريب
put up v شيد	**quell** v يقمع
put up with v تابع	**quench** v يطفئ
putrid adj عفِن	**quest** n تحقيق
puzzle n لغز	**question** v سأل
puzzling adj يُحيّر	**question** n سؤال
pyramid n هَرَم	**questionable** adj مريب
python n الأصَلة	**questionnaire** n اسْتِفْتاء

P
Q

queue n ضفيرة
quick adj سريع
quicken v نشط
quickly adv بسرعة
quicksand n الوَعْث
quiet adj هادئ
quietness n هدوء
quilt n لِحَاف
quit iv فعلاً
quite adv فعلاً
quiver v يهتزّ
quiz v يسخر
quotation n الاقتباس
quote v يقتبس
quotient n حاصل

Q
R

R

rabbi n الرّبّان
rabbit n الأرنب
rabies n الكَلَب
raccoon n الرّاكون
race v يُسابق
race n مسابقة . مباراة
racism n عنصرية

racist adj عنصري
racket n مضرب التنس
racketeering n مبتز للأموال
radar n الرادار
radiation n الإشعاع
radiator n المِشْعاع
radical adj جذريّ
radio n راديو
radish n فِجْلة
radius n نصف القطر
raffle n البيع اليانصيبيّ
raft n الرَّمَث
rag n خِرْقة
rage n غيظ
ragged adj مُمَزّق
raid n غارة, مداهمة
raid v يُغير على
raider n مغير
rail n حاجز . سياج
railroad n سكة حديدية
rain n مَطر
rain v تُمطِر
rainbow n قوس قُزَح
raincoat n المِمْطر
rainfall n هطول المطر
rainy adj مُمْطِر
raise n ارتفاع
raise v يَرفع , يثير

raisin n زبيب	rat n فأر
rake n المِدَمّة	rate n سعر , قيمة
rally n تجمع	rather adv بالأحرى
ram n كبش	ratification n إقرار
ram v ينطح	ratify v يصدّق على
ramification n تشعُّب	ratio n نسبة
ramp n انحدار	ration v حصص
rampage v ثور	ration n حصة
rampant adj متفش	rational adj معقول
ramson v بقرم	rationalize v يسوّغ
ranch n مزرعة كبيرة	rattle v يُقعقِع
rancor n ضغينة	ravage v يَنْهَب
randomly adv عَشْوائِيًّا	ravage n خراب
range n صفّ	rave v يهذي
rank n مرتبة, صف	raven n غراب أسود
rank v يرتّب	ravine n المسيل
ransack v يفتّش بتدقيق	raw adj نَيْء
rape v يَغْتَصِب	ray n شُعاع
rape n إغْتِصاب	raze v يُدمِّر
rapid adj سريع	razor n موسى الحلاقة
rapist n مغتصب	reach v يبلغ
rapport n علاقة	reach n مجال
rare adj نادر	react v يؤَثّر
rarely adv نادرًا	reaction n رد فعل
rascal n وَغْد	read iv قرأ
rash v اقتلع	reader n القارئ
rash n طفح جلدي	readiness n استعداد
raspberry n فراولة	reading n قراءة

R

ready adj مستعدّ	**rebuke** n توبيخ
real adj حقيقيّ	**rebut** v دفع بالحجة
realism n الواقعيّة	**recall** v استرداد
reality n حقيقة	**recant** v يستردّ
realize v يدرك	**recap** v لخص
really adv في الواقع	**recapture** v يستردّ
realm n مملكة	**recede** v تقهقر
realty n العِقار	**receipt** n استلام
reap v يَحصد	**receive** v تسلم
reappear v بدا	**recent** adj حديث
rear v يربّي	**reception** n الاستقبال
rear n مُؤخّرة	**receptive** adj تقبُّليّ
rear adj خلفيّ	**recess** n ارتداد
reason v يفكّر	**recession** n ارتداد
reason n صواب	**recharge** v شحن البطارية
reasonable adj معقول	**recipe** n وصفة
reasoning n استنتاج	**reciprocal** adj تَبادُليّ
reassure v طمأن	**recital** n تلاوة
rebate n خَصم	**recite** v يتلو
rebel v يتمرّد	**reckless** adj طائش
rebel n متمرّد	**reckon** v يعتبر
rebellion n تمرد	**reckon on** v اعتمد
rebirth n نهضة	**reclaim** v يُصلِح
rebound v يرتدّ	**recline** v يحني
rebuff v يَصُدّ	**recluse** n الناسك
rebuff n صدّ	**recognition** n تمييز
rebuild v أعاد بناءً	**recognize** v يميّز
rebuke v وبخ	**recollect** v يَذكُر

R

recollection n تذكُّر	recur v يعاود
recommend v يفوّض أمرَه إلى	recurrence n تكرار
recompense v يكافئ	recycle v أعاد تصنيع
recompense n مكافأة	red adj أحمر
reconcile v أصلح ذات البين	red tape n روتين
reconsider v أعاد البحث	redden v يُحمِّر
reconstruct v أعاد البناء	redeem v يفتدي
record v يدوّن , يسجّل	redemption n افتداء
record n تسجيل , مَحْضَر	red-hot adj ملتهب
recorder n المسجّل	redo v قام ثانية بـ
recording n تسجيل	redouble v يضاعف
recount n يَسْرد	redress v يُصْلِح
recoup v يستردّ	reduce v قلص
recourse v تواتر	redundant adj فائض
recourse n التجاء	reed n خَيْزُرَانة
recover v إستعاد	reef n ثَنية الشِّراع
recovery n استرداد	reel n بَكَرَة . مِكبّ
recreate v يُنْعِش	reelect v أعاد إنتخاب
recreation n استجمام	reenactment n تشريع قانون
recruit v يجنّد	reentry n استرداد الملك
recruit n مجنَّد	refer to v يحكم بين ًّ
recruitment n تجنيد	referee n حَكَّم ٌ
rectangle n المستطيل	reference n مَرْجع
rectangular adj مستطيلي	referendum n مذكّرة
rectify v يصحّح	refill v يملأ ثانية
rector n عميد	refinance v يمول ثانية
rectum n شرج	refine v يكرّر
recuperate v يعوّض	refinery n مِصْفاة

R

reflect v ينعكس	**regime** n النظام
reflection n انعكاس	**regiment** n حشد
reflexive adj انعكاسيّ	**region** n منطقة
reform v يعدّل	**regional** adj إقليميّ
reform n إصلاح	**register** v يسجّل
refrain v اللازمة	**registration** n تسجيل
refresh v يُنْعِش	**regret** v يأسف
refreshing adj منعش	**regret** n أسف
refreshment n انتعاش	**regrettable** adj مؤسف
refrigerate v يبرّد	**regularity** n النظاميّة
refuel v زود	**regularly** adv بانتظام
refuge n ملجأ	**regulate** v ينظّم
refugee n اللاجئ	**regulation** n مرسوم
refund v أعاد مالا	**rehabilitate** v يُصلِح
refund n إعادة مالِ	**rehearsal** n مراجعة
refurbish v رمم	**rehearse** v يدرّب
refusal n رفضٌ	**reign** v يحكم
refuse v يَرْفُضُ	**reign** n حُكم
refuse n نُفاية	**reimburse** v عوض
refute v يُفنّد	**rein** v يكبح
regain v يستردّ	**rein** n عِنان
regal adj فخم	**reindeer** n الرّنة
regard v يحترم	**reinforce** v يقوّي
regarding pre في ما يتّصل بـ	**reiterate** v يكرّر
regardless adv مهما يكن	**reject** v يرفض
regards n تحيّات	**rejection** n رَفْضٌ
regeneration n تجديد	**rejoice** v يُهج
regent n وصي العرش	**rejoin** v ينضم ثانيةً

R

rejuvenate v يجدّد	reluctantly adv على كره
relapse n انتكاس	rely on v أعتمد على
related adj متعلق	remain v يَبقى
relationship n علاقة	remainder n بقيّة
relative adj موصول	remaining adj متبق
relative n القريب	remains n بقايا
relax v يسترخي	remake v صنع ثانية
relax n استرخاء	remark v يلاحظ
relaxing adj مسترخ	remark n ملاحظة
relay v تناوب	remarkable adj جدير بالملاحظة
release v يُطْلِق	remarry v يتزوّج ثانيةً
relegate v يَنفي	remedy v يعالج
relent v يَرقّ	remedy n علاج
relentless adj قاس	remember v يَذْكُر
relevant adj مناسب	remembrance n ذكرى
reliable adj موثوق	remind v يُذكّر
reliance n تعويل	reminder n المذكّر
relic n تذكار	remission n غُفْران
relief n نجدة	remit v يَغْفِر
relieve v يُنْجد , يُسعف	remittance n إيداع
religion n دِيْن	remnant n بقيّة
religious adj دِينيّ	remodel v صاغ من جديد
relinquish v تخلى	remorse n ندامة
relish v يستمتع	remorseful adj نادم جداً
relive v يحيا	remote adj من بعد
relocate v رحيل	removal n انتقال
relocation n ترحيل	remove v يَنقل
reluctant adj مُقَاوم	remunerate v عوض

R

renew v يُجَدّد	**reply** n جواب
renewal n تجديد	**report** v يقدّم تقريراً
renounce v تخلى	**report** n تقرير
renovate v يحيي	**reportedly** adv كما يعتقد
renovation n إحياء	**reporter** n المُخْبِر
renowned adj مشهور	**repose** v استراح
rent v يؤجّر	**repose** n راحة
rent n إيجار	**represent** v يمثّل
reorganize v أعاد تنظيم	**repress** v كبح
repair v يُصلح	**repression** n كبح
reparation n إصلاح	**reprieve** n إرجاء
repatriate v شخص معاد لوطنه	**reprint** v يعيد الطبع
repay v جازى	**reprint** n طبعة ثانية
repayment n مجازاة	**reprisal** n انتقام
repeal v يلغي	**reproach** v يلوم
repeal n إلغاء	**reproach** n لوم
repeat v يكرّر	**reproduce** v أنتج ثانية
repel v صد	**reproduction** n إنتاج
repent v يتوب	**reptile** n زاحف
repentance n توبة	**republic** n جمهورية
repetition n تكرار	**repudiate** v تبرأ
replace v يستبدل	**repugnant** adj بغيض
replacement n تبديل	**repulse** v صد
replay n معادة	**repulse** n صدّ
replenish v يستكمل	**repulsive** adj كريه . بغيض
replete adj مُتْخَم	**reputation** n سُمعة
replicate v طوى	**reputedly** adv علي ما يقال
reply v يُجيب	**request** v يسأل

R

request n سؤال

require v يتطلّب

requirement n مَطلَب

rescue v يُنقِذ

rescue n إنقاذ

research v يبحث

research n بحث

resemblance n تشابه

resemble v شابه

resent v استاء

resentment n استياء

reservation n حَجْز

reserve v يحجز

reservoir n خزّان

reside v أقام

residence n إقامة

residue n رواسب

resign v استقال

resignation n اِسْتِقَالة

resilient adj مرن

resist v يقاوم

resistance n مقاومة

resolute adj مصمّم

resolution n حل

resolve v يحلّ

resort v يلجأ

resounding adj يُدَوّي

resource n مَورد

respect v يحترم

respect n احترام

respectful adj متسم بالاحترام

respective adj شخصيّ

respiration n تنفُّس

respite n إرجاء

respond v يجيب

response n إجابة

responsibility n مسؤوليّة

responsible adj مسؤول

responsive adj مستجيب

rest v يرقد

rest n نوم

rest room n حجرة التواليت

restaurant n مَطعَم

restful adj مُريح

restitution n إرجاع

restless adj ضَجِر

restoration n إرجاع

restore v يعيد

restrain v يكبح

restraint n كَبْح

restrict v حصر

result n نتيجة

resume v أوجز

resumption n استئناف

resurface v يظهر على السطح

resurrection n بَعْث

R

resuscitate v يُنعِش	**revert** v يعود
retain v يحتفظ بـ	**review** v إعادة نظر , مراجعة
retaliate v يثأر	**review** n إعادة نظر , نقد
retaliation n ثأر	**revise** v راجع
retarded adj يَعُوْق	**revision** n تنقيح
retention n احتفاظ	**revive** v ينتعش
retire v ينسحب , يتقاعد	**revoke** v يلغي
retirement n انسحاب , تقاعد	**revolt** v يثور
retract v يَسْحَب	**revolt** n ثورة
retreat v ينسحب	**revolting** adj ثائر
retreat n انسحاب , تراجع	**revolve** v يفكّر في
retrieval n استرداد	**revolver** v سدس
retrieve v استعاد	**revue** n عمل مسرحيّ
retroactive adj رجعي	**revulsion** n تغيُّر
return v يعود	**reward** v يكافئ
return n عودة	**reward** n مكافأة
reunion n اجتماع	**rewarding** adj مكافئ
reveal v إفشاء	**rheumatism** n الروماتزم
revealing adj موح	**rhinoceros** n الكركدَنّ
revel v استمتع	**rhyme** n سَجْع
revelation n وَحْي	**rhythm** n التناغم
revenge v يثأر	**rib** n ضِلع
revenge n ثأر	**ribbon** n وشاح
revenue n ربح	**rice** n رُزّ
reverence n تبجيل	**rich** adj غنيّ
reversal n انقلاب	**rid of** iv يتخلص من
reverse n عكس	**riddle** n احجية
reversible adj يُعْكَس	**ride** iv يركب . يمتطي

R

ridge n تلال سلسلة	rite n طَقْس
ridicule v سخر من	rival n المنافس
ridicule n سخرية	rivalry n تنافُس
ridiculous adj سخيف	river n نهر
rifle n بندقية	rivet v يُبرشم , لفت الانتباه
rift n صَدْع	riveting adj برشمة
right adv الي اليمين	road n طريق
right adj قويم , أيمن	roam v يطوف
right n يمين	roar v يَهْدر
rigid adj صلب	roar n هدير
rigor n صَرامة	roast v يشوي
rim n حافة	roast n مشويّ
ring iv يطوّق	rob v يَسْلب
ring n حلقة. طوق	robber n لص
ringleader n زعيم فتنة	robbery n لصوصيّة
rinse v يَشْطف	robe n ثوب
riot v شاغب	robust adj قويّ
riot n شَغَب	rock n صخر
rip v يَشُقّ	rocket n صاروخ
rip apart v مزق	rocky adj صخريّ
rip off v خادع	rod n قضيب
ripe adj يانع	rodent n القارض
ripen v يَنْضَج	roll v يُدَحْرج
ripple n تموّج	romance n الرومانسية
rise iv يَبْزغ	roof n سَقْف
risk v خاطر	room n حجرة , غرفة
risk n مخاطرة	roomy adj متّسِع
risky adj خطير	rooster n ديك

R

root n جِذر

rope n حَبْل

rosary n سُبْحَة

rose n وَرْد

rosy adj ورديّ

rot v يتعفّن

rot n تعفّن

rotate v يدور

rotation n دَوَران

rotten adj نَتِن

rough adj خشِن

round adj مستدير

roundup n جمع شمل

rouse v أثار

rousing adj مثير

route n مَسْلَك

routine n الروتين

row v يتشاجر

row n شجار

rowdy adj مشاكس

royal adj مَلَكيّ

royalty n المَلَكيّة

rub v يحتكّ بـ

rubber n مطاط

rubbish n نُفاية

rubble n دَبْش

ruby n ياقوت

rudder n دَفّة

rude adj خام

rudeness n خشونة

rudimentary adj بدائيّ

rug n سجادة

ruin v يخرّب

ruin n خراب

rule v يحكم

rule n حكم

ruler n الحاكم , المسطّر

rum n الرّمّ

rumble v يدمدم

rumble n دمدمة

rumor n إشاعة

run iv عَدْو

run away v يفرّ

run into v يصطدم بـ

run out v ينتهي

run over v تجاوز الحد

run up v يرتفع

runner n العَدّاء

runway n طريق

rupture n فَتْق

rupture v أصاب بالفتق

rural adj ريفيّ

ruse n خُدْعَة

rush v يندفع

Russia n روسيا

Russian adj روسيّ

R

rust v يَصْدَأ

rust n صَدأ

rustic adj ريفيّ

rust-proof adj بدون صدأ

rusty adj صَدِئٌ

ruthless adj قاس

rye n الجاوْدار

S

sabotage v يخرّب

sabotage n تخريب

sack v فصل, سرق

sack n كيس, نهب

sacrament n سر مقدس

sacred adj مكرّس

sacrifice n تضحية

sacrilege n تدنيس المقدسات

sad adj حزين

sadden v يُحْزِن

saddle n سَرْج

sadist n سادي

sadness n حُزْن

safe adj آمن

safeguard n حرَسٌ

safety n أمن

sail v يُبْحِر

sail n شراع

sailboat n مركب شراعي

sailor n بحّار

saint n قِدّيس

salad n سَلَطة

salary n راتب

sale n بَيْع

sale slip n قسيمة الشراء

salesman n البائع

saliva n لُعاب

salmon n السَّلمون

saloon n صالون

salt n مِلح

salty adj مالح

salvage v يُنقذ

salvation n إنقاذ

same adj عينُهُ

sample n عَيّنة

sanctify v يقدّس

sanction v يقرّر

sanction n إقرار

sanctity n قداسة

sanctuary n حَرَم

sand n رَمْل

sandal n خُفّ

sandpaper n ورق الزّجاج

R
S

sandwich n سندويتش

sane adj سليم العقل

sanity n سلامة العقل

sap n نُسْغُ

sap v أضعف

saphire n سفير

sarcasm n سُخْرَية

sarcastic adj سُخْريّ

sardine n السّردين

satanic adj إبليسيّ

satellite n قمرٌ صناعيّ

satire n هجاء

satisfaction n إشباع

satisfactory adj مُرْض

satisfy v يُشبع

saturate v يُشَبِّع بـ

Saturday n السبت

sauce n الصَّلْصَة

saucepan n الكَفْت

saucer n الصُّحَيْفَة

sausage n سُجُق

savage adj متوحّش

savagery n وحشيّة

save v ينقذ . يَدّخِر

savings n المدَّخَر

savior n المُنْقِذ

savor v يستطيب

saw iv يَنْشر

saw n مِنشار

say iv يقول

saying n قول

scald v يُحْرِق بُخار

scale v وزن

scale n كِفّة الميزان , سَفَطَة

scalp n فروة الرأس

scam n تَدْجيل

scan v يفحص بِدِقّة

scandal n فضيحة

scapegoat n كبش الفِداء

scar n النّدَب

scarce adj نادر

scarcely adv نادراً

scarcity n نُدرة

scare v يُفزع

scare n ذعرّ

scare away v ردع

scarf n لفاع

scary adj مروّع

scatter v يُبَعْثر

scenario n السيناريو

scene n مشهد مسرحيّ

scenery n جِهاز المسرح

scent n رائحة

sceptic adj النّزّاع إلى الشّك

schedule v يُدْرج

schedule n جدول , قائمة

scheme n برنامج	scrape v يَكْشط
schism n انقسام	scratch v يَخدش
scholar n تلميذ	scratch n خَدْش
scholarship n منحة تعليمية	scream v يصرخ
school n مدرسة	scream n صرخة
science n علم	screech v يصرخ
scientific adj عِلْمِيّ	screen n حاجز , وقاء
scientist n العالِم	screen v يحجب , يستر
scissors n مِقص	screw v يدير لولبيًا , يلوي
scoff v يهزأ	screw n لولب
scold v يوبّخ	screwdriver n مِفَكّ
scolding n توبيخ	scribble v يخربش
scooter n دراجة بخارية	script n مخطوطة المسرحيّة
scope n مَجال	scroll n الدّرْج
scorch v يَسْفَع	scrub v يفرك
score n عشرون	scruples n شكّ
score v يسجّل إصابةً	scrupulous adj شكّ
scorn v يزدري	scrutiny n تفحُّص
scornful n محتقِر	scuffle n يتشاجر
scorpion n عقرب	sculptor n النّحات
scoundrel n الوَغْد	sculpture n فنّ النحت
scour v طاف بالمكان مسرعا	sea n بحر
scourge n سَوْط	seagull n النورس
scout n الكشافة	seal v يَخْتِم
scramble v يخلط	seal n عَهْد . خَتْم
scrambled adj مخلوط	seal off v سدـ
scrap n قُصاصة	seam n دَرْزَة
scrap v يهجر	seamless adj غير ملحوم

S

seamstress *n* خيّاطة	seduce *v* يَغرّ
search *v* يفتّش	seduction *n* إغواء
search *n* تفتيش	see *iv* يرى
seashore *n* شاطئ البحر	seed *n* بزْرَة
seasick *adj* مصابٌ بدُوار البحر	seedless *adj* بدون بذر
seaside *adj* ساحِلي	seedy *adj* كثير البزور
season *n* فصل	seek *iv* يبحث عن
seasonal *adj* موسميّ	seem *v* يبدو
seasoning *n* إلتابل	segment *n* قطعة
seat *n* مقعد	segregate *v* يفصل
seated *adj* جالس	segregation *n* فَصْل
secede *v* إنشق على	seize *v* يستولي على
secluded *adj* منعزل	seizure *n* استيلاء
seclusion *n* عَزْل	seldom *adv* نادراً
second *n* الثاني	select *v* يختار
secondary *adj* ثانويّ	selection *n* اختيار
secrecy *n* تكتُّم	self-concious *adj* خجول
secret *n* سِرّ	self-esteem *n* احترام الذات
secretary *n* سكرتير	self-evident *adj* بديهيّ
secretly *adv* سِرّاً	selfish *adj* أنانيّ
sect *n* شيعة	selfishness *n* أنانية
section *n* مَقْطَع	self-respect *n* احترام النفس
sector *n* قِطاع	sell *iv* يبيع
secure *v* يصون	seller *n* سلعة رائجة
secure *adj* مصون	sellout *n* باع كل ما يملك
security *n* أمن	semblance *n* شكل
sedate *v* يسكن (الالام)	semester *n* نصف سنة
sedation *n* تسكين	seminary *n* بُوْرَة

S

senate n مجلس الشيوخ	**sergeant** n رقيب
senator n سناتور	**series** n سلسلة
send iv يقذف	**serious** adj جِدّيّ , خطير
sender n مُرسِل	**seriousness** n جِدّيّة , خطورة
senile adj شيخوخيّ	**sermon** n موعظة
senior adj أرشد	**serpent** n أفعى
seniority n الأرشدية	**serum** n المصل
sensation n حسّ	**servant** n خادم
sense v معنى	**serve** v يَخْدِم . ينفع
sense n معنى , حاسّة	**service** n خدمة
senseless adj مُعَمّى عليه	**service** v قام بصيانته
sensible adj مُدرك	**session** n جلسة
sensitive adj حسّاس	**set** n اتجاه
sensual adj جِسّيّ	**set** iv يُقْعِد
sentence v يحكم على	**set about** v ينشر إشاعةً
sentence n حكمٌ بعقوبة , جملة	**set off** v وضع، حدد
sentiment n عاطفة	**set out** v يشرع في
sentimental adj عاطفيّ	**set up** up يَنْصِب
sentry n حارس	**setback** n عقبة
separate v يَفْصِل	**setting** n وَضْع
separate adj منعزل	**settle** v يوطّد
separation n فَصْل	**settle down** v أهدأ
September n سبتمبر	**settle for** v اكتفى
sequel n نتيجة	**settlement** n توطيد
sequence n سلسلة	**settler** n المستوطِن
serenade n لحن	**setup** n قامة , قيافة
serene adj هادئ	**seven** adj سبع
serenity n هدوء	**seventeen** adj سَبعَ عشرة

S

seventh adj سابع	shameless adj مُخْزِ
seventy adj سبعون	shape v يصوغ
sever v يَفْصِل	shape n قالب
several adj منفصل	share v شاطر
severance n فَصْل	share n حصّة . نصيب
severe adj صارم , قاسٍ	shareholder n المساهم
severity n صرامة	shark n القِرْش
sew v يخيط	sharp adj ماضٍ , قاطع
sewage n مياه البوالع	sharpen v شحذ
sewer n بالوعة	sharpener n مِبْراة
sewing n خِياطة	shatter v يحطّم
sex n الجنس	shattering adj ساحق
sexuality n الجنسانية	shave v يَكْشط
shabby adj رثّ	she pro هي
shack n كوخ	shear iv يَجُزّ
shackle n غُلّ	shed iv يُريق
shade n ظليل , طيف	sheep n خروف
shadow n ظِلّ	sheets n المُلاءة
shady adj ظليل	shelf n رَفّ
shake iv يهتزّ	shell n صَدَفة
shaken adj مخلوط بالهزّ	shellfish n المَحار
shaky adj متزعزع	shelter v يَسْتر
shallow adj ضَحْل	shelter n مُلْتَجأ
sham n زائف	shelves n رَفّ
shambles n مَجْزَرٌ	shepherd n الراعي
shame v يُخجّل	sherry n خمرة
shame n خَجَلٌ	shield v يستر
shameful adj مُخْجل	shield n تُرْس

S

shift n فريق مناوبة	**shortcoming** n عيب
shift v يبدّل , يحوّل	**shortcut** n إختصار
shine iv لمع	**shorten** v يقصّر
shiny adj لامع	**shorthand** n اختزال
ship n سفينة	**shortlived** adj قصير الاجل
shipment n شَحْنة	**shortly** adv باختصار
shipwreck n سفينة غارقة	**shorts** n سروال قصير
shirk v يتجنّب	**shortsighted** adj حَسير
shirt n قميص	**shot** n إطلاق نار , لقطة
shiver v يرتعش	**shotgun** n بندقية رش
shiver n رعشة	**shoulder** n كِتف
shock v يَصدم	**shout** v يصيح
shock n صَدمَة	**shout** n صيحة
shocking adj فظيع	**shouting** n صيحة
shoddy adj رديء	**shove** v يَدْفع
shoe n حذاء	**shove** n دفع
shoelace n رِبَاطُ الجِذَاءِ	**shovel** n مِجْرَفة
shoepolish n خجول	**show** iv يَعْرض
shoestore n متجر أحذية	**show off** v يَتَبَاهَى
shoot iv أطلق , قذف	**show up** v ظهر
shoot down v يُطلِق	**showdown** n المكاشفة
shop v يتسوّق	**shower** n دُشّ
shop n مَتْجر	**shrapnel** n شظايا
shoplifting n سرق السلع	**shred** v يمزّق
shopping n دكّان	**shred** n خرقة
shore n شاطئ	**shrewd** adj قارس
short adj قصير , ناقص	**shriek** v يَصرُخ
shortage n نَقْص	**shriek** n صرخة

S

shrimp n الاربيان

shrine n مَقام

shrink iv انكمش

shroud n كَفَن

shrouded adj مُسَجّى

shrub n شجيرة

shrug v هز كتفيه

shudder n رعْدَة

shudder v يرتعد

shuffle v يُلَخْبط

shun v يجتنب

shut iv يُغلق

shut off v أوقف

shut up v يُسِكت

shuttle v يتحرّك جيئةً وذهوباً

shy adj جبان

shyness n جُبْن

sick adj مريض

sicken v يُمْرض

sickening adj مغث

sickle n مِنْجَل

sickness n مرض

side n جانب

sideburns n سالف الشعر

sidestep v تحرك بخفة

sidewalk n رصيف

sideways adv من الجَنْب

siege n حصار

siege v يحاصر

sift v يَنْخُل

sigh n تنهُّد

sigh v يتنهّد

sight n مَعلم

sightseeing v زار معالم

sign v يَسِم

sign n إشارة , إيماءة

signal n إشارة

signature n إمضاء

significance n دلالة

significant adj ذو معنى

signify v يَعْني

silence n هدوء

silence v أسكت

silent adj صامت

silhouette n المُسَلوَتَة

silk n حرير

silly adj أبله

silver n فِضّة

silverplated adj مطلى بالفضة

silversmith n صائغ الفضّة

similar adj متشابه

similarity n تَشابُةٌ

simmer v يغلي برفق

simple adj بسيط

simplicity n بساطة

simplify v يبسّط

simply adv ببساطة	**sister** n شقيقة
simulate v يتظاهر	**sit** iv يَجْلِس
simultaneous n متزامن	**site** n موقع
sin v يأتَمُر	**sitting** n جلوس
sin n إثم	**situated** adj واقع
since c بما أن	**situation** n موقع
since pre منذ	**six** adj ستّة
since then adv من قبل	**sixteen** adj ستّة عشر
sincere adj مخلص	**sixth** adj السادس
sincerity n إخْلاص	**sixty** adj ستّون
sinful adj مذنب	**sizable** adj كبير
sing iv يغنى	**size** n حَجْم
singer n مُغَن	**size up** v خمن
single n فرد	**skate** v يتزلّج
single adj أعزب . منفرد	**skate** n مزلج
singlehanded adj فردى	**skeleton** n هيكل
singleminded adj مخلص	**skeptic** adj الشُّكوكيّ
singular adj مُفْرَد	**sketch** v رسم
sinister n كارثة	**sketch** n مُخطَّط
sink iv يغرق	**sketchy** adj تخطيطى
sink in v غور	**ski** v يَتَزَحْلَق
sinner n الآثِم	**skill** n مهارة
sip v يَرشُف	**skillful** adj بارع
sip n رَشفَة	**skim** v يَقْشِد
sir n سيّدي	**skin** v يسلخ
siren n صفّارة الإنذار	**skin** n جلد
sirloin n قطعة لحم	**skinny** adj جلديّ
sissy adj مخنث	**skip** v طفر

S

skip n وثبة	**sleeveless** adj بلا أكمام
skirmish n مناوشة	**sleigh** n مَرْكبة الجليد
skirt n تنّورة	**slender** adj نحيل
skull n جُمْجُمَة	**slice** v قطع الى شرائح
sky n السّماء	**slice** n شريحة
skylight n المَنْوَر	**slide** iv ينزلق
skyscraper n ناطحة سحاب	**slightly** adv إلى حَدٍّ
slab n لوح	**slim** adj ممشوق، نحيل
slack adj رِخْو	**slip** v ينزلق
slacken v يُرْخي	**slip** n انسلال، زلّة
slacks n بنطلون واسع	**slipper** n خُفّ
slam v غلق بعنف	**slippery** adj زَلِق
slander n افتراء	**slit** iv يَشُقّ
slanted adj منحرف	**slob** adj قذر
slap n صفعة	**slogan** n شِعار
slap v يَصْفَع	**slope** n مُنحَدَر
slash n شَرْط	**sloppy** adj مُوحِل
slash v يَشْرُط	**slot** n اخدود
slate n الارِدواز	**slow** adj بطيء
slaughter v يذبح	**slow down** v يَخْفِضُ السرعة
slaughter n مَذْبَحَة	**slow motion** n بطيء الحركة
slave n العبد	**slowly** adv ببطء
slavery n استعباد	**sluggish** adj كسول
slay iv ذبح	**slum** n حيّ الفقراء
sleazy adj مهلهل	**slump** v هبط
sleep iv ينام	**slump** n هبوط
sleep n نوم	**slur** v يتغاضى عن
sleeve n كُمّ	**sly** adj ماكر

S

smack *n* طَعْم	snatch *v* امسك
smack *v* يتلمّظ	sneak *v* يَنْسَلّ
small *adj* صغير	sneeze *v* يَعْطُس
small print *n* فقرة صغيرة	sneeze *n* عَطْسة
smallpox *n* الجُدَريّ	sniff *v* يتنشّق
smart *adj* واخز	sniper *n* قناص
smash *v* يحطّم	snitch *n* نمّ
smear *n* لطخة	snooze *v* قفى
smear *v* يلطّخ , يلوّث	snore *v* غط
smell *iv* يَشُمّ	snore *n* غطيط
smelly *adj* ذو رائحة	snow *v* ثلجت
smile *v* يبتسم	snow *n* ثلج
smile *n* ابتسامة	snowfall *n* تساقُط الثلج
smith *n* الصائغ	snowflake *n* نُدْقَةُ الثَّلج
smoke *v* يَدْخِن	snub *v* يَزْجُرُ
smoked *adj* مدخن	snub *n* زَجْرة
smoker *n* المُدَخِّن	soak *v* يُنْقَع
smoking gun *n* دليل قاطع	soak in *v* نقع فى
smooth *v* يملّس	soak up *v* امتص
smooth *adj* أملس	soar *v* يحلّق
smoothly *adv* بنُعومَة	sob *v* يَنْشِج
smoothness *n* نعومة	sob *n* نَشيج
smother *v* يخنق	sober *adj* رزين
smuggler *n* المهرب	so-called *adj* المزعوم
snail *n* حَلَزُون	sociable *adj* اجتماعيّ النزعة
snake *n* حيّة	socialism *n* الاشتراكيّة
snare *v* نصب فخا	socialist *adj* اشتراكيّ
snare *n* شَرَكّ	socialize *v* إجتمع

S

society *n* جمعيّة

sock *n* السُّوْك

sod *n* مَرْج

soda *n* الصودا

sofa *n* الأريكة

soft *adj* مريح

soften *v* يُلَيّن

softly *adv* بلين

softness *n* نعومة

soggy *adj* نَدِيّ

soil *v* يلوّث

soil *n* لطخة

soiled *adj* مدنس

solace *n* عزاء

solar *adj* شَمْسِيّ

solder *v* يَلْحُمُ

soldier *n* جندي

sold-out *adj* مباعة

sole *n* أخمص القدم

sole *adj* وحيد

solely *adv* وَحدَهُ

solemn *adj* جليل

solicit *v* يَلْتَمِس

solid *adj* مُصْمَت

solidarity *n* تضامن

solitary *adj* معتزلٌ

solitude *n* انعزال

soluble *adj* ذواب

solution *n* حلّ

solve *v* يَحُلّ

solvent *adj* مِيْفاء

somber *adj* مُعتم

some *adj* بعض

somebody *pro* شخص ما

someday *adv* يوماً

somehow *adv* بطريقة ما

someone *pro* شخصٌ ما

something *pro* شيءٌ ما

sometimes *adv* أحياناً

someway *adv* بطريقةٍ ما

somewhat *adv* إلى حدّ ما

son *n* ابن

song *n* غناء

son-in-law *n* الصَّهر

soon *adv* قريباً

soothe *v* يهدئ

sorcerer *n* الساحر

sorcery *n* سِحْر

sore *n* قَرْح

sore *adj* مؤلم

sorrow *n* حزن

sorrowful *adj* حَزين

sorry *adj* آسِف

sort *n* نوع

sort out *v* شرح

soul *n* نَفْس

S

sound n صوت	**spanking** n رشيق
sound v يصوّت , يتردّد	**spare** v يصفح عن
sound out v يذيع	**spare** adj احتياطيّ
soup n حِساء	**spare part** n قطعة غيار
sour adj حامض	**sparingly** adv ببخل
source n منبع	**spark** n شرارة
south n الجنوب	**spark off** v أشعل
southbound adv متجه جنوبا	**spark plug** n شمعة الإشعال
southeast n الجنوب الشرقيّ	**sparkle** v أثّر ضئيل
southern adj جنوبيّ	**sparrow** n العصفور
southerner n الجنوبيّ	**sparse** adj متفرّق
southwest n الجنوب الغربيّ	**spasm** n تشنج
souvenir n تَذْكار	**speak** iv يتكلّم
sovereign adj مسيطر	**speaker** n المتكلّم , الخطيب
sovereignty n سيادة	**spear** n رمح
soviet adj سوفياتيّ	**spearhead** v يتقدم كرأس حربة
sow iv يَبْذُر الحَبّ	**special** adj خاص
spa n ينبوع معدني	**specialize** v يُخصّص
space n فُسحة	**specialty** n الخاصّيّة
space out v حدق	**species** n صِنف
spacious adj رَحْب	**specific** adj مميّز
spade n مِسْحاة	**specimen** n عيّنة
Spain n إسْبَانِيَا	**speck** n بُقْعَة
span v شبر	**spectacle** n مشهد
span n شِبْر . امتداد	**spectator** n المُشاهِد
Spaniard n الأسباني	**speculate** v يتأمّل
Spanish adj أسبانيّ	**speculation** n تأمّل
spank v يَصْفَع	**speech** n خطاب

S

speechless adj أبكم	**splendid** adj عظيم
speed iv يُسْرِع	**splendor** n روعة
speed n سرعة	**splint** n شريحة
speedily adv بسرعة	**splinter** n شَظِيّة
speedy adj سريع	**splinter** v يشظّي
spell iv يتهجّى	**split** n شِقّ . صدعٌ
spell n رُقْيَة	**split** iv يَشُقُّ
spelling n تهجئة	**split up** v انفصل
spend iv يُنْفِق	**spoil** v يسلب
spending n مصاريف	**spoils** n غنيمة
sperm n المَنِيّ	**sponge** n إسْفَنْج
sphere n كُرَة	**sponsor** n العَرّاب
spice n تابلٌ	**spontaneity** n العَفْويّة
spicy adj تابليّ	**spontaneous** adj عَفْوي
spider n عنكبوت	**spooky** adj شبحي
spiderweb n بيت العنكبوت	**spool** n مِكَبّ
spill iv يسفح	**spoon** n مِلعَقة
spill n لفافة ورقية	**spoonful** n مِلْء ملعقة
spin iv يَغْزل . يَنْسج	**sporadic** adj متقطّع
spine n العمود الفقري	**sport** n رياضة
spineless adj لا فقاري	**sportman** n الرياضى
spinster n الغَزّالة	**sporty** adj رياضي
spirit n روح	**spot** v ينقّط
spiritual adj روحيّ	**spot** n بُقعة , نقطة
spit iv يَبْصُق	**spotless** adj نظيف
spite n نِكاية	**spotlight** n ضوءٌ كشّاف
spiteful adj حاقد	**spouse** n الزوج
splash v رشش	**sprain** v التوى

S

sprawl v انبطح	**stability** n استقرار
spray v يَرُشّ	**stable** adj مستقرّ
spread iv ينشر , يبسط	**stable** n إسْطَبل
spring iv ينبثق , يطلُع	**stack** v يكوّم
spring n نبْعٌ , ينبوع	**stack** n كوْمَة
springboard n مِنَصّة الوثب	**staff** n عصا
sprinkle v نثر	**stage** n دَرَجَة
sprout v يَشطَأ	**stage** v نظم, خطف
spruce up up نظم	**stagger** v يترنّح
spur v يَنْخَس	**staggering** adj مربك
spur n مِهماز , غصنٌ ناتئ	**stagnant** adj راكد
spy v يستطلع	**stagnate** v يَرْكُد
spy n الجاسوس	**stagnation** n ركود
squalid adj قَذِر	**stain** v يُبقّع
squander v يُشتّت	**stain** n وصمة
square adj مربّع	**stair** n سُلّم
square n المُرَبّع . الخانَة	**staircase** n بَيْتُ السّلّم
squash v يسحق	**stairs** n سلَالِم
squeak v يَصِرّ	**stake** n وَتد . سِناد
squeaky adj حاد	**stake** v علم
squeamish adj سريع الغثيان	**stale** adj مبتَذَل
squeeze v يضغط	**stalemate** n مأزق
squeeze in v انحشر	**stalk** v يمشي بتشامخ
squeeze up v ضغط	**stalk** n ساق
squid n الحَبّار	**stall** n مربط الجواد
squirrel n السّنجاب	**stall** v يُمَاطِل
stab v يَطعن	**stammer** v يتمتم
stab n طعنة	**stamp** v يدوس

S

stamp n مِسْحَقَة	**state** v يعيّن
stamp out v سك العملة	**statement** n تعبير
stampede n فرارٌ جماعيّ	**station** n مَوْقِف
stand iv يقف	**stationary** adj ثابت
stand n مَوْقِف	**stationery** n القِرْطاسِيّة
stand for v يمثّل	**statistic** n إحصائى
stand out v يبرز	**statue** n نُصُب
stand up v يقف	**status** n وَضْع . منزلة
standard n عَلَم . راية	**statute** n تشريع
standardize v عاير, إختبر بمعيار	**staunch** adj لا ينفذ
standing n وقوف	**stay** v يدعم
standpoint n وجهة نظر	**stay** n دعامة
standstill adj تجميدى	**steady** adj ثابت , راسخ
staple v شبك	**steak** n شريحة من لحم
staple n رَزَّة	**steal** iv يتحدّر
stapler n دَبّاسَة	**stealthy** adj مُسْتَرَق
star n نجم	**steam** n بُخار
starch n نَشاء	**steel** n الفولاذ
starchy adj نَشَوِيّ	**steep** adj شاهق
stare v يُحدِّق	**stem** n ساقُ النبات
stark adj متصلّب	**stem** v حجز التيار
start v يبدأ	**stench** n نَتانة
start n بداية	**step** n دَرَجَة , خطوة
startle v يروّع فجأة	**step down** v تنازل
startled adj مروع	**step out** v يَخْرُجُ
starvation n جوع	**step up** v اذداد
starve v يجوع	**stepbrother** n أخ غير شقيق
state n دولة , ولاية	**step-by-step** adv بالتدريج

S

stepdaughter n ربيبة	stimulate v ينبّه
stepfather n زوج الأمّ	stimulus n المنبّه
stepladder n السَّبْيَة	sting iv يَلسَع
stepmother n زوجة الأب	sting n لَسْعَة , حُمَة
stepsister n أخت غير شقيقة	stinging adj لاذع
stepson n ربيب	stingy adj شحيح
sterile adj عقيم	stink iv يُنتِن
sterilize v يُعقّم	stink n نَتَنّ
stern n الكوثل	stinking adj منتن
stern adj صارم	stipulate v يشترط
sternly adv قوى كالفولاذ	stir v يحرّك , يثير
stew n يخنة	stir up v يثير
stewardess n مضيفة	stitch v يدرز
stick v يطعن	stitch n دَرزَة
stick iv غرز	stock v يختزن
stick around v بقي	stock n مواش , المخزون
stick out v برز	stocking n جورب
stick to v لزم	stockroom n مخزن
sticker n لاصقة	stoic adj رواقيّ
sticky adj لزج	stomach n مَعِدَة
stiff adj متبيّس	stone n حَجَر
stiffen v يُبيّس	stone v يرجم
stiffness n صلابة	stool n مقعد
stifle v يخنق , يُخمد	stop v يُوقِف
stifling adj خانق	stop n توقُّف
still adj ساكن	stop by v يزور
still adv لا يزال	stop over v توقف
stimulant n المنبّه	storage n مَخْزَن

S

store v يخزن

store n مخزون

stork n اللَّقْلَق

storm n عاصفة

stormy adj عاصف

story n حكاية , قصّة

stove n مَوْقِد

straight adj مستقيم

straighten out v سوى

strain v يَشُدّ

strain n إجهاد

strained adj مرهق

strainer n مِصفاة

strait n مَضيق

stranded adj محصور

strange adj أجنبيّ

stranger n الغريب

strangle v يَشْنُق

strap n رباط

strategy n الاستراتيجيّة

straw n قشّ

strawberry n الفريز

stray adj ضالّ

stray v يضِلّ

stream n نهر , جدول

street n شارع

streetcar n ترامواي

streetlight n مصباح الشارع

strength n قوّة

strengthen v يُقَوّي

strenuous adj نشيط

stress n ضَغْط , إجهاد

stressful adj مرهق للأعصاب

stretch n امتداد

stretch v يمدّد

stretcher n الموسّعة

strict adj صارم

stride iv خطا بخطوه واسعه

strife n نزاع

strike n ضَرَبة

strike iv يذهب , ينطلق

strike back v انتقم

strike out v سدد ضربات

strike up v استهل

striking n ضَرْب

string n خيط . سِلك

stringent adj صارم

strip n قطاع

strip v يزيل

stripe n ضربة

striped adj مخطَّط

strive iv كافح

stroke n ضَرَبة

stroll v يتمشّى

strong adj قويّ

structure n بناء

struggle v يكافح	**subscribe** v يكتتب
struggle n كفاح	**subscription** n اكتتاب
stub n جذل الشجرة	**subsequent** adj لاحِقّ
stubborn adj عنيد	**subsidiary** adj مُساعِد
student n الطالب	**subsidize** v دعم
study v يدرس	**subsidy** n إعانة ماليّة
stuff n أمتعة	**subsist** v يبقى
stuff v يحشو	**substance** n خلاصة
stuffing n حَشْوَة	**substandard** adj دومعيارى
stuffy adj مزكوم	**substantial** adj جوهري
stumble v يتعثر	**substitute** v يستبدِل
stun v يدوّخ	**substitute** n بديل
stunning adj مذهِل	**subtitle** n عنوان فرعيّ
stupendous adj مُذهِل	**subtle** adj رقيق
stupid adj أحمق	**subtract** v طرح
stupidity n حماقة	**subtraction** n الطّرْح
sturdy adj قويّ	**suburb** n الضاحية
stutter v يتمتم	**subway** n نَفَقّ
style n أسلوب	**succeed** v نجح
subdue v يُخضِع	**success** n نجاح
subdued adj مكبوح	**successful** adj ناجح
subject v يعرّض	**successor** n وريث
subject n مسند , موضوع	**succulent** adj عصاري
sublime adj سامٍ	**succumb** v يخضع
submerge v يغمر	**such** adj مِثل
submissive adj خاضع	**suck** v يمصّ
submit v يُسلِم إلى	**sucker** adj مَصّاص
subpoena n مذكرة إحضار	**sudden** adj فُجائيّ

S

suddenly adv فجأةً

sue v يقاضي

suffer v يعاني

suffer from v يعاني من

suffering n متألِّم

sufficient adj كافٍ

suffocate n اختناق

sugar n سُكَّر

suggest v يقترح

suggestion n اقتراح

suggestive adj مُوحٍ

suicide n انتحار

suit n التماس

suitable adj ملائم

suitcase n حقيبة سفر

sullen adj متجهِّم

sulphur n الكبريت

sum n مبلغ

sum up v قدر بسرعة

summarize v يُلخِّص

summary n مُوجَز

summer n الصيف

summit n ذِرْوَة

summon v استدعى

sumptuous adj سَخِيّ

sun n الشمس

sunblock n كريمة

sunburn n سَفْعَة

Sunday n الأحد

sundown n الغروب

sunglasses n نَظَّارَةٌ شَمْسِيَّة

sunken adj مغمور

sunny adj مُشْمِس

sunrise n الشروق

sunset n الغروب

superb adj جليل

superfluous adj فائض

superior adj متفوق

superiority n التَّفوّق

supermarket n مَتْجَرٌ كَبير

superpower n القوى العظمى

supersede v يخلف

superstition n خُرافَة

supervise v أشرف على

supervision n إشراف

supper n العَشاء

supple adj مِطواع

supplier n مزود

supplies n مخزون

supply v يزوّد

support v يحتمل

supporter n المؤيّد،

suppose v يعتقد

supposing c إفرض

supposition n فرضية

suppress v يقمَع

supremacy n سيادة	**suspense** n تَرَقُّب قَلِق
supreme adj الأسمى	**suspension** n تعطيل موقت
surcharge n عِبء ثقيل	**suspicion** n اشتباه
sure adj واثق	**suspicious** adj مشبوه
surely adv بثقة	**sustain** v يساند
surf v يسبح	**sustenance** n قوت
surface n سَطْح	**swallow** v ابتلع
surge n طُمُوّ	**swamp** n مستنقَع
surgeon n الجرّاح	**swamped** adj مغمور
surgical adv جراحيّ	**swan** n التّمّ
surname n كُنْيَة	**swap** v يقايض
surpass v فاق	**swap** n مقايضة
surplus n الفائض	**swarm** n الخَشْرَم
surprise v يفاجئ	**sway** v يتمايل
surprise n مفاجأة	**swear** iv يُقسِمُ
surrender v يُسلّم	**sweat** n عَرَق
surrender n تَسْليم	**sweat** v يَعْرق
surround v يطوّق	**sweater** n السترة المعرقة
surroundings n محيط	**Sweden** n السُّويد
surveillance n مراقبة	**Sweedish** adj سويدى
survey n فحص	**sweep** iv يكنس
survival n البقاء	**sweet** adj حُلو
survive v يبقى حيًّا	**sweeten** v يحلّي
survivor n ناجي	**sweetheart** n الحبيب
susceptible adj حسّاس	**sweetness** n حلاوة
suspect v يرتاب	**sweets** n حلوى
suspect n المشبوه	**swell** iv ينتفخ
suspend v يعطّل موقّتا	**swelling** n منتفخ

S

swift adj سريع
swim iv يَسْبَح
swimmer n السابح
swimming n سباحة
swindle v يخدع
swindle n خِداع
swindler n مشعوذ
swing iv يؤرجح
swing n تأرجُح , تمايُل
Swiss adj سويسريّ
switch v يضرب بالسّوط
switch n سَوط
switch off v قطع تيار
switch on v أشعل
Switzerland n سُويسرَا
swivel v دار على محور
swollen adj متورم
sword n سَيْف
swordfish n سمك أبو سيف
syllable n مَقْطَعٌ لَفْظيّ
symbol n رَمْز
symbolic adj رَمزيّ
symmetry n تناظر
sympathize v يتعاطف
sympathy n تعاطف
symphony n السّمفونيّة
symptom n عَرض
synagogue n كَنِيس

synchronize v يتزامَن
synod n السّنودس
synonym n المرادف
synthesis n تأليف
syphilis n السِّفْلس
syringe n مِحقَنة
syrup n شراب
system n نظام
systematic adj نِظاميّ

T

table n طاولة
tablecloth n السّماط
tablespoon n ملعقة المائدة
tablet n لوحة تذكارية
tack n المُسَيْمير
tackle v يعالج
tact n ذوق
tactful adj لبِق
tactical adj تكتيكيّ
tactics n التكتيك
tag n شريط الحذاء
tail n ذَيل
tail v يتعقّب

S
T

tailor n الخيّاط

tainted adj تالف

take iv يأخذ

take apart v يفكّك

take away v ينقل

take back v يستردّ

take in v يَسْتَوعِبُ

take off v ينزع

take out v يَقْتَلِعُ

take over v يتولّى الأمر

tale n إشاعة

talent n الطالب

talk v يتكلّم

talkative adj ثرثار

tall adj طويل

tame v يُدجّن

tangent n المماس

tangerine n اليُوسُفِيّ

tangible adj ملموس

tangle n تعقّد

tank n حوض

tanned adj مدبوغ

tantamount to adj مساو

tantrum n نَوْبَة غضب

tap n سِدادة

tap into v قرع

tape n شريط

tapestry n بساط حائط مزخرف

tar n قطران

tarantula n عنكبوت ذئبي

tardy adv بطيء

target n تُرس . هدف

tariff n تعريفة

tarnish v يُفسِد

tart n التُّرْتَة

tartar n التتاري

task n مهمّة

taste v يذوق , يتذوّق

taste n حاسة الذوق

tasteful adj حَسَنُ الذّوْق

tasteless adj تَفِهٌ

tasty adj لذيذ المَذاق

tavern n حانة

tax n ضريبة

tea n شاي

teach iv يعلّم

teacher n المعلّم

team n فريق

teapot n إبريق الشاي

tear iv يمزّق , ينتزع

tear n دمعة

tearful adj دامع

tease v يمشّط

teaspoon n ملعقة شاي

technical adj تِقْنيّ

technicality n التّقْنيّة

technician *n* فني

technique *n* تكتيك

technology *n* التكنولوجيا

tedious *adj* مُضجِر

tedium *n* ضَجَر

teenager *n* المراهق

teeth *n* أسنان

telegram *n* برقية

telepathy *n* التُّخاطر

telephone *n* الهاتف

telescope *n* المِقْراب

televise *v* يُتَلِفز

television *n* تلفزيون

tell *iv* يروي

teller *n* الرّاوي

telling *adj* شديد الأثر

temper *n* مِزاج

temperature *n* درجة الحرارة

tempest *n* عاصفة

temple *n* هيكل

temporary *adj* مؤقّت

tempt *v* يُغْري

temptation *n* إغراء

tempting *adj* مُغْر

ten *adj* عَشَرة

tenacity *n* تماسُك

tenant *n* المستأجِر

tendency *n* نزعة

tender *adj* غضّ , ضعيف

tenderness *n* رقة, حنان , طراوة

tennis *n* التِّنِس

tenor *n* مَغزَى

tense *adj* متوتّر

tension *n* توتر

tent *n* خَيْمَة

tentacle *n* مِجَسّ

tentative *adj* تجريبيّ

tenth *n* العاشر

tenuous *adj* رقيق

tepid *adj* فاتر

term *n* نهاية

terminate *v* ينتهي

terminology *n* المصطلَحات

termite *n* النمل الأبيض

terms *n* نهايات

terrace *n* دَكّة

terrain *n* أرض

terrestrial *adj* أرضيّ

terrible *adj* رهيب

terrific *adj* هائل

terrify *v* يروّع

terrifying *adj* مرعب

territory *n* إقليم

terror *n* رُعْب

terrorism *n* إرهاب

terrorist *n* الإرهابيّ

terrorize v أرهب	**thermostat** n ترموستات
terse adj جامع	**these** adj هؤلاء
test v يختبر	**thesis** n الفَرْضيّة
test n اختبار	**they** pro هم
testament n عهد	**thick** adj ثخين , سميك
testify v يَشْهَد	**thicken** v يُثخّن
testimony n شهادة	**thickness** n ثخانة
text n المتن	**thief** n لِصّ
textbook n الكتاب المدرسيّ	**thigh** n فَخِذ
texture n نسيج	**thin** adj رقيق , نحيل
thank v يشكر	**thing** n حادثة
thankful adj شاكر	**think** iv يعتقد
thanks n شكرا	**thinly** adv بضَعْف
that adj كَيْ	**third** adj ثالث
thaw v يذيب	**thirst** v يظمأ
thaw n ذوبان	**thirsty** adj ظامئ
theater n مسرح	**thirteen** adj ثلاثة عَشَر
theft n سَرقة	**thirty** adj ثلاثون
theme n موضوع	**this** adj بهذا القدر
themselves pro أنْفُسهم	**thorn** n الزُّعرور
then adv آنئذٍ	**thorny** adj شائك
theologian n اللاهوتيّ	**thorough** adj شامل
theology n اللاهوت	**those** adj أولئك
theory n نظرية	**though** c رَغْمَ ذَلِكَ
therapy n مداواة	**thought** n تفكير
there adv هناك	**thoughtful** adj عميق التفكير
therefore adv لذلك	**thousand** adj ألف
thermometer n المِحَرّ	**thread** v لولب

thread n سنّ اللولب	**thwart** v يعارض
threat n تهديد	**thyroid** n الغدّة الدَّرَقيّة
threaten v يهدِّد	**tickle** v يدغدغ
three adj ثلاثة	**tickle** n دغدغة
thresh v يَدْرس	**ticklish** adj حساس للدغدغة
threshold n عَتَبة	**tidal wave** n موجة عارمة
thrifty adj مزدهر	**tide** n المدّ والجزْر
thrill v يهزّ	**tidy** adj مرتّب
thrill n اهتزاز	**tie** v يربط . يعقد
thrive v ازدهر	**tie** n رباط . صلة
throat n حنجرة	**tiger** n نَمِر
throb n نَبْض	**tight** adj كتِيْم
throb v ينبض	**tighten** v يشدّ
thrombosis n الخَثّر	**tile** n آجُرة . قرميدة
throne n عرش	**till** adv حتّى
throng n حَشْد	**till** v يحرث
through pre خلال	**tilt** v يُميل
throw iv يرمي	**timber** n أشجار
throw away v ينبذ	**time** n وقت
throw up v تقيّأ	**time** v يُوقّت
thug n السَّفّاح	**timeless** adj سرمدي
thumb n بهام اليد	**timely** adj في حينه
thumbtack n دبوس طبعة	**times** n مواعيد
thunder n رَعْد	**timetable** n جَدْوَلٌ زَمَنيّ
thunderbolt n صاعقة	**timid** adj خجول
thunderstorm n عَاصِفَةٌ رَعْدِيّة	**timidity** n خجل
Thursday n الخميس	**tin** n قَصْدير
thus adv هكذا	**tiny** adj صغير جدّاً

tip n أسْلَة , طرفٌ مستدقّ	**tomb** n قبر
tiptoe n رأس إصبع القدم	**tombstone** n بلاطة ضريح
tired adj مُتْعَب	**tomorrow** adv غداً
tiredness n تعب	**ton** n طنّ
tireless adj لا يتعب	**tone** n نَبَرَة
tiresome adj مُتْعِب	**tongs** n مِلْقَط
tissue n نسيج	**tongue** n لسان
title n عنوان	**tonic** n مقو
to pre إلى	**tonight** adv هذه الليلة
toad n العُلْجُوْم	**tonsil** n اللوزة
toast v يحمّص الخبزَ , يدفّئ	**too** adv أيضاً
toast n شُرْب النخب	**tool** n أداة
toaster n مِحْمَصَة	**tooth** n سِنّ
tobacco n تبغ	**toothache** n وجع السنّ
today adv اليومَ	**toothpick** n الخِلال
toddler n طفل يبدأ المشي	**top** n قمّة
toe n إصبع القَدَم	**topic** n موضوع مقالةٍ
toenail n ظفر الرجل	**topple** v ينقلب
together adv معاً	**torch** n مشعل
toil v يكدَح	**torment** v يُعذِّب
toilet n مرحاض	**torment** n تعذيب
token n علامة	**torrent** n سَيْل
tolerable adj محتَمَل	**torrid** adj حارّ
tolerance n احتمال	**torso** n جذع التمثال
tolerate v يحتمل	**tortoise** n سُلَحْفاة
toll n مَكْسٌ , قَرْع الناقوس	**torture** v يعذِّب
toll v يقرع	**torture** n تعذيب
tomato n طماطِم	**toss** v يتقاذف

total *adj* إجماليّ	**tractor** *n* الجَرّارة
totalitarian *adj* ديكتاتوريّ	**trade** *n* مهنة
totality *n* مجموع كلّيّ	**trade** *v* يقايض
touch *n* مس, هيئة	**trademark** *n* علامة تجارية
touch *v* يلمِس	**trader** *n* التاجر
touch on *v* استعرض	**tradition** *n* التَّحدار
touch up *v* نقح	**traffic** *n* تجارة
touching *adj* مؤثّر	**traffic** *v* يتاجر بـ
tough *adj* متين	**tragedy** *n* التراجيديا
toughen *v* يمتّن	**tragic** *adj* تراجيديّ
tour *n* رحلة	**trail** *v* يتجرجر
tourism *n* السياحة	**trail** *n* ذَيْل
tourist *n* السائح	**trailer** *n* المُتَنَشِّرَة
tournament *n* مباراة	**train** *n* قطار
tow *v* يَقطُر	**train** *v* درب
towards *pre* نَحْو	**trainee** *n* متدرب
towel *n* مِنْشفة	**trainer** *n* المدرّب
tower *n* بُرْج	**training** *n* تدريب
towering *adj* شاهق	**trait** *n* مَسْحَة
town *n* بلدة	**traitor** *n* الخائن
town hall *n* دار البلدية	**trajectory** *n* مسار
toxic *adj* سُمّيّ	**tram** *n* تُرام
toxin *n* السُّمِّين	**trample** *v* يطأ
toy *n* دُمْيَويّ	**trance** *n* غَشْيَة
trace *v* يرسم	**tranquility** *n* هدوء
track *n* أثر	**transaction** *n* صفقة
track *v* يتعقّب	**transcend** *v* يتجاوز
traction *n* جَرّ	**transcribe** *v* ينسخ

transfer v يحوّل	treat v يفاوض
transfer n تحويل	treat n دعوة
transform v يتحوّل	treatment n معاملة , معالجة
transformation n تحوُّل	treaty n معاهدة
transfusion n نقل الدم	tree n شجرة
transient adj زائل	tremble v يرتجف
transit n عبور	tremendous adj مروّع
transition n انتقال	tremor n رجفة
translate v يترجم	trench n خَندق
translator n المترجم	trend n نزعة
transmit v بث	trendy adj شائع
transparent adj شفّاف	trespass v يأثم
transplant v يزدرع	trial n تجربة , اختبار
transport v ينقل	triangle n مُثلّث
trap n الطُّراب	tribe n قبيلة
trash n نُفاية	tribulation n بليّة
trash can n سلة النفايات	tribunal n محكمة
traumatic adj جرحي	tribute n جزية
traumatize v جرح	trick v يخدع
travel v يسافر	trick n حيلة , خدعة
traveler n المسافر	trickle v يَقْطُر
tray n صينيّة	tricky adj مُخادع
treacherous adj خائن	trigger v شن
treachery n خيانة	trigger n المِقْداح
tread iv يدوس	trim v يزيّن
treason n الخيانة العظمى	trimester n الفصل
treasure n كنز	trimmings n زَرْكَشَة
treasurer n الخازن	trip n زلة

trip v يتعثّر	**tuberculosis** n السُّلّ
triple adj ثلاثيّ	**Tuesday** n الثُّلاثاء
tripod n ثلاثيّ القوائم	**tuition** n تعليم
triumph n نَصْر	**tulip** n التُّوليب
triumphant adj منتصِر	**tumble** v يَتَشَقلَب
trivial adj مبتذل	**tummy** n بطن بلغة الأطفال
trivialize v جعله تافها	**tumor** n ورَم
trolley n الترولي	**tumult** n شَغَب
troop n جماعة	**tumultuous** adj مشاغِب
trophy n نُصب تذكاري	**tuna** n التُّنّ
tropic n المدار الاستوائي	**tune** n تناغم
tropical adj استوائيّ	**tune** v تناغم
trouble n ضِيق	**tunic** n التُّنْك
trouble v يُوجِع	**tunnel** n نفَق
troublesome adj مزعج	**turbine** n التُّربينة
trousers n سروال	**turbulence** n تمرُّد
trout n التُّروْتَة	**turf** n طبقة عشب
truce n هدنة	**Turk** adj التركيّ
truck n عربة نقل	**Turkey** n الديك الروميّ
trumped-up adj لفق	**turmoil** adj هياج
trumpet n بوق	**turn** n دَوَران
trunk n ساق . البدن	**turn** v يدير
trust v يثق	**turn back** v يرجع
trust n ثِقة	**turn down** v يطوي
truth n صِدق	**turn in** v ينعطف ويدخل
truthful adj صادق	**turn off** v يطفئ
try v يحاكم	**turn on** v يُشعِل
tub n حوض	**turn out** v انتهى

T

turn over v يَقْلِب

turn up v يقوّي

turret n البُرَيْج

turtle n سُلَحفاة

tusk n نابٌ

tutor n معلّم خصوصيّ

tweezers n مِلْقاط صغير

twelfth adj ثاني عَشَر

twelve adj اثنا عَشَر

twentieth adj العشرون

twenty adj عشرون

twice adv مرتين

twilight n شفق

twin n التَّوْأم

twinkle v يتلألأ

twist v يَجْدِل

twist n حَبْل , كعكة هلاليّة

twisted adj متشابك

twister n إعصار

two adj اثنان

tycoon n مليونير

type n نموذج , سِمَة

type v يمثّل

typical adj نَموذَجيّ

tyranny n جور

tyrant n المستبدّ

U

ugliness n بشاعة

ugly adj بشِع

ulcer n قَرْحَة

ultimate adj أقصى

ultimatum n إنذار

ultrasound n مغال في الصوت

umbrella n مِظَلّة

umpire n حَكَّمٌ

unable adj عاجز

unanimity n إجماع

unarmed adj أعزل

unassuming adj متواضع

unattached adj مستقلّ

unavoidable adj محتوم

unaware adj جاهل

unbearable adj لا يُطاق

unbeatable adj لا يُقْهَر

unbelievable adj لا يُصدَّق

unbiased adj عادل

unbroken adj متواصل

unbutton v يفكّ

uncertain adj ملتبس

uncle n العمّ

uncomfortable adj مزعج

uncommon adj غير مألوف

T
U

unconscious *adj* لا واع

uncover *v* يعرّي

undecided *adj* متردّد

undeniable *adj* لا يُجْحَد

under *pre* دون

undercover *adj* سرّي

underdog *n* خاسر

undergo *v* يتحمّل

underground *adj* تحأرضي

underlie *v* تخفى خلف

underline *v* أكد

underlying *adj* ضمني

undermine *v* قوض

underneath *pre* تحت

underpass *n* طريق تحتية

understand *v* يَفْهم

understandable *adj* معقول

understanding *adj* عاطف

undertake *v* يباشر

underwear *n* ثوب تحتيّ

underwrite *v* يُذَيّل

undeserved *adj* غير مستوجب

undesirable *adj* غير مرغوب فيه

undisputed *adj* مسلم به

undo *v* يفك

undoubtedly *adv* يقيناً

undress *v* يعرّي

undue *adj* غير ضروري

unearth *v* يكتشف

uneasiness *n* قلق

uneasy *adj* مرتبك

uneducated *adj* غير مثقّف

unemployed *adj* عاطل عن العمل

unemployment *n* البطالة

unending *adj* سرمدي

unequal *adj* غير متساوٍ

unequivocal *adj* بيّن

uneven *adj* وَتْرِيّ

uneventful *adj* هادئ

unexpected *adj* فجائيّ

unfailing *adj* ثابت

unfair *adj* جائر

unfairly *adv* ظُلْمًا

unfairness *n* ظلم

unfaithful *adj* خائن

unfamiliar *adj* غريب

unfasten *v* يفك

unfavorable *adj* سلبي

unfit *adj* غير كفؤ

unfold *v* يكشِف

unforeseen *adj* مفاجئ

unforgettable *adj* لا يُنْسَى

unfounded *adj* لا اساس له

unfriendly *adj* معاد

unfurnished *adj* غير مجهز

ungrateful *adj* عاقّ

unhappiness n تعاسة	**unload** v يُفرِّغ الحمولة
unhappy adj تعيس	**unlock** v يفتح
unharmed adj سالم	**unlucky** adj مشؤوم
unhealthy adj مريض	**unmarried** adj عازب
unheard-of adj جديد	**unmask** v يخلع القناع
unhurt adj غير ضار	**unmistakable** adj جليّ
unification n توحيد	**unnecessary** adj غير ضروريّ
uniform n منتظم	**unnoticed** adj غير ملحوظ
uniformity n انتظام	**unoccupied** adj شاغر
unify v يُوَحِّد	**unofficially** adv بصفة شخصية
unilateral adj آحادي الجانب	**unpack** v فضا
union n اتحاديّ	**unpleasant** adj كريه
unique adj وحيد	**unplug** v نزع القابس
unit n وحدة	**unpopular** adj غير شعبيّ
unite v يوحِّد	**unprofitable** adj غير مُربح
unity n وحدة	**unprotected** adj غير مقاوم
universal adj شامل	**unravel** v ينحلّ
universe n الكون	**unreal** adj مصطنَع
university n جامعة	**unrealistic** adj غير واقعى
unjust adj جائر	**unreasonable** adj غير عاقل
unjustified adj مستدل عليه	**unrelated** adj غير متصل
unknown adj مجهول	**unreliable** adj غير جدير بالثقة
unlawful adj محرّم	**unrest** n اضطراب
unleash v يحرِّر	**unsafe** adj خطِر
unless c إلّا إذا	**unselfish** adj إيثاريّ
unlike adj متخالف	**unspeakable** adj لا يُوصَف
unlikely adj بعيد الإحتمال	**unstable** adj مُزَعْزَع
unlimited adj مُطلَق	**unsteady** adj مُقلَقل

U

unsuccessful *adj* مخفق

unsuitable *adj* غير ملائم

unsuspecting *adj* غير مرتاب

unthinkable *adj* لا يُتَصَوَّر

untie *v* يفك

until *pre* إلى

untimely *adj* مبكّر

untouchable *adj* لا يمس

untrue *adj* خائن

unusual *adj* نادر

unveil *v* يَبْسط

unwillingly *adv* كرها

unwind *v* يحلّ

unwise *adj* أحمق

unwrap *v* فض

upbringing *n* تنشئة

upcoming *adj* وشيك

update *v* عصر

upgrade *v* حسن

upheaval *n* جَيَشان

uphill *adv* صُعُداً

uphold *v* يدعم

upholstery *n* تنجيد

upkeep *n* صيانة

upon *pre* على

upper *adj* عُلويّ

upright *adj* عموديّ

uprising *n* ثورة

uproar *n* اضطراب

uproot *v* يَجْتَثّ

upset *v* يَقْلِب

upstairs *adv* فوق

uptight *adj* عصبي

up-to-date *adj* عصري

upturn *n* اضطراب

upwards *adv* إلى فوق

urban *adj* مَدينيّ

urge *n* إلحاح

urge *v* يُلحّ

urgency *n* الإلحاحيّة

urgent *adj* مُلِحّ

urinate *v* يَبُوْل

urine *n* بَوْل

urn *n* جرة تحفظ رماد الوتى

us *pre* نا

usage *n* استعمال

use *v* يَسْتَعْمِل

use *n* استعمال

used to *adj* معتاد

useful *adj* نافع

usefulness *n* منفعة

useless *adj* عديم الجدوى

user *n* المستعمِل

usher *n* الحاجب

usual *adj* معتاد

usurp *v* يغتصب

utensil n إناء	**value** n قيمة
uterus n الرَّحِم	**valve** n صِمام
utilize v انتفع	**vampire** n الهامّة
utmost adj أعظم	**van** n مِروحة
utter v يلفظ	**vandal** n الوندالي
	vandalism n الوَنْدَلَة
	vandalize v يونلد
	vanguard n طليعة الجيش
	vanish v يتلاشى
V	**vanity** n تكبر
	vanquish v يهزم
	vaporize v يبخِّر
vacancy n شغور	**variable** adj متقلّب
vacant adj شاغر	**varied** adj معدَّل , متنوّع
vacate v يُبطِل	**variety** n تنوُّع
vacation n إبطال	**various** adj متنوّع
vaccinate v لقح	**varnish** v يصقل
vaccine n لِقاح	**varnish** n البَرْنْيق
vacillate v يتذبذب	**vary** v ينوّع
vagrant n المُتَشَرِّد	**vase** n الزَّهرية
vague adj غامض	**vast** adj فسيح
vain adj فارغ	**veal** n عِجْل
vainly adv عَبَثًا	**veer** v ينحرف
valiant adj شجاع	**vegetable** v نبات
valid adj صالح	**vegetarian** v نباتى
validate v جعله شرعيا	**vegetation** n الحياة النباتية
validity n شرعية	**vehicle** n مركبة
valley n وادٍ	**veil** n حِجاب
valuable adj نفيس	

U
V

vein n وَرِيد	**vestige** n أثر
velocity n سُرعة	**veteran** n جندي عريق
velvet n مُخْمَل	**veterinarian** n طبيب بيطريّ
venerate v بجل	**veto** v نقض
vengeance n انتقام	**viaduct** n جسر
venison n لحم الطرائد	**vibrant** adj مُتذبذب
venom n حقد	**vibrate** v يُذَبذب
vent n ثُقْب	**vibration** n ذبذبة
ventilate v يُهَوّي	**vice** n رذيلة
ventilation n تهوية	**vicinity** n قُرب
venture v يغامر	**vicious** adj فاسدٌ
venture n مغامرة	**victim** n ضَحيّة
verb n فعل	**victimize** v يضحّي
verbally adv لفظيًّا	**victor** n المنتصر
verbatim adv نَصًّا	**victorious** adj منتصر
verdict n قرار محكمة	**victory** n نَصْر
verge n صولجان	**view** n رؤية
verification n تحقيق	**view** v يشاهد
verify v يُثْبت	**viewpoint** n وجهة نظر
versatile adj متعدّد الجوانب	**vigil** n عشية العيد
verse n آية	**village** n قرية
versed adj متمكّن	**villager** n القَرَويّ
version n ترجمة	**villain** n النذل
versus pre ضدّ	**vindicate** v يبرئ
vertebra n فَقارَة	**vindictive** adj حقود
very adv جدًّا	**vine** n الكَرْمَة
vessel n وعاء	**vinegar** n خَلّ
vest n صُدْرَة	**vineyard** n كَرم

violate v يغتصب	vivid adj حيّ
violence n اغتصاب	vocabulary n المعجَم
violent adj عنيف	vocation n النداء الباطنيّ
violet n بنفسـج	vogue n موضة
violin n الكمان	voice n صَوْت
violinist n الكمانيّ	void adj شاغر , خِلْوٌ من
viper n الأفعى الخبيثة	volatile adj متطاير
virgin n العذراء	volcano n بركان
virginity n عُذْرَة	volleyball n الكرة الطائرة
virile adj رجوليّ	voltage n جهد كهربائى
virility n رجولة	volume n مقدار , كتلة
virtue n فضيلة	volunteer n المتطوّع
virtually adv واقعيًّا	vomit v يتقيّأ
virtuous adj خلقي	vomit n قَيْء
virulent adj خبيث	vote v يقترع
virus n الفيروس	vote n اقتراع
visibility n جلاء	voting n اقتراع
visible adj مَرْئيّ	vouch for v يؤكد
vision n رؤيا	voucher n وَصْل
visit n زيارة	vow v يُقْسم
visit v يزور	vowel n صوتُ لِيْن
visitor n الزائر	voyage v سافر
visual adj بَصَريّ	voyager n مسافر
visualize v يتصوَّر	vulgar adj مألوف
vital adj حيويّ	vulgarity n السُّوقيّة
vitality n حيوية	vulnerable adj قابل للعطب
vitamin n الفيتامين	vulture n نَسْر
vivacious adj نشيط	

V

W

wafer n الرُّقاقة

wag v يهتزّ

wage n أجر

wagon n سيّارة مقفلة

wail v يُعْول

wail n عويل

waist n خَصْر

wait v ينتظر

waiter n النادل

waiting n انتظار

waitress n النادلة

waive v يهجر

wake up iv يَسْتَيْقِظُ

walk v يمشي

walk n مَشْي

walkout n إضرابٌ عماليّ

wall n سُوْر

wallet n محفظة

walnut n جوز

walrus n الفَظّ

waltz n الفالس

wander v يتجوّل

wanderer n المتجوّل

wane v يتضاءل

want v يريد

war n حرب

ward n حراسة

warden n الحافظ

wardrobe n خزانة الثياب

warehouse n مستودع

warfare n نضال

warm adj دافئ

warm up v يُدَفِّئُ

warmth n دِفء

warn v يُحْذِّر

warning n تحذير

warp v يَفْتِل

warped adj ملتو

warrant v يضمن

warrant n ضمانة

warranty n ضمانة

warrior n المحارب

warship n سفينة حربيّة

wart n ثُؤلول

wary adj يَقِظ

wash v يَغْسِل

washable adj يغسل

wasp n زُنْبُوْر

waste v يخرّب

waste n قَفْر

waste basket n سلة المهملات

wasteful adj مخرّب

watch n تَيَقُّظ

watch v ينتبه	weapon n سلاح
watch out v إحترس من	wear n ملابس , بلى
watchful adj مؤرّق	wear iv يلبس , يتقلّد
watchmaker n الساعاتي	wear down v أبلى
water n ماء	wear out v تآكل, استمر
water v ينضح	weary adj منهك
water down v تزود بالماء	weather n الطقس
waterfall n شلال	weave iv يَنْسُج
waterheater n مسخن مائى	web n نَسْج العنكبوت
watermelon n البطّيخ الأحمر	wed iv يتزوّج
waterproof adj صامدٌ للماء	wedding n عُرْس
watershed n نقطة تحول	wedge n إسفين
watertight adj مَسِيْك	Wednesday n الأربعاء
watery adj مائيّ	weed n عشبة ضارّة
watt n الواطّ	weed v يزيل العشب الضارّ
wave n موجة , تموّج	week n أسبوع
waver v يتردّد	weekday adj أسبوعي
wavy adj مائج	weekend n نهاية الأسبوع
wax n شَمْع	weekly adv أسبوعيًّا
way n طريق , سبيل	weep iv يبكي
way in n مدخل	weigh v يَزِن
way out n مخرج	weight n وَزْن
we pro نَحْنُ	weird adj عجيب
weak adj ضعيف	welcome v يرحّب بـ
weaken v يُضْعف	welcome n ترحيب
weakness n ضَعْف	weld v يَلْحَم
wealth n غنى	welder n اللحامة
wealthy adj غنيّ	welfare n خير

W

well n وعاء لسائل

well-known adj معروف

well-to-do adj غَنِيّ

west n الغرب

westbound adv متجه نحو الغرب

western adj غربيّ

westerner adj الغربيّ

wet adj بَليل

whale n حوت

wharf n رصيف الميناء

what adj أَيّ

whatever adj أيّما

wheat n قَمْح

wheel n عَجَلة

wheelbarrow n عجلة اليد

wheeze v يَصْفِر

when adv متى

whenever adv في أي وقت

where adv أين

whereabouts n مُسْتَقِرّ

whereas c حيث أن

whereupon c وإذ ذاك

wherever c بماذا

whether c سواء

which adj أَيّ

while c بينما

whim n نزوة

whine v يَعْوي

whip v جلد، خطف

whip n سَوْط

whirl v يُدَوِّم

whirlpool n دُرْدُوْر

whiskers n شَارِب القط

whisper v يَهْمِس

whisper n هَمْس

whistle v يَصْفِر

whistle n صَفّارة

white adj أبيض

whiten v يُبَيِّضَ

whittle v يبري

who pro من

whoever pro كلّ مَن

whole adj سالم

wholehearted adj صادق

wholesale n البيْع بالجُملة

wholesome adj صحّيّ

whom pro من

why adv لِمَا

wicked adj شرّير

wickedness n خبث

wide adj واسع

widely adv على نحو واسع

widen v يوسّع

widespread adj ممتدّ

widow n أرملة

widower n الأرمل

width n عَرْض	wine n خَمْر
wield v دبر الأمر	winery n مصنع الخمرة
wife n زوجة	wing n جَناح
wig n اللُّمّة	wink n غمزة
wiggle v يتذبذب	wink v غمز
wild adj بَرّيّ	winner n الفائز
wild boar n خنزير بري	winter n الشتاء
wilderness n قَفْر	wipe v يَمْسَح
wildlife n حيوانات ضارية	wipe out هزم
will n مَيْل , رغبة	wire n سِلْك , برقيّة
willfully adv عَمْدًا	wireless adj لاسلكيّ
willing adj مستعدّ	wisdom n حكمة
willingly adv طوعا	wise adj حكيم
willingness n استعداد	wish v يتمنّى
willow n شجر الصَّفصاف	wish n أُمْنيَة
wily adj ماكِر	wit n عقل
wimp adj واهن	witch n السّاحرة
win iv يفوز	witchcraft n سِحر
win back v يَسْتَعِيدُ	with pre ضد
wind n ريح	withdraw v ينسحب
wind iv يستروح , يجفف	withdrawal n انسحاب
wind up عبأ الساعة	withdrawn adj يستردّ .
winding adj لَولبيّ	wither v يَذْبُل
windmill n طاحونة هوائية	withhold iv يكبح
window n نافذة	within pre فى
windpipe n الرُّغامى	without pre خارجَ كذا
windshield n الزجاج الأمامي	withstand v يقاوم
windy adj عاصف	witness n الشاهد

W

witty adj بارع	**worm** n دودة
wives n زوجة	**worn-out** adj رَثّ
wizard n العَرّاف	**worrisome** adj مقلق
wobble v يتذبذب	**worry** v يقلَق
woes n ويل	**worry** n قلَقٌ
wolf n ذئب	**worse** adj أسوأ
woman n امرأة	**worsen** v يجعله أسوأ
womb n الرَّحِم	**worship** n سيادة
women n نِسَاء	**worst** adj أسوأ
wonder v يَعجَب	**worth** adj ما يساوي كذا
wonder n عجيب	**worthless** adj تافه.
wonderful adj مدهش	**worthwhile** adj ذو شأن
wood n خشبٌ	**worthy** adj مستحق ل
wooden adj متخشّب	**would-be** adj راغب
wool n صُوف	**wound** n جُرْح
woolen adj صوفيّ	**wound** v يَجْرَح
word n كلمة	**woven** adj منسوج
wording n الصّياغة	**wrap** v يغطّي
work n عمل	**wrap up** v لف
work v يعمل	**wrapping** n غلاف
work out v تدرب	**wrath** n حَنَقّد
workable adj عمليّ	**wreath** n إكليل
workbook n دفتر العمل	**wreck** v يحطّم
worker n الشّغّيل	**wreckage** n حُطام
workshop n وَرْشَة	**wrench** n مفتاح رَبْط
world n العالم	**wrestle** v يكافح
worldly adj دنيويّ	**wrestler** n مُصَارع
worldwide adj عالميّ	**wrestling** n كِفاح , صِراع

W

wretched adj بائس	**yarn** n حكاية
wring iv يَعْصُر	**yawn** n تثاؤب
wrinkle v يتجعّد	**yawn** v يَنفَغِر
wrinkle n جَعْدَة	**year** n عام
wrist n المِعْصَم	**yearly** adv سنويًّا
write iv كتب	**yearn** v يتوق إلى
write down v يسجِّل	**yeast** n خميرة
writer n الكاتب	**yell** v صرْخة
writhe v غاضب جدا	**yellow** adj أصفر
writing n كتابة	**yes** adv نعمل
written adj مَكْتُوب	**yesterday** adv أمس
wrong adj خاطئ	**yet** c أيضاً
	yield v يمنَح , يَهَب
	yield n غلّة
	yoke n نِيْر

X

X-mas n شجرة عيد الميلاد	**yolk** n آلمُحّ
X-ray n الاشعة السينية	**you** pro أنْتَ
	young adj صغير
	youngster n شابّ
	your adj مِلكُكَ
	yours pro لكَ
	yourself pro نفسك
	youth n الشّباب
	youthful adj شابّ

Y

yacht n اليَخْت	
yam n اليام	
yard n يارد	

X
Y

Z

zap v يمحو يحذف

zeal n حماسة

zealous adj متحمّس

zebra n حمار الزَّرد

zero n صِفْر

zest n المُنَكّه

zinc n الزّنك

zip code n الرمز البريدي

zipper n الزِّمام ٱنمنزلق

zone n مِنْطقة

zoo n حديقة الحيوانات

zoology n عِلم الحيوان

Arabic-English

ا

الدّرْج n scroll	اتفاقية n convention
ابتداء n beginning	اتهام n accusation
ابتدائي adj initial	اثنا عَشَر adj twelve
ابتز v extort	اثنان adj two
ابتزاز n extortion	اجتماع n assembly
ابتزاز المال n blackmail	اجتماعي adj gregarious
ابتسامة n smile	اجتنابٌ n avoidance
ابتكار n innovation	اجرة الشحن n freight
ابتلع v ingest, swallow	اجهض v abort
ابتهاج n cheers, joy	احتاج v need
ابعد adv beyond	احتجاج n outcry, protest
ابليس n devil	احتجاز n detention
ابن n son	احترار n heat
ابن الأخ n nephew	احترام n respect, honor
ابن آوى n jackal	احترام الذات n self-esteem
ابن زنا n bastard	احترام النفس n self-respect
ابنة n daughter	احتشام n decency
اتجاه n set	احتشد v huddle
اتجه v head for	احتضن v clinch
اتحاد n alliance, merger	احتفاء n ovation
اتحاديّ n union	احتفاظ n retention
اتساع n immensity	احتفالي adj festive
اتفاق n agreement, accord	احتكار n monopoly
	احتكاك n friction
	احتمال n likelihood
	احتياط n provision

احتياطيّ spare adj	ارتاب distrust v
احجية riddle n	ارتباط liaison n
احد الامرين either adv	ارتباك clumsiness n
احياء animation n	ارتجاعيّ backward adj
اختار choose, opt for v	ارتجل improvise v
اختبار test, trial n	ارتداد recess n
اختبر examine v	ارتسم loom v
اختراق breakthrough n	ارتشاح infiltration n
اخترق permeate v	ارتشف gulp v
اختزال shorthand n	ارتطام hit n
اختصر outline; abbreviate v	ارتفاع elevation, raise n
اختطاف kidnapping n	ارتفع lift off v
اختطف grab v	ارتكب perpetrate v
اختفاء disappearance n	ارتياب distrust n
اختفى disappear v	ارق insomnia n
اختلاط chaos n	ازدحام jam, congestion n
اختلاف difference n	ازدراء disdain, contempt n
اختلال malfunction n	ازدرائيّ derogatory adj
اختلس embezzle, pilfer v	ازدرى look down v
اختناق suffocate n	ازدهار prosperity n
اختيار option, selection n	ازدهر flourish, thrive v
اختياريّ optional adj	استاء resent v
اخدود slot n	استأصل eradicate v
اخطف abduct v	استبعد exclude v
ادعاء allegation n	اِسْتِتار coverup n
اذداد step up v	استثمار investment n

استثمر invest v	استعباد slavery n
استثناء exception n	استعجل hasten v
استثنائيّ particular adj	استعداد readiness n
استجمام recreation n	استعرض touch on v
استجمع قواه brace for v	استعلام inquiry n
استجوب interrogate v	استعمار application n
استحالة impossibility n	استعمال usage, use n
استحسان approbation n	استعمال خاطئ misuse n
استحقاق merit n	استغاثه appeal n
استحقاقات dues n	استغل exploit v
استحواذ hangup n	استغلال explotation n
استخدم employ, engage v	اسْتِفْتاء questionnaire n
استخلص debrief v	استقال resign v
استدعى summon v	اِسْتِقَالَة resignation n
استراح repose v	استقامة bluntness n
استرخاء relax n	استقبال desk n
استرد get back v	استقرار stability n
استرداد retrieval, recovery n	استقلال independence n
استرداد الملك reentry n	استقلاليّ autonomous adj
استرضائيّ conciliatory adj	استلام receipt n
استرق eavesdrop v	استلزم entail v
استسلم capitulate v	استمتع gratify, revel v
استشارة consultation n	استمر keep on v
استشهاد martyrdom n	استمرار continuation n
استضاف entertain v	استنتاج conclusion n
استعاد retrieve v	استنتج infer v

اشـتراكيّ socialist adj	استند v lean on
اشـترى v purchase	استنسـاخ n cloning
اشـتعال n inflammation	استنسـخ v clone
اشمئزاز n loathing	استنشـق v inhale
اصطاد v hunt	استنطاق n inquest
اصطدام n clash	استنكار n disapproval
اصطدم v impact	استنكر v censure
اصطناعي adj artificial	استهجن v disapprove
اضطراب n unrest, uproar	استهدافي adj allergic
اضطراب عنيف n convulsion	استهل v strike up
اضطرب v flicker	استهلاك n consumption
اضطهاد n oppression	استهلالي n initials
اطلاق المدافع n gunfire	استوائيّ adj tropical
اعتباطيّ adj arbitrary	استورد v import
اعتداء n outrage	استياء n displeasure
اعتذار n apology	استيراد n importation
اعتراض n challenge	استيعاب n intake
اعتراف n confession	استيلاء n seizure
اعترض v interrupt	استئناف n appeal
اعترف v grant	اسـم n name
اعتزاز, n appreciation	اسـم العائلة n last name
اعتسافيّ adj abusive	اسـم الفاعل n participle
اعتقاد n opinion	اسـمنت n concrete
اعتقل v lock up	اشـتاق v long for
اعتلال جسدي n ailment	اشـتباه n suspicion
اعتمد v reckon on	اشـتراك n participation

attend, care v اعتنى	shrimp n الاربيان
habitual adj اعتيادي	slate n الاردواز
immigration n اغتراب	strategy n الاستراتيجيّة
emigrate v اغترب	reception n الاستقبال
assault, rape, violence n اغتصاب	continuity n الاستمرارية
assassination n اغتيال	allergy n الاستهداف
faint v اغمى عليه	pseudonym n الاسم المستعار
redemption n افتداء	socialism n الاشتراكيّة
calumny n افتراء	X-ray n الاشعة السينية
presumption n افتراض	aberration n الاضطراب
motion, proposal n اقتراح	moderation n الاعتدال
ballot, vote n اقتراع	quotation n الاقتباس
propose v اقترح	bronchitis n الالتهاب الشُعَبيّ
frugality n اقتصاد	merger n الاندماج
economize v اقتصد	harmony n الانسجام
extract v اقتلع	noun n الإ سم
below adv اقل من	mugging n الإبلاغ عن سطو
subscription n اكتتاب	pear n الإجّاص
acquisition n اكتساب	heartfelt adj الإخلاص
discovery n اكتشاف	hindsight n الإدراك المتأخر
discover, find out v اكتشف	articulation n الإرتباط بمفاصل
settle for v اكتفى	terrorist n الإرهابيّ
parishioner n الابرشى	diarrhea n الإسهال
Monday n الاثنين	radiation n الإشعاع
abbreviation n الاختصار	framework n الإطار
choice n الاختيار	clergy n الإكليروس

الأسقف pontiff n	الإلحاحيّة urgency n
الأسمى supreme adj	الإنجليكاني Anglican adj
الأصَلة python n	الإنفلونزا flu n
الأصيل afternoon n	الأ حدب hunchback n
الأعْراف purgatory n	الأ فق horizon n
الأعزَب bachelor n	الأبْرَشِيّة diocese n
الأفعى الخبيثة viper n	الأبله moron, idiot adj
الأكثرية majority n	الأبوة fatherhood n
الأكسجين oxygen n	الأحد Sunday n
الأكورديون accordion n	الأحفور fossil n
الألعاب نارية fireworks n	الأخلاقيّة morality n
الألف باء alphabet n	الأدنى least adj
الألومينيوم aluminum n	الأربعاء Wednesday n
الأمومة motherhood n	الأربعون forty adj
الأناناس pineapple n	الأرستقراطي aristocrat n
الأنيميّة anemia n	الأرستقراطية aristocracy n
الأوركسترا orchestra n	الأرشدية seniority n
الأولِمْبياد olympics n	الأرغني organist n
الأوّلية primacy n	الأرمل widower n
الآثم sinner n	الأرنب rabbit n
الآليّة mechanism n	الأريكة sofa n
الآمر commander n	الأزرق البحري navy blue adj
الآن here adv	الأسباني Spaniard n
البابا Pope n	الأسبرين aspirin n
البابويّة papacy n	الأسبقية priority n
البارومتر barometer n	الأستاذ professor n

aggressor *n* الباغي	unemployment *n* البطالة
grown-up *n* البالغ	penguin *n* البطريق
panorama *n* البانوراما	abdomen *n* البطن
builder *n* الباني	watermelon *n* البطّيخ الأحمر
pound *n* الباوند	chimpanzee *n* البَعام
baseball *n* البايسبول	survival *n* البقاء
pint *n* البايْنت	parsley *n* البَقْدُونس
salesman *n* البائع	midair, maid *n* البكر
petroleum *n* البترول	bell *n* البل
petal *n* البَتَلة	platinum *n* البلاتين
pelican *n* البَجَع	plastic *n* البلاستيك
novelty *n* البِدْع	balm *n* البَلْسَم
trunk *n* البدن	anchovy *n* البَلَم
brandy *n* البراندي	blouse *n* البُلُوزة
Portugal *n* البُرتُغال	oak *n* البلّوط
barge *n* البَرج	acorn *n* البلّوطة
parliament *n* البرلمان	puberty *n* البلوغ
varnish *n* البَرْنِيْق	billiards *n* البليارد
protocol *n* البروتوكول	hatchet *n* البليطة
protein *n* البروتين	billion *n* البليون
prostate *n* البروستات	mason *n* البنّاء
bronze *n* البرونز	fingertip *n* البنانة
turret *n* البُرَيْج	pentagon *n* البنتاغون
precursor *n* البشير	pendulum *n* البندول
onion *n* البَصَل	penny *n* البنس
potato *n* البطاطا	pancreas *n* البنكرياس

penicillin *n* البنيسيلين	tragedy *n* التراجيديا
porter *n* البوّاب	turbine *n* التُّربينة
pudding *n* البودنْغ	tart *n* التُّرْتَة
polish *n* البولندية	collarbone *n* التَّرْقُوَة
next door *adj* البيت المجاور	abandonment *n* التّرك
bureaucracy *n* البيروقراطيّة	Turk *adj* التركيّ
beret *n* البيْرِيه	trout *n* التُّرْوْتَة
bison *n* البيسون	trolley *n* الترولي
raffle *n* البيْع اليانصيبيّ	climbing *n* التسلق
wholesale *n* البيْع بالجُملة	diagnosis *n* التشخيص
seasoning *n* التابل	clearance *n* التصفية
dealer, trader *n* التاجر	premeditation *n* التعمُّد
ninth *adj* التاسع	optimism *n* التفاؤل
tartar *n* التتاري	superiority *n* التّفوُّق
recourse *n* التجاء	technicality *n* التِّقنيّة
commerce *n* التِّجَارَة	tactics *n* التكتيك
blasphemy *n* التجديف	frequency *n* التكرر
freezing *adj* التجليد	technology *n* التكنولوجيا
equipment *n* التجهيزات	swan *n* التمّ
cohesion *n* التحام	suit *n* التماس
tradition *n* التّحْدار	crocodile *n* التمساح
masterpiece *n* التحفة	tuna *n* التُّنّ
attainment *n* التحقيق	abdication *n* التّنازل
arbitration *n* التحكيم	rhythm *n* التناغم
telepathy *n* التُّخاطر	tennis *n* التِّنس
pheasant *n* التدرج	tunic *n* التُّنْك

notation *n* التّنويت	smallpox *n* الجُدَريّ
arthritis *n* التهاب المفاصل	surgeon *n* الجرّاح
pneumonia *n* الْتِهَاب رِئَويّ	tractor *n* الجَرّارة
meningitis *n* التهاب سحايا	cliff *n* الجُرُف
gobble, guzzle *v* التهم	butcher *n* الجزّار
bow *n* التواء	parsnip *n* الجزر الأبيض
twin *n* التّوأم	Greenland *n* الجزيرة الخضراء
imposition *n* التوجب	molecule *n* الجُزَيئ
tulip *n* التُّوليب	hanger *n* الجلاد
sprain *v* التوى	Friday *n* الجمعة
avalanche *n* التيهور	everybody *pro* الجميع
eight *adj* الثامن	heaven, paradise *n* الجنة
second *n* الثاني	sex *n* الجنس
consistency *n* الثبات على مبدإ	humankind *n* الجنس البشرى
mammal *n* الثَدْيّ	sexuality *n* الجنسانية
bereavement *n* الثكل	nationality *n* الجنسيّة
Tuesday *n* الثُّلاثاء	south *n* الجنوب
eighty *adj* الثمانون	southeast *n* الجنوب الشرقيّ
drunk *adj* الثمل	southwest *n* الجنوب الغربيّ
collector *n* الجابي	southerner *n* الجنوبيّ
spy *n* الجاسوس	atmosphere *n* الجوّ
eastern *adj* الجانب الشرقي	jeweler *n* الجوهريّ
rye *n* الجاوْدار	pilgrim *n* الحاجّ
cataclysm *n* الجائحة	usher, janitor *n* الحاجب
coward *n* الجبان	eleventh *adj* الحادي عشر
algebra *n* الجَبْر	motive *n* الحافز

warden n الحافظ	father-in-law n الحمو
magistrate n الحاكم	larynx n الحَنْجَرة
bearer n الحامل	palate n الحَنَك
squid n الحَبّار	vegetation n الحياة النباتية
pulse n الحبوب	treasurer n الخازن
sweetheart n الحبيب	loser n الخاسر
partridge n الحَجَل	specialty n الخاصّيّة
minimum n الحدّ الأدنى	God, Creator n الخالق
blacksmith n الحدّاد	five adj الخامس من
kite n الحَدَأة	square n الخانَة
juvenile n الحَدَث	traitor n الخائن
fringe n الحدود	baker n الخبّاز
consonant n الحرف الساكن	thrombosis n الخَثّر
artisan, craftsman n الجِرَفي	autumn n الخريف
backlash n الحركة الارتجاعية	ceramic n الخِزافة
asylum n الحرم المقدس	lettuce n الخس
piggy bank n الحصالة الخنزيرية	poppy n الخَشْخاش
civilization n الحِضارة	swarm n الخَشْرم
attendance n الحضور	contour n الخط كفافي
arbiter n الحَكَم	speaker n الخطيب
autonomy n الحكم الذاتيّ	toothpick n الخِلال
bit n الحَكَمة	Thursday n الخميس
haircut n الحلا قة	choir n الخُوْرس
barber n الحَلّاق	tailor n الخيّاط
nipple n الحلمة	treason n الخيانة العظمى
mother-in-law n الحماة	benevolence n الخيرية

dime *n* الدَّايم	rabbi *n* الرَّبّان
creditor *n* الدائن	fourteen *adj* الربع عشر
outsider *n* الدَّخيل	men *n* الرّجال
cyclist *n* الدَّرّاج	uterus, womb *n* الرّحِم
auctioneer *n* الدلّال	livelihood *n* الرّزق
guidelines *n* الدليل الموجز	newsletter *n* الرسالة الاخبارية
Denmak *n* الدنمارك	painter *n* الرسّام
bureaucrat *n* الدواويني	mileage *n* الرسم بالميل
diabetes *n* الديابيتس	messenger *n* الرسول
diplomacy *n* الديبلوماسيّة	machine gun *n* الرّشّاش
Turkey *n* الديك الروميّ	plumber *n* الرّصاص
dictatorship *n* الديكتاتوريّة	kneecap *n* الرّضفة
democracy *n* الديموقراطيّة	cure *n* الرعاية الروحيّة
dinosaur *n* الديناصور	windpipe *n* الرُّغامى
climax *n* الذروة	mate *n* الرفيق
posterity *n* الذُّرِّية	wafer *n* الرُّقاقة
gold *n* الذهب	knee *n* الرُّكبة
four *adj* الرابع	rum *n* الرّم
radar *n* الرادار	pomegranate *n* الرُّمّان
major *n* الراشد	raft *n* الرّمَث
patron *n* الراعي	zip code *n* الرمز البريدي
raccoon *n* الرّاكون	reindeer *n* الرّنة
marksman *n* الرامي	novelist *n* الرّوائيّ
teller *n* الرّاوي	routine *n* الروتين
herald, pioneer *n* الرائد	rheumatism *n* الروماتزم
capitalism *n* الرأسماليّة	romance *n* الرومانسية

sportman n الرياضى	liquid n السائل
athlete n الرياضيّ	Saturday n السبت
math n الرياضيات	sweater n السترة المعرقة
countryside n الريف	jailer n السّجّان
clown n الريفيّ	prisoner n السجين
presidency n الرئاسة	belly button, navel n السرة
chief n الرئيس	sardine n السّردين
appendix n الزائدة الدودية	cypress n السّرْو
visitor n الزائر	burglary n السطو
windshield n الزجاج الأمامي	facet n السطيح
thorn n الزُّعْرور	thug n السّفّاح
zipper n الزمام المنزلق	syphilis n السّفْلس
colleague n الزميل	population n السّكّان
zinc n الزّنك	drunkenness n السكر
vase n الزهرية	tuberculosis n السُّلّ
spouse n الزوج	salmon n السّلمون
swimmer n السابح	greyhound n السلوقي
magician n السّاحر	quail n السّلْوَى
witch n السّاحرة	sky n السّماء
sixth adj السادس	tablecloth n السّماط
watchmaker n الساعاتي	symphony n السّمفونيّة
bartender n الساقى في حانة	bleak n السمك الابيض
butler n الساقي	toxin n السُّمّين
barman n الساقي في حانة	centimeter n السّنتيمتر
barmaid n الساقية في حانة	squirrel n السّنجاب
tourist n السّائح	synod n السّنودس

الشُّكوكيّ skeptic adj	السُّوقيّة vulgarity n
الشَكِيمة bit n	السُّوك sock n
الشمّاس deacon n	السُّويد Sweden n
الشمال north n	السياحة tourism n
الشّماليّ northerner adj	السياسة politics n
الشمس sun n	السياسي politician n
الشّهر month n	السيانيد cyanide n
الشّيهم porcupine n	السّيّبة stepladder n
الشيوعيّة communism n	السّيرة biography n
الصائغ smith n	السيكوباتي psychopath n
الصّبا boyhood n	السيكولوجيا psychology n
الصباح morning n	السيناريو scenario n
الصحافيّ journalist n	الشارب mustache n
الصحة health n	الشارع lawmaker n
الصُّحَيْفة saucer n	الشّاعر poet n
الصّرصور cockroach n	الشاغل occupant n
الصقر buzzard n	الشاليه chalet n
الصّلْصَة sauce n	الشاهد gravestone n
الصليبيّ crusader n	الشّباب youth n
الصّليبيّة crusade n	الشتاء winter n
الصّندَقة boxing n	الشحيح miser n
الصّهر son-in-law n	الشّذوذ abnormality n
الصودا soda n	الشرطة police n
الصوم الكبير Lent n	الشروق sunrise n
الصّياغة wording n	الشّعر poetry n
الصيدليّ pharmacist n	الشّغّيل worker n

الصيف n summer	العالِم n scientist
الضاحية n suburb	العامل n laborer
الضمير n conscience	العامية n informality
الضوء الومضي n flashlight	العائش n liver
الطاغية n despot, dictator	العبد n slave
الطافية n buoy	العد التنازلي n countdown
الطالب n student	العَدّاء n runner
الطالِن n talent	العَدْو n pace
الطاهي n cook	العذراء n maiden, virgin
الطاووس n peacock	العَرّاب n sponsor
الطبّ n medicine	العَرّاف n wizard
الطبعة الزرقاء n blueprint	العَروس n bride
الطِّراب n trap	العريس n bridegroom
الطِّرْح n subtraction	العريف n corporal
الطفولة n childhood	العُرْبيّ n nudist
الطُّفَيْليّ n parasite	العَشاء n supper
الطقس n weather	العشرون adj twentieth
الطنان n buzzer	العصفور n sparrow
الطيّار n aviator	العصور القديمة n antiquity
الطَيَران n aviation	الْعَظاءة n lizard
الظبي n antelope	العظم الوَجْنيّ n cheekbone
الظُّلّة n awning	العَفَن الفُطْريّ n mildew
الظُّهر n noon	العَفْويّة n spontaneity
الظّهور الأوّل n debut	العِقار n realty
العاشر n tenth	العقل الموجه n mastermind
العاصمة n metropolis	العُلْجُوْم n toad

العلكة bubble gum n	الفائز winner n
العلوم الأدبية humanities n	الفائض surplus n
العمّ uncle n	الفحم charcoal n
العماد baptism n	الفَرَس mare n
العُمْر lifetime adj	الفُرسان cavalry n
العمل التحضيري groundwork n	الفَرْضِيّة thesis n
العمل بالزراعة farming n	الفريز strawberry n
العمود الفقري backbone n	الفُشار popcorn n
العناوين الرئسية highlight n	الفصل trimester n
العناية الإلهية providence n	الفضائي cosmonaut, astronaut n
العندليب nightingale n	الفُطر mushroom n
العِيار caliber n	الفَطور breakfast n
الغازولين gasoline n	الفَظّ walrus n
الغدّة الدَّرَقيّة thyroid n	الفلّاح peasant n
الغرب west n	الفَلَكِيّ astronomer n
الغربيّ westerner adj	الفلوت flute n
الغروب sundown n	الفِلّين cork n
الغريب stranger n	الفناء الخلفى backyard n
الغَزّالة spinster n	الفَنّان artist n
الغسق dusk n	الفَنّائيّة mortality n
الغَسُول lotion n	الفندق hotel n
الغَوْغاء mob n	الفوترغرافي photography n
الفاتح conqueror n	الفُوسـفُور phosphorus n
الفاصِلة comma n	الفول السـوداني peanut n
الفاصلة العليا apostrophe n	الفولاذ steel n
الفالس waltz n	الفيتامين vitamin n

القُنْدُس n beaver	الفيروس n virus
القُولُون n colon	الفيزياء n physics
القوى العظمى n superpower	الفيشة n chip
القيادة العامة n headquarters	الفيلسوف n philosopher
القيراط n carat	القابلة n midwife
القيصر n czar	القاتل n assassin, killer
القَيِّم n custodian	القاتل, قتل n homicide
الكاتب n writer	القارض n rodent
الكاتب العدل n notary	القارئ n reader
الكاحل n ankle	القاطع n cutter
الكازينو n casino	القالون n gal
الكبريت n sulphur	القُدّ n cod
الكتاب المدرسيّ n textbook	القدرة n ability
الكتاب المقدّس n bible	القِرْش n shark
الكُتُبي n bookseller	القِرْطاسِيّة n stationery
الكرة الارضية n globe	القرن n century
الكرة الأرضية n ball	القَرَويّ n villager
الكرة الطائرة n volleyball	القريب n relative
الكَرَز n cherry	القُرَيْدِس n prawn
الكَرْكَدَنّ n rhinoceros	القرينة n context
الكَرْمة n vine	القِسْمَة n destiny
الكَرَنْك n crank	القَصَبة n borough
الكشافة n scout	القُضاعَة n otter
الكِظامَة n clue	القُطْر n diameter
الكَفْت n saucepan	القَفّال n locksmith
الكفيل n guarantor	القمر n moon

stork *n* اللَّقْلَق	rabies *n* الكَلَب
wig *n* اللَّمّة	cynic *adj* الكَلْبيّ
launch *n* اللَّنْش	violin *n* الكمان
maker *n* الله	violinist *n* الكمانيّ
tonsil *n* اللوزة	daughter-in-law *n* الكَنّة
leukemia *n* اللوكيميا	abbey *n* الكنيسة
materialism *n* الماديّة	stern *n* الكوثل
giant *n* المارد	cocaine *n* الكوكايين
marshal *n* المارشال	planet *n* الكوكب
masochism *n* الماسوشية	cocktail *n* الكوكتيل
pedestrian *n* الماشي	comedy *n* الكوميديا
cattle *n* الماشية	universe *n* الكون
mahagony *n* الماهوغانية	kilogram *n* الكِيلُوغْرام
hundred *adj* المائة	kilometer *n* الكيلومتر
plug *n* المأخذ	kilowatt *n* الكيلووات
missionary *n* المبشِّر	chemistry *n* الكيمياء
ovary *n* المَبيض	chemist *n* الكيميائي
conspirator *n* المتآمر	agnostic *n* اللاأدري
contributor *n* المتبرّع	refugee *n* اللاجئ
wanderer *n* المتجوّل	laser *n* اللازر
correspondent *n* المتراسِل معه	refrain *v* اللازمة
translator *n* المترجم	player *n* اللاعب
vagrant *n* المُتَشَرّد	theology *n* اللاهوت
intruder *n* المتطفل	theologian *n* اللاهوتيّ
volunteer *n* المتطوّع	welder *n* اللحامة
bigot *adj* المتعصّب	plaster *n* اللّصوق

organism n المتعضي	المدّ والجزْر n tide
learner n المتعلّم	المدار الاستوائي n tropic
bystander n المتفرّج	المُدّخِر n savings
speaker n المتكلّم	المُدَّخِّن n smoker
apprentice n المتمهن	المدرب n trainer
text n المتن	المدرس n master
trailer n المُتَنَشِّرة	المُدَّعَى عليه n defendant
culprit n المُتّهم	المدّعي n plaintiff
metaphor n المجاز	المِدفعيّة n artillery
arena n المجتلد	المدلّك n masseur
leper n المجذوم	المدلّكة n masseuse
freezer n المجمد	المِدَمّة n rake
madman n المجنون	director, manager n المدير
yolk n آلمُحّ	المَدين n debtor
oyster, shellfish n المَحار	المَذْبَح n altar
warrior n المحارب	المذكّر n reminder
accountant n المحاسِب	المُذَنّب n comet
mayor n المحافظ	المرادف n synonym
lawyer n المحامي	المراهق n teenager
lover n المُحِبّ	المراهقة n adolescence
juggler n المحتال	المُربّع n square
thermometer n المِحَرّ	المربّى n conserve
motor n المحرّك	المرسِل إليه n addressee
portable adj المحمول	المركّب n composer
reporter n المُخْبِر	المَرْمَلاد n marmalade
stock n المخزون	المريء n esophagus

Mars n آلْمِرِّيخ	ravine n المسيل
follower n المريد	tack n المُسَيْمِير
outpatient n المريض الخارجي	infantry n المشاة
so-called adj المزعوم	onlooker, spectator n المشاهد
hairdresser n المزين	suspect n المشبوه
helper n المساعد	buyer n المشتري
passenger n المسافر	orient n المَشرق
shareholder n المساهِم	radiator n المِشْعاع
lessee, tenant n المستأجِر	bonfire n المَشْعَلَة
tyrant n المستبدّ	lantern n المِشْكاة
employee n المستخدم	apricot n المشمش
pawnbroker n المسترهِن	marshal n المشير
rectangle n المستطيل	terminology n المصطلَحات
user n المستعمِل	serum n المصل
beneficiary n المستفيد	photographer n المصوّر
settler n المستوطِن	bigamy n المضارَّة
chimney n المستوقد	amplifier n المضخم
mosque n المسجد	accelerator n المُعاجِل
marker, recorder n المسجل	healer n المعالج
ruler n المسطّر	coefficient n المُعامِل
gunman n المسلح ببندقية	aide n المعاون
silhouette n المُسَلْوَتة	confessor n المعترف
earphones n المسماع	admirer n المعجَب
contributor n المُسْهِم	vocabulary n المعجَم
Messiah n المسيح	average n المعدل
Christianity n المسيحية	miner n المعدّن

المعزّي comforter n	المليونير millionaire adj
المِعْصَم wrist n	المماس tangent n
المعضول incurable adj	المِمْطَر raincoat n
المعلّم teacher n	الممول investor n
المغايرة contrast n	المنافِس competitor, rival n
المغنطيسيّة magnetism n	المنامة nightgown n
المفجّر detonator n	المُنبّه alarm clock; stimulant n
المقاتل fighter n	المنتصر victor n
المقام denominator n	المنجّم astrologer n
المِقْداح trigger n	المُنجّمة asterisk n
المِقْراب telescope n	المَنْخِر nostril n
المِقرأ lectern n	المنظفة cleanser n
المقصّر delinquent n	المُنْقِذ savior n
المكاشـفة showdown n	المُنَكّه zest n
المكتبة bookstore n	المنْوَر skylight n
المكربن carburetor n	المَنِيّ sperm n
المكسيكيّ Mexican adj	المهاجِر migrant n
المكعّب cube n	المُهاجِم assailant n
المُلاءة sheets n	المَهْبِط airfield n
الملاكم boxer n	المهتدي convert n
الملحد atheist n	المهجع dormitory n
الملصق poster n	المهرب smuggler n
الملكية monarch n	المُهيّج agitator n
الملومية culpability n	الموتيل motel n
المِلّيمتر millimeter n	المَوْحَى oracle n
المليون million n	المُورْفِين morphine n

الموسّعة	stretcher *n*	النداء الباطنيّ	vocation *n*
الموسيقيّ	musician *n*	النّدب	scar *n*
الموظفين	personnel *n*	النذل	villain *n*
الموعد الأخير	deadline *n*	النّرد	dice *n*
الموقف	park *n*	النرويج	Norway *n*
الموكّل	client *n*	النّسَمة	asthma *n*
المُونُولُوج	monologue *n*	النّسناس	monkey *n*
المؤنث	feminine *adj*	النّشّال	pickpocket *n*
المؤيّد،	supporter *n*	النصير	patron, champion *n*
الميكانيكيّ	mechanic *n*	النظّاراتيّ	optician *n*
الميكروسكوب	microscope *n*	النّظام	regime *n*
الميكروفون	microphone *n*	النظاميّة	regularity *n*
النادل	waiter *n*	النّظير	peer *n*
النادلة	waitress *n*	النُّقْطَتان	colon *n*
الناس	people *n*	النّقيض	opposite *n*
الناسك	hermit, recluse *n*	النُّكاف	mumps *n*
الناشر	publisher *n*	النمل الأبيض	termite *n*
الناصح	adviser *n*	النموذج	prototype *n*
النبات الحبي	cereal *n*	النورس	seagull *n*
النبّوت	bat *n*	النيكوتين	nicotine *n*
النبيل	nobleman *adj*	الهاتف	telephone *n*
النتروجين	nitrogen *n*	الهادم	destroyer *n*
النّثر	prose *n*	الهادي	conductor *n*
النجّار	carpenter *n*	الهامّة	vampire *n*
النّجارة	carpentry *n*	الهُرْي	barn *n*
النّحّات	sculptor *n*	الهمجيّ	barbarian *n*

lagoon *n* الهَوْر	Japan *n* اليابان
monster *n* الهُوْلَة	earth, land *n* اليابِسة
divinity *n* الهوية	yam *n* اليام
heroin *n* الهيرويين مخدر	yacht *n* اليَخْت
cholera *n* الهَيْضَة	caterpillar *n* اليُسْرُوع
homework *n* الواجب المنزلي	Jew *n* اليهوديّ
incoming *adj* الوارد	Judaism *n* اليهوديّة
watt *n* الواطّ	iodine *n* اليُوْد
preacher *n* الواعظ	tangerine *n* اليُوسُفِيّ
newcomer *n* الوافد	today *adv* اليومَ
realism *n* الواقعيّة	diary *n* اليوميّات
parents *n* الوالدان	expand *v* امتد
heathen *n* الوثني	span *n* امتداد
idolatry *n* الوثنية	soak up *v* امتص
means *n* الوَسَط	prerogative, privilege *n* امتياز
mediator *n* الوسيط	woman *n* امرأة
curator *n* الوصيّ	snatch *v* امسك
page *n* الوصيف	emerge *v* انبثق
pose *n* الوضْعَة	extroverted *adj* انْبِساطِيّ
patriot *n* الوطنيّ	flat *adj* انبطاحا
quicksand *n* الوَعْث	sprawl *v* انبطح
scoundrel *n* الوَغْد	emanate *v* انبعث
attorney *n* الوكيل	attention *n* انتباه
vandal *n* الوندالي	suicide *n* انتحار
vandalism *n* الوَنْدَلَة	election *n* انتخاب
right *adv* الي اليمين	elect *v* انتخب

انتشر propagate v	انحنى lean, incline v
انتظار waiting n	انخفاض depreciation n
انتظام uniformity n	اندفاع impulse n
انتظر hang on v	اندلاع outbreak n
انتعاش pickup n	اندماج coalition n
انتفاخ bulge n	اندمج incorporate v
انتفاضة insurrection n	انذهال amazement n
انتفع utilize v	انسجام compatibility n
انتقاد criticism n	انسحاب withdrawal, retreat n
انتقاديّ critical adj	انسلال slip n
انتقال removal n	انصرف get out v
انتقام reprisal n	انضباط discipline n
انتقل hand down v	انطباع effect n
انتقم strike back v	انطلق get away v
انتكاس relapse n	انطوائي introvert adj
انتهازي pushy adj	انعزال solitude n
انتهى turn out v	انعطاف detour n
انجذب gravitate v	انعكاس reflection n
انجرف drift v	انعكاسيّ reflexive adj
انحدار ramp n	انغمار immersion n
انحراف deviation n	انغمس dive v
انحرف divert v	انفتاح openness n
انحشر squeeze in v	انفجار explosion, outburst n
انحلال degeneration n	انفجار دولاب blowout n
انحناء bow n	انفجاري explosive adj
انحناءة inclination n	انفجر erupt v

break away v انفصل
excitement n انفعال
passionate adj انفعاليّ
schism n انقسام
onslaught n انقضاض
elapse v انقضى
reversal n انقلاب
shrink v انكمش
go under, plummet v انهار
downpour, outpouring n انهمار
preoccupation n انهماك
collapse n انهيار
thrill n اهتزاز
heed v اهتمّ
interest n اهتمام
fuss n اهتياج
affirmative adj ايجابى

إ

hurricane n إعصار مداري
blackout n إالتعتيم
genocide n إبادة جماعية
expression n إبانة
graft v إبتز المال
navigation n إبحار
creativity, ingenuity n إبْداع
needle n إبرة
jug, mug n إبريق
teapot n إبريق الشاي
buckle n إبزيم
armpit n إبْطّ
vacation n إبطال
exile n إبعاد
communication n إبْلاغ
satanic adj إبليسيّ
perfection n إتقان
completion n إتمام
indict v إتهم
aggravation n إثارة
entrenched adj إثْباتِيّ
guilt, sin n إثم
dozen n إثنا عشر

إدارة حسابات bookkeeping n	إجابة response n
إدانة damnation n	إجبار constraint n
إدخال insertion n	إجباريّ obligatory adj
إدراك perception n	إجتمع socialize v
إدغام diphthong n	إجْحاف prejudice n
إدلاء بشهادة hearing n	إجراءات procedure n
إدمان الكحول alcoholism n	إجلال obedience n
إدْمانيّ addictive adj	إجماع consensus n
إذاعة publication n	إجماليّ total adj
إرَباً asunder adv	إجهاد strain, stress n
إرباك confusion n	إجهاض miscarriage n
إربط الحزام buckle up v	إحباط frustration, defeat n
إرتد defect v	إحترس من watch out v
إرث inheritance n	إحترق burn v
إرجاء reprieve, respite n	إحتفظ ببقائه exist v
إرجاع restoration n	إحراق combustion n
إرشاد guidance n	إحراق المباني arson n
إرهاب terrorism n	إحصاء count n
إزعاج disturbance n	إحصائى statistic n
إزميل chisel n	إحياء renovation n
إساءة استعمال abuse n	إختصار shortcut n
إسبانى Hispanic adj	إختطاف طائرة hijack n
إسْبَانيَا Spain n	إخفاق failure, miss n
إستشاط غضبا flare-up v	إخلاص fidelity n
إستعاد recover v	إخوة في الدين brethren n
إسْطبل stable n	إدارة conduct, direction n

sponge n إسْفَنْج	frame n إطار
wedge n إسفين	flat n إطار ضارب
abortion n إسقاط	flattery, praise n إطراء
Islamic adj إسلاميّ	firefighter, fireman n إطْفائيّ
anonymity n إسم مستعار	delivery n إطلاق سراح
gesture, sign n إشارة	gunshot, shot n إطلاق نار
dial tone n إشارة صوتية	refund n إعادة مالٍ
rumor, hearsay n إشاعة	review n إعادة نظر
satisfaction n إشباعّ	review v إعادة نظر
bridesmaid n إشْبينةُ العَروس	handicap n إعاقة
buy v إشترى	subsidy n إعانة ماليّة
supervision n إشراف	embrace n إعتناق
notice n إشعار	embrace v إعتنق دينا
compassion n إشفاق	admiration n إعجاب
gruelling adj إشْكاليّ	concoction n إعداد
hit n إصابة	fondness n إعزاز
finger n إصبع	twister n إعصار
toe n إصبع القَدَم	exemption, acquittal n إعفاء
emission n إصدار	notification n إعلام
insistence n إصرار	advertising n إعلان
reform, reparation n إصلاح	exhaustion n إعياء
floodlight n إضاءة	temptation n إغراء
additional adj إضافيّ	closure n إغلاق
overtime adv إضافيّا	faint n إغماء
dossier, file n إضبارة	enticement n إغواء
walkout n إضرابٌ عماليّ	premises n إفتراض

إفترض مسبقا presuppose v	إلى الأمام onwards adv
إفرض supposing c	إلى الشاطئ ashore adv
إفشاء reveal v	إلى الوراء backwards adv
إفلاس bankruptcy n	إلى حَدٍّ slightly adv
إقالة dismissal n	إلى حد كاف enough adv
إقالة lay off v	إلى حدّ ما somewhat adv
إقامة residence n	إلى فوق upwards adv
إقرار ratification n	إلى مكان farther adv
إقليم county, province n	إماتة الجسد mortification n
إقليميّ regional adj	إمبراطور emperor n
إقناع persuasion n	إمبراطورة empress n
إكراه constraint n	إمبراطوري imperial adj
إكليل wreath n	إمبراطورية empire n
إكليلي coronary adj	إمرأة فاتنة mermaid n
إلا except pre	إمساك constipation n
إلّا إذا unless c	إمضاء signature n
إلحاح urge n	إمكانيّة possibility n
إلحاد heresy n	إناء utensil n
إلحاق annexation n	إنتاج reproduction n
إلزاميّ compulsory adj	إنتشار الجند deployment n
إلغاء repeal n	إنتصر عليه beat v
إلغاء قيمته depreciate v	إنتظار طويل long-standing adj
إلكتروني electronic adj	إنتظم في صف line up v
إلهاء distraction n	إنجاز accomplishment n
إلى to, until pre	إنجلترا England n
إلى الأبد forever adv	إنجيل gospel n

notice *n* إنذار	belief *n* إيمان
alarm *n* إنذار بخطر	
human being *n* إنسان	
buildup *n* إنشاء	
secede *v* إنشق على	آ
expenditure *n* إنفاق	
burst *v* إنفجر	
influenza *n* إنفلونزا	dad, father *n* أبٌ
rescue, salvation *n* إنقاذ	childless *adj* أبتر
incontinence *n* إنقياد للشهوة	never *adv* أبداً
contradiction *n* إنكار	endless *adj* أبدي
English *adj* إنكليزي	parochial *adj* أبرشيّ
affront, insult *n* إهانة	parish *n* أبرشية
neglect *n* إهمال	April *n* أبريل
unselfish *adj* إيثاريّ	exonerate *v* أبرئ
positive *adj* إيجابيّ	hate *v* أبغض
rent *n* إيجار	dumb, idiotic *adj* أبكم
concise *adj* إيجازي	silly *adj* أبله
inspiration *n* إيحاء	wear down *v* أبلى
remittance *n* إيداع	niece *n* أبنة الأخ
Ireland *n* إيرلندا	paternity *n* أبوّة
Irish *adj* إيرلندي	fatherly *adj* أبوي
Italian *adj* إيطاليّ	blank, white *adj* أبيض
Italy *n* إيطاليا	harmonize *v* أتلف
arrest *n* إيقاف	rouse, excite *v* أثار
sign *n* إيماءة	vestige, track *n* أثر

أثر القدم n footprint	أخرق awkward, clumsy adj
أثرٌ ضئيل v sparkle	أخزى v disgrace
أثم v err	أخصب v fertilize
أثيم adj atrocious	أخطأ v goof
أجداد n grandparents	أخطبوط n octopus
أجر n wage	أخطئ v mistake
أجرة البريد n postage	أخفى v hide
أجرد adj empty	أخلاق n moral
أجش adj hoarse, husky	أخلاقي adj ethical, moral
أجل v glorify	أخمص القدم n sole
أَجَمَة n brush	أُخُوّة n brotherhood
أجنبي adj foreign	أخَوِيّ adj brotherly, fraternal
أجنبي n foreigner	أخير adj latest, last
أحد عشر adj eleven	أخيرا adv eventually, lastly
أحدث v make	أداة n tool
أحرف كبير n capital letter	أداة تنكير a a, an
أحسر adj myopic	أدخل v insert
أحمر adj red	أدرك v overtake
أحمق adj inept, stupid	أدركه v catch up
أحياناً adv occasionally, sometimes	أدغال n jungle
أحيائيّ adj biological	أدلى v hang
أخ n brother	أدْنَى n bottom
أخ غير شقيق n stepbrother	أدنى adj lower
أخدود n furrow, groove, pothole	أدوات n material
أخرج n drawback	أدوات منزلية n hardware
أخرس adj dumb	أذن ب v foreshadow

أزمة حرجة n crisis

أساء التفسير v misinterpret

أساس n base, basis

أساسيّ adj grassroots, basic

أسبانيّ adj Spanish

أسبوع n week

أسبوعي adj weekday

أسبوعيًّا adv weekly

أسَد n lion

أسْر n capture

أسرع v hurry

أسس v establish

أسطوانة n cylinder, disk

أسطورة n fable, legend

أسطول n fleet, navy

أسف n regret

أسقط v let down

أسْقُف n bishop

أسكت v silence

أسلاف n antecedents

أسَلَة n tip

أسلوب n manner, style

أسلوب الحياة n lifestyle

أسمر adj brown

أسمنت n cement

أسمى adj paramount

---

damage, harm n أذى

herald v أذيع

earnings n أرباح

embarrass v أربك

groin n أربية

orthodox adj أرثوذكسيّ

fragrant adj أرج

purple adj أرجواني

mail v أرسل بالبريد

brief, guide v أرشد

archive n أرشيف

terrain n أرض

height n أرض مرتفعة

terrestrial adj أرضيّ

dismay, horrify v أرعب

widow n أرملة

hare n أرنب الوحشية

terrorize, dread v أرهب

armchair n أريكة

dislodge, dispel v أزاح

grease v أزال الشحم

defrost v أزال الصقيع

dehydrate v أزال الماء

blue adj أزرق

disrupt v أزعج

infested adj أزعج

أصلاً originally adv	أسمى من above pre
أصلح ذات البين reconcile v	أسنان teeth n
أصلع bald adj	أسنان إصطناعية dentures n
أصلي fundamental, original adj	أسهم pool v
أصم deaf adj	أسوأ worse, worst adj
أصهار in-laws n	أسود black adj
أصيص pot n	أسير captive n
أصيص ورود flowerpot n	أشار connote v
أضاء enlighten v	أشاع popularize v
أضاء بضعف gleam v	أشجار timber n
أضاع lose v	أشرف على supervise v
أضحوكة laughing stock n	أشرق light v
أضعف impair, sap v	أشعل fire, ignite v
أطر frame v	أشقر blond adj
أطراف الجسم extremities n	أشكلي formal adj
أطفأ extinguish v	أشلاء carnage n
أطلق fire, shoot v	أشيب gray adj
أطلق سراح discharge v	أصاب hit, inflict v
أعاد البحث reconsider v	أصاب بالفتق rupture v
أعاد البناء reconstruct v	أصالة authenticity n
أعاد إنتخاب reelect v	أصبح become v
أعاد بناء rebuild v	أصبح باردا cool down v
أعاد تصنيع recycle v	أصدر امرا الى bid v
أعاد تنظيم reorganize v	أصغر junior adj
أعاد مالا refund v	أصفاد handcuffs n
أعتق emancipate v	أصفر yellow adj

rely on *v* أعتمد على	endorse *v* أقرّ
marvel *n* أعجوبة	lend *v* أقرض
miraculous *adj* أعجوبيّ	ultimate *adj* أقصى
electrocute *v* أعدم بالكهرباء	less, lesser *adj* أقلّ
single *adj* أعزب	obsess *v* أقلق
unarmed *adj* أعزل	induce *v* أقنع
give in *v* أعطى	more *adj* أكثر
better *adj* أعظم	underline *v* أكد
pronounce *v* أعلن	grieve *v* أكمد
exclaim *v* أعلن بقوة	insist *v* ألح
maximum *adj* أعلى	thousand *adj* ألف
head *n* أعلى الشئ	millennium *n* ألف عام
blind *v* أعمى	cast *v* ألقى
blind *adj* أعمى	pain *n* ألم
namely *adv* أعني	earache *n* ألم الأذن
entice *v* أغرى	German *adj* ألماني
August *n* أغُسْطُس	Germany *n* ألمانيا
carol *n* أغنية مَرِحَة	inspire *v* ألهم
prospect *n* أفاق	auto *n* ألى
divulge *v* أفشى سرا	mom, mother *n* أمّ
best *adj* أفضل	mortify *v* أمات
advantage *n* أفضليّة	before *pre* أمامَ
serpent *n* أفعى	foreground *n* أمامَ
impoverished *adj* أفقر	forward *adv* أمامي
horizontal *adj* أفقي	front *adj* أمامي
erect *v* أقام	baggage, luggage *n* أمتعة

أمْر bid; commandment n	أنبوب duct n
أمس last night adv	أنْتَ you pro
أمسك بـ catch v	أنتج ثانية reproduce v
أمسك بقوة hold on to v	أنتج محاصيل diversify v
أمعاء bowels n	أنثى الطير hen n
أمعاء مفرد intestine n	أنسباء المرء folks n
أمل hope n	أنشـودة chant n
أملَس smooth adj	أنف nose n
أمن insure v	أنفُسـهم themselves pro
أمن safety, security n	أنفق disburse v
أُمْنِيَة wish n	أنفق ماله بطيش lash out v
أموال funds n	أنهى end up v
أمومة maternity n	أنيس affable adj
أمومية maternal adj	أنيق fashionable, neat adj
أمي illiterate adj	أنين groan n
أمير prince n	أهان debase, insult v
أميرال admiral n	أهدأ cool down v
أميرة princess n	أهلا hello e
أميركي American adj	أهمل leave out v
أمين الصندوق cashier n	أهمل مهمة fall down v
أمين المكتبة librarian n	أو or c
أنّ groan v	أوبرا opera n
أنا myself pro	أوتوماتيكي automatic adj
أناني egoist n	أوجز resume v
أنانيّ selfish, greedy adj	أوروبا Europe n
أنانية selfishness n	أوروبي European adj

أوز goose, geese n	آرتشاء bribery n
أوقف shut off v	آسر enthralling adj
أوقف السيارة park v	آسف sorry adj
أوّل premier adj	آص ace n
أولاً primarily adv	آكل لحم البشر cannibal n
أولي first, prime adj	آلة machine n
أولَئِك those adj	آلة تصوير copier n
أومض glance v	آلة حاسبة calculator n
أونصة ounce n	آلة صغيرة gadget n
أيّ which, what adj	آمن safe adj
أيّ إنسان anybody pro	آنية زجاجية glassware n
أيّ شخص anyone pro	آنية فخّاريّة crockery n
أيّ شيء anything pro	آنئذٍ then adv
أي لحظة hourly adv	آية verse n
أيديولوجية ideology n	
أيضاً also, too adv	
أيقونة icon n	
أيما whatever adj	
أيمن right adj	
أين where adv	
آجرّة tile, brick n	
آحادي الجانب unilateral adj	
آخَر other, another adj	
آداب اللغة literature n	
آدمي human adj	
آذى harm v	

rather *adv* بالأحرى

adoptive *adj* بالتَّبنّي

step-by-step *adv* بالتدريج

barely, hardly *adv* بالجهد

conversely *adv* بالعَكْس

exaggerate *v* بالغ

nine *adj* بالغ عدده تسعة

overestimate *v* بالغ في التقدير

inside out *adv* بالمقلوب

sewer *n* بالوعة

regularly *adv* بانتظام

lonely *adv* بانفراد

faded *adj* باهِت

glamorous *adj* باهر

exorbitant *adj* باهظ

helpless *adj* بائس

neatly *adv* بإتْقان

closely *adv* بإحكام

highly *adv* بإرتفاع مبالغ

ceaselessly *adv* بإستمرار

exceedingly *adv* بإفراط

hopefully *adv* بأمل

anyhow *pro* بأية حال

sparingly *adv* ببخل

initially *adv* ببداية

simply *adv* ببساطة

ب

aloud *adv* ب جِهاراً

door *n* باب

backdoor *n* بابٌ خلفيّ

joyfully *adv* بابْتِهاج

broadly *adv* باتساع

humbly *adv* باحتشام

nut-shell, briefly, shortly *adv* باختصار

initiate *v* بادر

prefix *n* بادئة

battleship *n* بارجة

chilly, cold *adj* بارد

cool *adj* بارد باعتدال

frosty *adj* بارد جداً

memorable *adj* بارز

skillful, witty *adj* بارع

gunpowder *n* بارود

pea *n* بازلّا

barring *pre* باستثناء

bus *n* باص

null, invalid *adj* باطل

inside *adj* باطن

sellout *n* باع كل ما يملك

balance *n* باقي الحساب

slowly adv ببطء	inception, start n بداية
parrot n بَبغاء	primitive, rudimentary adj بدائيّ
parakeet n ببغاء صغير	begin v بدأ
justly adv بتبرير	knowingly adv بدراية
fluently adv بتدفق	nicely adv بِدِقّة
amputation n بتر	exchange v بدل
mutilate v بتر	instead adv بدلا من
dock v بتر ذيلا	corporal adj بدنيّ
transmit v بثّ	cordless adj بدو حبل
pimple n بَثْرة	seedless adj بدون بذر
surely adv بثقة	defenseless adj بدون حماية
alongside, by pre بجانب	rust-proof adj بدون صدأ
cowardly adv بجُبْن	jobless adj بدون عمل
gravely adv بجدية	substitute n بديل
venerate v بجل	fatty, obese adj بدين
madly adv بجنون	self-evident adj بديهيّ
sailor n بحّار	axiom n بديهية
explore v بحث	dissipate v بذر
sea n بحر	grain n بذرة
marine adj بحريّ	exert v بذل
lake n بحيرة	habit n بذلة ركوب الخيل
fumes, steam n بخار	improper adj بذيء
harshly adv بخشونة	honesty n براءة
incense n بخور	proficiency n براعة
reappear v بدا	Portuguese adj برتغاليّ
owing to adv بداعي	orange n برتقالة

برْج tower n	بريء heal v
برج الحرس belfry n	بريء blameless adj
برد hail n	بريد post, mail n
برد قارس nip n	بريدُ الطُّرُود parcel post n
برز heighten v	بريد جوّي airmail n
برز للعيان arise v	بريطانيّ British adj
برشمة riveting adj	بريطانيا Britain n
برعم germinate v	برئ honest, innocent adj
برعم bud n	بز excel v
برعم despite c	بز excellence n
برغوث flea n	بزرة seed n
برفق lightly adv	بزود بالطعام cater to v
برق lightning n	بساطة simplicity n
برقوق plum, prune n	بسبب because of pre
برقية telegram, wire n	بستان orchard n
بركان volcano n	بستاني gardener n
برم impatience n	بسرعة quickly adv
برمائيّ amphibious adj	بسعر berserk adv
برميل barrel n	بسْكويت biscuit n
برميل صغير keg n	بسهولة easily adv
برنامج agenda, program n	بسيط simple adj
برنامج إذاعي broadcast n	بشاعة ugliness n
برنس bathrobe n	بشأن about pre
برهان proof n	بشَجاعة bravely adv
بروز ocurrence n	بشرط providing that c
برّي wild adj	بشِع ugly adj

anew adv بشكل جديد	tardy, slow adv بطيء
expressly adv بشكل معبر	melon n بطيخ
eyesight n بصر	dispatch v بعث
frankly adv بصراحة حقا	resurrection n بَعْث
optical, visual adj بَصَريّ	hereafter adv بعد
unofficially adv بصفة شخصية	dimension n بُعْد
fingerprint n بصمة	afterwards adv بعدئذ
loudly adv بصَوْتٍ عالٍ	few, some adj بعض
currently adv بصورة عامة	kindly adv بعطف
foresight n بصيرة	in depth adv بعمق
goods n بضاعة	mosquito n بَعُوْضَة
merchandise n بضائع	distant adj بعيد
properly adv بضبط	far adv بعيد
noisily adv بضجّة	unlikely adj بعيد الإحتمال
thinly adv بضَعْف	off adv بعيداً
duck n بط	away adv بعيدا جانبا
postcard n بطاقة بريدية	furiously adv بغضب
patriarch n بطريرك	proudly adv بغَطْرَسَة
else adv بطريقة أخرى	mule n بَغْل
someway, somehow adv بطَريقةٍ ما	hateful, odious adj بغيض
likewise adv بطريقة مماثلة	conquer v بفتح بلداً
heroic adj بطل	bug n بَقّ
belly n بطن	leftovers, remains n بقايا
tummy n بطن بلغة الأطفال	cow n بقرة
heroism n بطولة	ramson v بقرم
slow motion n بطىء الحركة	patch, speck, spot n بقعة

stick around v بقي	misfortune n بليّة
stub, remainder n بقية	wet adj بَليل
much adv بكثير	softly adv بلين
pulley, reel n بَكَرة	since c بما أن
compel v بُكره	wherever c بماذا
huge adj بكل ضخامة	grudgingly adv بمرارة
how adv بكم	jokingly adv بمزاح
sleeveless adj بلا أكمام	coffee n بُنّ
nonstop adv بلا توقف	bricklayer, construction n بنّاء
flawless adj بلا عيب	constructive adj بنائيّ
aimless adj بلا هدف	item, article n بند
plague n بلاء	hazelnut n بندق
palace n بَلاط	nut n بندقة
tombstone n بلاطة ضريح	rifle n بندقية
bulletin n بلاغ	shotgun n بندقية رش
Belgian adj بلجيكيّ	gas n بنزين
country n بلد ريف	forcibly adv بنشاط
town n بلدة	pants n بنطلون
city hall n بلدية	slacks n بنطلون واسع
balmy adj بَلسَمِيّ	smoothly adv بنُعُومَة
plush adj بلشي	violet n بنفسج
gulp n بلعة	build v بنى
amount to v بلغ	base v بنى على أساس
plutonium n بلوتونيوم	built-in adj بني في
crystal n بلّور	format n بنية
wear n بلّى	thumb n بهام اليد

بهت dim v	بَياض البَيض egg white n
بهجة delight v	بيان catalog n
بهجة delight n	بيان موجز briefing n
بهذا القدر this adj	بيانو piano n
بهلوان acrobat n	بيبلوغرافيا bibliography n
بهمّة busily adv	بيت house, home n
بهيمة beast n	بيتُ السّلّم staircase n
بهيميّ bestial adj	بيّت العنكبوت cobweb, spiderweb n
بهيمية bestiality n	بيت ريفي hall n
بواسطة per pre	بيتي homely adj
بُؤرة seminary n	بيداغوجيا pedagogy n
بورجوازيّ bourgeois adj	بيضة egg n
بوصة inch n	بيْضويّ oval adj
بوضوح clearly, plainly, obviously adv	بيْع sale n
بوق honk v	بين between pre
بوق cornet n	بين explicit, unequivocal adj
بوقة horn n	بينة evidence n
بول evacuate v	بينما while c
بوْل urine n	بيئة environment n
بُولَنْدَا Poland n	
بولندي Polish adj	
بوليس سرى detective n	
بومة owl n	
بُؤرة focus n	
بُؤس misery n	

ت

تآكُل wear out v	تابع disciple n
تآمُر conspiracy n	تابع put up with v
تبادل interchange n	تابع أمين henchman n
تَبادُليّ reciprocal adj	تابل condiment, spice n
تباهي pomposity n	تابليّ spicy adj
تبأر gauge v	تابوت casket, coffin n
تبجيل reverence n	تاج crown, garland n
تبخر evaporate v	تاجر merchant n
تبديل replacement n	تاريخ date; chronicle n
تبذير extravagance n	تافه worthless, petty adj
تبرأ repudiate v	تالٍ next adj
تبرأ من disown v	تالف tainted adj
تبرج flaunt v	تامّ outright, complete adj
تبرّع contribution n	تأثيث furnishings n
تبطين lining n	تأثير impact n
تبع follow v	تأجيل postponement n
تبغ tobacco n	تأخر hold back v
تَبَن adoption n	تأخير delay n
تبنى foster v	تأرجُح swing n
تبين discern v	تألق glitter, outshine v
تتقاطع intersect v	تأليف synthesis n
تتمّة complement n	تأمل meditation, speculation n
تتويج coronation, crowning n	تأمين insurance n
تثاؤب yawn n	
تثبيط discouragement v	
تثقيب perforation n	

appraisal, estimation n تثمين	outfit n تجهيزات
dispute v تجادل	underground adj تحأرضيّ
traffic n تجارة	down adv تحت
commercial adj تجاريّ	underneath pre تحت
against pre تجاه	defiance, dare n تحدّ
disregard v تجاهل	limitation n تحديد
encroach, exceed v تجاوز	caution, warning n تحذير
run over v تجاوز الحد	freedom n تحرر
force v تجبر	sidestep v تحرك بخفة
regeneration n تجديد	liberation n تحرير
experiment, trial n تجربة	disillusion n تحرير من الوهم
tentative adj تجريبيّ	incitement n تحريض
conviction n تجريم	distortion n تحريف
espionage n تجسس	prohibition n تحريم
burp v تجشأ	improvement n تحسين
burp n تجشؤ	crash n تحطُّم
congregation, rally n تجمع	close to pre تحفظ
gather v تجمع	ascertain v تحقق من
make up v تجمل	demeaning adj تحقير
mob v تجمهر	investigation, quest n تحقيق
standstill adj تجميدك	analysis n تحليل
cosmetic n تجميلي	enthuse v تحمس
duck, evade v تجنب	endure, incur v تحمل
enormous adj تجنيد	firmness n تحمل
recruitment n تجنيد	harden v تحمل المشاق
miscarry v تُجْهِض	mutate v تحول

transformation n تحوُّل	graduate v تدرج
conversion, transfer n تحويل	training n تدريب
regards n تحيّات	drill n تدريب عسكري
odds n تحيز	piecemeal adv تدريجيًّا
coagulate v تخثر	inauguration n تدشين
coagulation n تخثر دمه	massage n تدليك
numbness n تخدير	annihilation n تدمير
sabotage n تخريب	sacrilege n تدنيس المقدسات
lace n تخريم	relic, souvenir n تذكار
drawing n تخطيط	recollection n تذكُّر
sketchy adj تخطيطى	memento n تَذْكِرَة
underlie v تخفى خلف	nag, grouch v تذمر
disposal n تخلص من	complaint, murmur n تذمّر
escape v تخلص من	correlate v ترابط
give away v تخلص منه	move back v تراجع
fall behind v تخلف عن	retreat n تراجع
relinquish v تخلى	tragic adj تراجيديّ
boundary n تَخْم	tram n تُرام
assessment n تخمين	streetcar n ترامواي
envisage v تخيل	chair v ترأس جلسة
overlap v تداخل	dust n تربة
get by v تدبر	pat n تربيتة
scam n تَدْجيل	arrangement n ترتيب
intervene v تدخل	dismount v ترجل
intervention n تدخل	drop n ترجل
work out v تدرب	interpretation n ترجمة

welcome n ترحيب	تزود بالماء v water down
greetings n ترحيبات	تزوير n forgery
relocation n ترحيل	تساقُط الثلج n snowfall
authorization n ترخيص	تساهل v indulge
hesitation n تردد	تساهل n leniency!
تردد الى مكان v frequent	تساو adv fifty-fifty
تردد على v haunt	تسجيل n enrollment
hesitant adj ترددي	تسرُّب n leak, leakage
تُرس n target, shield	تسرع n haste
precipitate v ترسب	تسريحة n hairdo
candidacy n تَرَشُّح	تسعون adj ninety
appeasement v ترضية	تسكع v hang around
expect v ترقب	تسكين n sedation
تَرَقُّب قَلِقٌ n suspense	تسلق v get up
promotion n ترقية	تسلم v receive
leave v ترك	تسلم n extradite
composition n تركيب	تسلية n pastime
condensation n تركيز	تَسْليم n surrender
thermostat n ترموستات	تسليم بقضية n admission
halt v ترنح	تسليم مجرم n extradition
hymn n ترنيمة	تسميم n poisoning
anthem n ترنيمة دينية	adjustment, compromise;
antidote n تِرْياق	intercession n تسوية
increase v تزايد	likeness, similarity, analogy n تشابه
ice skate v تزلج على الجليد	تشاجر v hassle
adulation n تزلف	تَشارُك n communion

conference n	تشاوُر	declension n	تصريف الأسماء
pessimism n	تشاؤم	look into v	تصفح
hug v	تشبث	liquidation n	تصفية
dispersal n	تشتيت	applause n	تصفيق
cramp n	تشجّج	design, plan n	تصميم
lubrication n	تشحيم	mannerism n	تصنع
emphasis n	تشديد	assortment n	تصنيف
autopsy n	تشريح الجثة	conceive v	تصور
statute n	تشريع	picturesque adj	تصويري
reenactment n	تشريع قانون	dwindle v	تضاءل
October n	تشرين الأول	discord n	تضارب
ramification n	تشعّب	solidarity n	تضامن
intercede v	تشفع	sacrifice n	تضحية
formation n	تشكيل	expansion n	تضخم
spasm n	تشنج	dishonesty n	تضليل
muddle n	تشوُّش ذهني	have v	تضمن
look forward v	تشوق	coincidence n	تطابق
deformity n	تشوُّه	medication n	تطبيب
mayhem n	تَشْويه	application n	تطبيق
hazard n	تصادف	blink v	تَطْرَف العينُ
collision n	تصادُم	embroidery n	تطريز
correction n	تصحيح	graft n	تطعيم النبات
dole out v	تصدق	intrusion n	تطفُّل
foreword n	تصدير	look through v	تطلع الى
certificate n	تصديق	purification, purge n	تَطْهير
fend v	تصرف	enclosure n	تطويق

تظاهر *v* feign, pretend	تعقُّد *n* tangle
تعادل *n* draw	تعقيد *n* complication
تعارض *v* disagree	تعلم *v* learn
تعارض *n* discrepancy	تعلُّم *n* learning
تعاسة *n* unhappiness	تعليق *n* comment
تعاطف *n* sympathy	تعليم *n* tuition
تعامل *n* dealings	تعليم مسيحى *n* catechism
تعاون *n* collaboration	تعهد *n* engagement
تعاونيّ *adj* cooperative	تعْويذة *n* charm
تعب *n* tiredness	تعويض *n* compensation
تعبير *n* statement	تعويل *n* reliance
تعبير ساخر *n* cynicism	تعيس *adj* unhappy
تعدّد *n* multitude	تعيش *v* freshen
تعدُّد الزوجات *n* polygamy	تعيين *n* appointment
تعديل *n* amendment	تغذية *n* nourishment, nutrition
تعذيب *n* torment, torture	تغرغر بالماء *v* gargle
تعرُّق *n* perspiration	تغطية *n* coverage
تعريفة *n* tariff	تغلب *v* get over, outdo
تعزية *n* consolation	تغيُّر *n* revulsion
تعزيز *n* reinforcements	تغيير *n* change
تعصب *n* intolerance	تُفّاحة *n* apple
تعصّب أعمى *n* bigotry	تفاهة *n* banality
تَعَطُّل *n* breakdown	تفاوت *n* disparity
تعطيل موقت *n* suspension	تفاوض *n* negotiation
تعفّن *n* rot	تفتُّح *n* opening
تعقب *v* pursue	تفتيش *n* search

explode v تفجر	drip n تقطر
detonation n تفجير	imitation n تقليد
scrutiny n تفحّص	technical adj تِقْنِيّ
gory adj تفرج	recede v تقهقر
gaze v تفرس	devotion, piety n تقوى
decadence, disintegration n تفسّخ	confirmation n تقوية
exude v تفصد	almanac n تقويم
detail n تفصيل	holy, pious adj تقي
come apart v تفكك	throw up v تقيأ
consideration n تفكير	fester v تقيح
tasteless adj تَفِهٌ	confinement n تَقْيِيد
outperform v تفوق	generation n تكاثر
delegation n تفويض	parity n تكافؤ
retirement n تقاعد	arrogance, vanity n تكبّر
receptive adj تقبُّليّ	secrecy n تكتُّم
advance, go ahead, pull ahead v تقدم	technique n تكتيك
headway n تقدم	tactical adj تكتيكيّ
advance, course, progress n تقدّم	duplication n تكرار
progressive adj تقدميّ	consecration n تكريس
appreciation n تقدير قيمة	pose v تكلف
almost adv تقريباً	foretell v تكهن
approximate adj تقريبيّ	adaptation n تكييف
report n تقرير	heap n تل
division n تقسيم	manipulate v تلاعب
delinquency n تقصير	recital n تلاوة
bleach n تقصير مادة	damage v تلف

تلفزيون television n	تمطر رذاذا drizzle v
تلفون phone n	تملص elude v
تلفيق invention n	تملق court n
تلميح allusion n	تمهيد preamble n
تلميح insinuation v	تمهيديّ preliminary adj
تلميذ pupil n	تموج fluctuate v
تلويث contamination n	تموُّج ripple n
تلويح بـ wave n	تَمْويه camouflage n
تماثل identify v	تميز distinction n
تماسك cling v	تمييز recognition n
تماسُك tenacity n	تنازل step down v
تماماً altogether adj	تنازل عن back down v
تماماً completely adv	تناظر symmetry n
تماما entirely, fully adv	تناغم tune n
تمايُل swing n	تنافُس rivalry n
تمثال نصفيّ bust n	تنافسيّ competitive adj
تمثيل assimilation n	تناوب relay v
تمثيلي exemplary adj	تناول مخدرات dope v
تمثيلية farce n	تنبُّؤ prediction n
تمدد lie v	تنجيد upholstery n
تمرُّد mutiny n	تنحنح hem n
تمرد disobedience n	تندلع الحربُ break out v
تمرد disobey v	تنزه hike v
تمرين coaching n	تنزيل رتبة degradation n
تمساح إستوائي alligator n	تنسيق coordination n
تُمطِر rain v	تَنْشِيط activation n

تنشـئة upbringing n	توتر n tension
تنصيب installation n	توثيق documentation n
تنضيد composition n	توجيه control n
تنظيم organization n	توحيد conjunction, integration n
تنَفُّس aspiration n	تودد ingratiate v
تنفس breathing, respiration n	تودُّد courtship n
تنقيح revision n	تورد flush v
تنكر disguise v	تورط involvement n
تنهُّد sigh n	تورط في جريمة complicity n
تنّورة skirt n	توريط implication n
تنوع diversity n	توزيع distribution n
تنوُّع variety n	توسط mediocrity n
تنين dragon n	توسل entreat, beseech v
تهجئة spelling n	توسيع development n
تهديد threat, menace n	توصية commendation n
تهريب contraband n	توضيح clarification n
تهشـُّم crash n	توطيد settlement n
تهكّمّي ironic adj	توظيف appointment n
تهنئة congratulations n	توفير economy n
تهوية ventilation n	تَوْق longing n
توابل flavor n	توقع expect v
تواتر recourse v	توقع expectancy n
توازن equilibrium, poise n	توقف cut off, stop over v
تواضع humility n	توقُّف stop n
توبة repentance n	توقُّف على dependence n
توبيخ rebuke n	توقف فجأة cut out v

adoration n توقير	frustrate v ثبط
autograph n توقيع	discourage v ثبط العزيمة
assertion n توكيد	thickness n ثخانة
assumption n تولّ	thick adj ثخين
officiate v تولى منصب	breast n ثَدْي
glow v توهج	talkative adj ثرثار
flow, influx n تيار	gossip v ثرثر
availability n تيسير	opulence n ثروة
watch n تَيَقُّظ	chandelier n ثُرَيّا
fig n تين	fox n ثعلب
hesitate v تثنىئ	culture n ثقافة
	cultural adj ثقافيّ
	educational adj ثقافي
	hole, puncture n ثقب
	drill v ثقب
	trust n ثِقة
	educate v ثقف
	burdensome adj ثقيل
	barracks n ثُكْنَة
	three adj ثلاثة
	thirteen adj ثلاثة عَشَر
	thirty adj ثلاثون
	triple adj ثلاثيّ
	tripod n ثلاثيّ القوائم
	icebox n ثلاجة
	snow n ثلج

ث

steady adj ثابت	
eighth adj ثامن	
latter adj ثانٍ	
inferior, secondary adj ثانوي	
twelfth adj ثاني عَشَر	
revolting adj ثائر	
retaliation n ثأر	
constancy n ثبات	
fasten v ثبت	

ثلجت snow v

ثُلمة break n

ثماني عشر eighteen adj

ثمر العُلّيْق blackberry n

ثمر الورد البرى hip n

ثمرة gain n

ثمرة الجهد harvest n

ثمل high adj

ثمن esteem v

ثمن cost n

ثمن التذكرة fare n

ثنائي dual adj

ثنائيّ اللغة bilingual adj

ثنى bend, flex; hire v

ثَنْية الشّراع reef n

ثوب dress, robe n

ثوبٌ تحتِيّ underwear n

ثور bull n

ثور heat; rampage v

ثَوْر ox n

ثور البركان erupt v

ثوران eruption n

ثورة revolt, uprising n

ثوم garlic n

ثُؤلول wart n

ثيران oxen n

ج

جاء come v

جادة boulevard n

جاذبية الارض gravity n

جارٍ current adj

جارٌ neighbor n

جارور drawer n

جارية ongoing adj

جازى repay v

جافّ arid, dry adj

جافة dried adj

جالس seated adj

جامع terse adj

جامعة university n

جامعيّ academic adj

جاموس buffalo n

جانب side n

جانب التل hillside n

جانباً aside adv

جانبيّ lateral adj

جاهل unaware adj

جائر unfair, unjust adj

جائزة award, prize n

جائع hungry adj

جدير بالملاحظة remarkable adj	جبار mighty adj
جديلة braid n	جبان heartless adj
جذاب attractive, appealing, desirable adj	جبل mountain n
جذام leprosy n	جبل جليد iceberg n
جذب haul v	جبلي hilly, mountainous adj
جذب attraction n	جُبْن shyness n
جِذر root n	جبهة forehead, front n
جذريّ radical adj	جُثّة corpse, carcass n
جذع التمثال torso n	جُحْر burrow n
جذل exult v	جحود disbelief n
جذل hilarious adj	جحيم hell n
جذل الشجرة stub n	جد grandfather n
جرّ drag v	جدًّا very adv
جرّ traction n	جداب eye-catching adj
جراثيم bacteria n	جدة grandmother n
جراحيّ surgical adv	جدل intertwine v
جَراد locust n	جدل controversy n
جرأة audacity n	جدول schedule n
جرثومة germ n	جَدْوَلٌ زَمَنِيّ timetable n
جرح injure, traumatize v	جدي kid n
جُرح wound n	جدّي serious adj
جرح بليغ gash n	جديا earnestly adv
جرحي traumatic adj	جدّية seriousness n
جرد inventory n	جديد fresh, new adj
جرد disqualify v	جديد تماماً brand-new adj
جَرَسُ الباب doorbell n	جدير بالإطراء praiseworthy adj

جُرعة dosage n	حُسَيمة corpuscle n
جرعة مفرطة overdose n	جشاء belch n
جُرُف precipice n	جَشَعٌ avarice n
جرّم incriminate v	جَشِع avaricious adj
جِرْو puppy n	جَعَة beer n
جرى flow v	جعجع clamor v
جريء intrepid, daring adj	جعد الشعر curly adj
جريدة newspaper n	جَعْدة wrinkle, crease n
جريمة felony, crime n	جعله أكثر وضوحا sharpen v
جِزّ clipping n	جعله تافها trivialize v
جزء part n	جعله رسميا formalize v
جزء حيوي linchpin n	جعله شرعيا validate v
جزة صوف fleece n	جعله يانعا mellow v
جَزر carrot n	جغرافية geography n
جَزمة boot n	جف drain v
جزية tribute n	جفاف coldness n
جزيرة island, isle n	حفف dry v
جزئيّ partial adj	جفن eyelid n
جُزْئيّا partially, partly adv	جلاء visibility n
جسد body n	جلالة majesty n
جسد embody v	جَلَبة racket n
جَسَديّ carnal adj	جَلد constant adj
جسر viaduct, bridge n	جلد flog, whip v
جِسم body n	جلدٌ مدبوغ leather n
جَسُور bold adj	جَلْدة lash n
جُسَيم particle n	جلديّ skinny adj

جلسة session n	جميل beautiful adj
جلوس sitting n	جن fairy n
جلوكوز glucose n	جناح pavilion n
جليّ unmistakable adj	جَناح wing n
جليد ice n	جنائيّ criminal adj
جليدي icy adj	جنباً إلى جنب abreast adv
جليسة أطفال babysitter n	جْنَة batch n
جليل solemn, superb adj	جُنْحة misdemeanor n
جَمَارك customs n	جند enroll, enlist v
جماعة troop n	جندي soldier n
جماعة الكَهَنة priesthood n	جندي عريق veteran n
جماليّ aesthetic adj	جنرال general n
جُمْجُمة skull n	جنس gender n
جمد immobilize v	جنوبيّ southern adj
جَمْرة brand n	جنون craziness n
جمرة coal n	جنى earn v
جمرة embers n	جنين embryo, fetus n
جَمْع collection n	جهاراً publicly adv
جمع شمل roundup n	جهارة الصوت volume n
جمعية association n	جهاز المسرح scenery n
جمعيّة society n	جهد effort n
جَمَل camel n	جهد كهربائى voltage n
حمل embellish v	جهز furnish v
جملة sentence n	جهل ignorance n
جُمَلةٌ مُعْتَرَضة parenthesis n	جواب answer, reply n
جمهورية republic n	جواب بارع comeback n

ج

ح

جوار proximity n	حاجب brow n
جوارب طويلة pantyhose n	حاجب العين eyebrow n
جواز سفر passport n	حاجب المحكمة bailiff n
جور tyranny n	حاجز barrier, screen n
جورب hose n	حاد intense; squeaky adj
جوز walnut n	حادّ acute adj
جوزة nut n	حادث incident n
جوزة الهند coconut n	حادثة happening, event n
جوع hunger n	حارّ cordial adj
جوقة chorus n	حارس guard, sentry n
جَوْن cove, creek n	حارس المرمى goalkeeper n
جوهر core n	حاز possess v
جوهرة gem n	حازوقة hiccup n
جوهري essential adj	حاسّة sense n
جوّي atmospheric adj	حاسة الذوق taste n
جَيْب pocket n	حاسم crucial adj
جيش army n	حاشية annotation n
جيش ردع deterrence n	حاصر besiege v
جَيَشان upheaval n	حاصل quotient n
جينة gene n	حاضر attendant n
	حاضر present adj
	حافة fringe, rim n
	حافر hoof n

حافظ v maintain	حجب الحقائق v cover up
حَافِظةُ أَوْرَاقٍ n briefcase	حجّة n argument
حافي القدمين adj barefoot	حِجّة n pilgrimage
حاقد adj spiteful	حِجْر n lap
حاكم n governor	حَجَر n stone
حال n adverb	حجر الزاوية n cornerstone
حالة n case	حجر الكلس n limestone
حالم adj faraway	حجرة n room
حالَما c once	حجرة التواليت n rest room
حامض adj sour	حجرة الجلوس n living room
حامل adj pregnant	حجرة الطعام n dining room
حامل البكالوريا n bachelor	حجرة المؤن n pantry
حانة n tavern	حُجرة النوم n bedroom
حاول v endeavor	حَجْز n attachment; reservation
حبة دواء n pill	حجز v impound
حبة صغيرة n pellet	حجز التيار v stem
حبّة قمح n corn	حجْم n bulk, size
حبر n ink	حجم n mass
حبل n cord, rope	حد n border, frontier
حَبْل n twist	حدّ n compass
حبّي adj amicable	حدّ n limit
حبيب adj darling	حِداد n mourning
حتى adv till	حدث n episode
حتى لو c even if	حدث v happen
حتى هنا adv hitherto	حَدَث adj juvenile
حِجاب n veil	حدد v itemize, mark

حَدْس conjecture n	حرَسّ safeguard n
حدق space out v	حرض incite, provoke v
حُدُودِيّ borderline adj	حرف distort v
حديث recent adj	حَرْف brink n
حديثاً lately adv	حرف letter n
حديد iron n	حرف جرّ preposition n
حديقة garden n	حَرْفيَّاً literally adv
حديقة الحيوانات zoo n	حَرْفيّاً literal adj
حذاء footwear, shoe n	حُرق burn n
حذر discreet adj	حرقة في المعدة heartburn n
حذر discretion n	حرك nod v
حذر exhort v	حرك باليد manhandle v
حذَر prudence n	حركة move n
حذِر prudent adj	حرَم sanctuary n
حَذَر precaution n	حِرْم من الكنيسة ban n
حذف omission n	حرم من الوراثة disinherit v
حذلقي pedantic adj	حرمان deprivation n
حراثة cultivation n	حريّة liberty n
حراسة ward n	حرير silk n
حِرام blanket n	حزازة hatred n
حرب war n	حِزام belt n
حرب العصابات guerrilla n	حزر estimate v
حربة bayonet n	حزمة bundle n
حربون harpoon n	حزن affliction, sorrow, sadness n
حرر كتب edit v	حزين sad, sorrowful adj
حرر, تخلص من free v	حسّ sensation n

soup *n* حِساء		horse *n* حصان	
account *n* حساب		impunity *n* حصانة	
predisposed; sensitive *adj* حساس		dividend, ration, share *n* حصة	
ticklish *adj* حساس للدغدغة		restrict *v* حصر	
calculation *n* حُسبان		ration *v* حصص	
envy *n* حسد		fort, bulwark *n* حصن	
envy *v* حسد		immunize *v* حصن	
discount *v* حسم		gravel *n* حصى	
deduction *n* حَسْم		mat *n* حصير	
upgrade, improve *v* حسن		outcome *n* حصيلة	
tasteful *adj* حَسَنُ الذّوْق		by-product *n* حصيلة ثانية	
alright, okay *adv* حسنا		nursery *n* حضانة	
handout *n* حسنة		present *v* حضر	
envious *adj* حسود		bosom, lap *n* حِضْن	
sensual *adj* حسّيّ		presence *n* حضور	
nearsighted, shortsighted *adj* حسير		wreckage *n* حُطام	
fill *v* حشا السن		firewood *n* حطب	
regiment; throng *n* حشد		fortune, chance, luck *n* حظ	
crowd *n* حَشْد من الناس		forewarn *v* حظر	
insect *n* حشرة		diaper *n* حفاظ الطفل	
stuffing, padding *n* حَشْوَة		drill, excavate *v* حفر	
filling *n* حشوة السن		pit *n* حفرة	
hashish *n* حشيش مخدر		committed *adj* حفظ	
pebble *n* حصاة		memorize *v* حفظ	
cobblestone *n* حصاة كبيرة		graduation *n* حفل التخرج	
blockade, siege *n* حِصار		celebration *n* حفلة	

حفلة التعميد christening n	حكمٌ بعقوبة sentence n
حفلة أنس وسَمَر party n	حكمة wisdom n
حفلة شواء barbecue n	حكومة government n
حفنة handful n	حكيم physician n
حفيد grandchild n	حكيم judicious, wise adj
حقّ الانتخاب franchise n	حل disentangle v
حقّ النشر copyright n	حل resolution, solution n
حقا indeed adv	حل clear-cut adj
حقارة meanness n	حل جمعية disband v
حقد venom, malice n	حل محل displace v
حقق implement v	حلاوة sweetness n
حقل ألغام minefield n	حلبة arena n
حقن inject v	حَلَزُون snail n
حقنة injection n	حِلْف league n
حقود malignant adj	حلق earring n
حقيبة handbag n	حلقة circle, ring n
حقيبة سفر suitcase n	حلم dream n
حقيبة ظهر backpack n	حلو honey n
حقير despicable, pitiful adj	حُلو sweet adj
حقيقة certainty n	حلوى sweets, candy n
حقيقي factual, real adj	حليب milk n
حك friction, itch n	حِلْية jewel n
حكاية story, anecdote n	حَليم meek adj
حكم govern v	حمار donkey n
حَكَّم referee, umpire n	حمار الزَّرد zebra n
حكم rule, reign n	حماسة enthusiasm n

fervent *adj* حماسي	nostalgia *n* حنين
stupidity *n* حماقة	homesick *adj* حنين للوطن
suspenders *n* حمالة البنطلون	money order *n* حوالة بريديّة
bathroom *n* حمّام	whale *n* حوت
dove, pigeon *n* حمامة	basin, tub, pool *n* حوض
sting *n* حُمَة	aquarium *n* حوض السمك
acid *n* حَمْض	around *pro* حَوْل
burden *n* حِمْل	about *adv* حول
lamb *n* حَمَل	endorse *v* حول شيك
lift *v* حَمْل	petrified *adj* حول لمادة صلبة
campaign *n* حملة	alive, vivid *adj* حيّ
manhunt *n* حملة البحث	slum *n* حيّ الفقراء
glare *n* حملقة	greet, hail *v* حيا
acidity *n* حُمُوضة	life *n* حياة
load *n* حُمُوْلَة	possession *n* حيازة
cargo *n* حمولة السفينة	snake *n* حيّة
fever *n* حمى	whereas *c* حيث أن
feverish *adj* حمى	maze *n* حيرة
intimate *adj* حميم	trick *n* حيلة
perjury *n* حنث باليمين	animal *n* حيوان
throat *n* حنجرة	lynx *n* حيوان الوَشَق
faucet *n* حنفية	pet *n* حيوان مدلل
fury *n* حنق	wildlife *n* حيوانات ضارية
wrath *n* حَنَّقْد	brute *adj* حَيَوَانيّ
kind *adj* حنون	vital *adj* حيويّ
genuflect *v* حنى الركبة تعبدا	energy *n* حيوية

خ

immortal *adj* خالد	
pure *adj* خالص	
dissent *v* خالف	
crude, rude *adj* خام	
ore *n* خامة	
stifling *adj* خانق	
fearful, afraid *adj* خائف	
disloyal *adj* خائن	
wickedness *n* خبث	
inform *v* خبر	
news *n* خبَر	
batch *n* خَبْزَة	
virulent *adj* خبيث	
expert *adj* خبير	
circumcision *n* خِتان	
seal *n* خَتْم	
timidity, shame *n* خجل	
ashamed *adj* خَجِل	
shoepolish *n* خجول	
timid *adj* خجول	
cheek *n* خدّ	
fraud, swindle *n* خِداع	
drug *v* خدر	
numb *adj* خَدِر	
scratch *n* خَدْش	
deception *n* خَدْع	

conclusion *n* خاتمة	
dishonest, deceptive *adj* خادع	
fool, rip off *v* خادع	
servant *n* خادم	
abroad *adv* خارجَ البلد	
without *pre* خارجَ كذا	
out, outside *adv* خارجاً	
exterior, outer *adj* خارجي	
underdog *n* خاسر	
special *adj* خاص	
especially *adv* خاصة	
our *adj* خاصّتنا	
his *pro* خاصته	
own *adj* خاصّتهُ	
hers *pro* خاصتها	
flank, loin *n* خاصرة	
attribute *v* خاصيّة	
property *n* خاصيّة	
submissive *adj* خاضع	
hijacker *n* خاطط	
risk *v* خاطر	
kidnapper *n* خاطف	
erroneous *adj* خاطئ	

dupe v خدع	disgrace n خزي
hoax, ruse, trick n خدعة	go down v خسر
duty, service n خدمة	loss n خُسْران
havoc, ravage n خراب	lumber, wood n خشب
myth, superstition n خرافة	hardwood n خشب قاس
fictitious adj خرافي	coarse, rough adj خشن
dilapidated adj خَرِب	rudeness n خشونة
go out, give out v خرج	fertility n خصب
derail v خرج عن الخط	lush adj خصب
junk n خردة	waist n خَصْر
mustard n خَرْدَل	earmark v خصص
artichoke n خُرْشوف	discount; adversary, opponent n خصم
cartridge n خرطوشة	chiefly adv خصوصاً
breach n خرق	confidential; peculiar adj خصوصي
go over v خرق القانونة	hostility n خصومة
rag, shred n خرقة	fertile adj خصيب
derailment n خروج عن الخط	equator n خط الاستواء
sheep n خروف	longitude n خطّ الطول
chart, map n خريطة	latitude n خطّ العرض
fall n خريف	pipeline n خط أنابيب
reservoir n خزّان	airline n خط جوي
cabinet n خزانة	coastline n خط ساحلى
wardrobe n خزانة الثياب	speech n خطاب
bookcase n خزانة كتب	crook n خُطّاف
dresser n خزانة مطبخ	error, mistake n خطأ
hoard v خزن	blunder n خطأ فاضح

misprint n خطأ مطبعيّ	compendium n خلاصة وافية
design n خِطّة	blender n خَلّاطٌ
danger, peril n خَطَرٌ	mixer n خلاطة
importance n خطر	controversial adj خِلافيّ
perilous, dangerous adj خطِر	over, through pre خلال
project v خطط	meanwhile adv خلال ذلك
lay-out n خطط	extricate v خلص
abduction n خَطْف	after, behind pre خَلف
kidnap, hijack v خطف	back adv خَلْفَ
engagement n خطوبة	rear adj خلفيّ
footstep n خطوة	background n خلفيّة
trip n خطوة رشـيقة	creation n خَلْق
seriousness n خطورة	virtuous adj خلقي
fiancé n خطيب	fault, defect n خلل
hazardous adj خطير	devoid adj خِلْوٌ من
sandal, slipper n خُفّ	careless adj خلو من الهموم
patrol n خَفْر	eternity n خلود
depression n خَفْض	let v خلى
minimize v خفض	beehive n خلية النحل
downsize v خفض العمالة	cape n خليج
flunk v خفق	alloy n خليط معدني
fall through v خفق في التفاوض	muffler n خمار
hidden, invisible adj خفي	ferment v خمر
light adj خفيف	wine n خَمْر
vinegar n خَلّ	sherry n خمرة
substance n خلاصة	fifth adj خمس

خ

خمسة عشر fifteen *adj*

خمّن evaluate *v*

خميرة ferment, yeast *n*

خناق angina *n*

خِنْجَر dagger *n*

خندق ditch, trench *n*

خنزير pig, hog, boar *n*

خنزير بري wild boar *n*

خَنْفَساء beetle *n*

خنق asphyxiation *n*

خَوْخ peach *n*

خوف fear *n*

خوف frighten *v*

خيار alternative *n*

خِياطة sewing, seamstress *n*

خيال fantasy *n*

خيال اللمبة lampshade *n*

خيالي fantastic *adj*

خيانة betrayal *n*

خيانة double-cross *v*

خيب الأمل disappoint *v*

خيبة أمل disappointment *n*

خيّر benevolent *adj*

خير welfare *n*

خيزران bamboo *n*

خَيْزُرَانة reed *n*

خيط fiber, string *n*

خَيْمة tent *n*

د

داء الصرع epilepsy *n*

دابّ creepy *adj*

داخل inside *pre*

داخلا inwards *adv*

داخلي interior, inner, inward *adj*

داخلي indoor *adv*

دار dwelling *n*

دار البلدية town hall *n*

دار العدل courthouse *n*

دار على محور swivel *v*

دافئ cozy, warm *adj*

دامع tearful *adj*

دائرة المعارف encyclopedia *n*

دائم lasting *adj*

دائما ever, always *adv*

دُبّ bear *n*

دبّاسة stapler *n*

دبر الأمر wield *v*

دَبْش rubble n	دس insinuate v
دبلوم diploma n	دستور constitution n
دبلوماسي diplomat n	دُشّ shower n
دبوس طبعة thumbtack n	دشن inaugurate v
دجاجة chicken n	دعابة humor n
دجّن domesticate v	دعامة pier n
دخل enter, go in v	دعاية propaganda n
دخل كافٍ competence n	دعم subsidize v
دخن fumigate v	دعوة call, invitation n
دخول entrée, entry n	دعوى litigation n
درابزون handrail n	دغدغة tickle n
دَرّاجَة bike n	دِفء warmth n
دراجة بخارية scooter n	دَقّة rudder n
دراجة نارية motorcycle n	دفتر الحسابات ledger n
دراجة هوائية bicycle n	دفتر العمل workbook n
درب train v	دفتر شيكات checkbook n
درج متحرك escalator n	دفع shove n
دَرَجَة degree, stage n	دفع بالحجة rebut v
درجة الباب doorstep n	دفع دفعة جزاء down payment n
درجة الحرارة temperature n	دفعة payment n
دردار elm n	دفعة واحدة lump sum n
دُرْدُور whirlpool n	دفن funeral n
دَرْزة seam, stitch n	دفيئة greenhouse n
درس lesson n	دَقّة precision n
دِرْع armor n	دقيق flour, oatmeal n
دريل نسيج drill n	دقيق precise, punctual adj

دقيقة n minute	دهن n fat
دكّان n shopping	دَهْن n painting
دَكّة n terrace	دواجن n poultry
دلالة n indication	دوار n dizziness
دلالة منذرة n foretaste	دواري adj dizzy
دلفين n dolphin	دوّاسة n pedal
دلو n bucket, pail	دوام n duration
دليل n guidebook	دودة n worm
دليل قاطع n smoking gun	دَوْر n cycle
دم n blood	دور سفلي n basement
دماغ n brain	دَوَران n turn, rotation
دمث adj gentle	دوق n duke
دمج v combine	دوقة n duchess
دمج n affiliation	دولار n dollar
دمدم v grumble	دولة n state
دمدمة n rumble	دولة بلْجيكا n Belgium
دمعة n tear	دولة حليفة n ally
دموّي adj bloody	دومعياری adj substandard
دمى v bleed	دونَ pre beneath, under
دمية n doll, puppet	ديبلوماسيّ adj diplomatic
دُمْيَوِيّ n toy	دير n cloister
دندرمة n ice cream	دَيْر n monastery
دنوّ n approach	ديسمبر n December
دنيوّي adj profane	ديك n cock, rooster
دهاء n ploy	ديكتاتوريّ adj dictatorial
دهان n dye, paint	ديموقراطيّ adj democratic

د

دين n faith, religion	دَقْن n chin
ديناميكي adj dynamic	ذَكَر n male
دِيني adj religious	ذِكْر n mention
	ذكَر الإوزّ n cob
ذ	ذكرى n remembrance
	ذكرى سنوية n anniversary
ذاب v dissolve	ذكي adj intelligent, astute, clever
ذاكرة n memory, mind	ذل v humiliate
ذاهل adj distraught	ذهب v go away
ذبابة n fly	ذهبي adj golden
ذبح v slay	ذو رائحة adj smelly
ذبذبة n vibration	ذو شأن adj worthwhile
ذبل v fade	ذو لقب adj hereditary
ذبول n decline	ذو معنى adj meaningful
ذخائر n munitions	ذو نمش adj freckled
ذخيرة حربيّة n ammunition	ذواب adj soluble
ذراع n arm	ذوبان n thaw
ذراع التطويل n boom	ذوق n tact
ذراع المِرفاع n boom	ذَيل n tail
ذرائعي adj pragmatist	ذَيْل n trail
ذرّة n atom	ذئب n wolf
ذروة n peak, summit	
ذرّي adj atomic	
ذريعة n plea	
ذعر n scare	

ر

rآئحة n odor, scent	رابح adj lucrative
رائع adj fabulous	رابط n couple
رائي adj divine	رابط الجأش adj composed
رأس إصبع القدم n tiptoe	رابع adj fourth
رأس مال n capital	رأتب n pay, salary
رأساً على عَقِب adv upside-down	راجع v revise
رأسمال n fund	راحة n ease, repose
رأسية n heading	راديو n radio
رباط n ligament, strap, tie	راسخ adj steady
رِبَاطُ الحِذَاءِ n shoelace	راشد adj major
رباطة جأش n coolness	راعي البقر n cowboy
ربّان الطائرة n pilot	راغب adj would-be
ربة الاهة n goddess	رافض adj disobedient
ربة المنزل n housewife	رافعة n hoist
ربح n revenue, proceeds	راقب v monitor, oversee
ربط v bind, connection	راكد adj stagnant
ربطة عنق n necktie	راهب n friar, monk
رُبْع n quarter	راهبة n nun
ربما adv may-be, perhaps	راهن v gage
ربَوي adj asthmatic	راهن على v bet
ربى v breed	راوغ v dodge
ربيب n stepson	راوية n informant
ربيبة n stepdaughter	راية n flag, banner
رَتابَة n monotony	
رتاج n bar	
رتب n hierarchy	

broom *n* رَتَمٌ	bad, shoddy *adj* رديء
monotonous *adj* رتيب	drizzle *n* رذاذ
shabby *adj* رث	vice *n* رذيلة
outweigh *v* رجح	rice *n* رزّ
retroactive *adj* رجعي	staple *n* رزّة
tremor *n* رجفة	bale *n* رزمة ضخمة
leg *n* رِجل	sober *adj* رزين
businessman *n* رجُل أعمال	epistle, letter *n* رسالة
clerk *n* رجُل دِين	ordination *n* رسامة الكاهن
manliness *n* رجولة	exhibit, sketch *v* رسم
virile *adj* رجوليّ	diagram *n* رسم بيانيّ
spacious *adj* رحْب	fee *n* رسم دخول
pull out *v* رحل	official *adj* رسميّ
journey, tour *n* رحلة	formally *adv* رسميا
flight *n* رحلة جوية	leash *n* رَسَن
clemency *n* رحمة	apostle *n* رسول
relocate *v* رحيل	apostolic *adj* رَسوليّ
merciful *adj* رحيم	infiltrate *v* رشح
marble *n* رُخام	splash *v* رشش
patent, permission *n* رخصة	sip *n* رَشفَة
slack *adj* رِخْو	hurl *v* رشق
inexpensive, cheap *adj* رخيص	corruption, bribe *n* رشوة
reaction *n* رد فعل	agile, brisk *adj* رشيق
defection *n* ردّة	spanking *n* رشيق
scare away *v* ردع	fund *v* رصد مبلغا
lobby *n* رَدْهة	alignment *n* رصف

boost *n* رفعٌ	sidewalk *n* رصيف
companionship *n* رفْقَة	wharf *n* رصيف الميناء
comrade, buddy *n* رفيق	mall *n* رصيف للمشاة
classmate *n* رفيق الصف	ground *n* رض
chip *n* رُقاقة	foul, damp, humid *adj* رطب
tenderness *n* رقة	humidity *n* رطوبة
dance, dancing *n* رقْص	custody *n* رعاية
label *n* رُقعة	horror, fright, consternation *n* رعب
number *n* رقم	thunder *n* رَعْد
digit *n* رقم تحت العشرة	shudder *n* رعْدة
promote *v* رقى	shiver *n* رعشة
sergeant *n* رقيب	pastoral *adj* رعوي
spell *n* رُقْية	graze *v* رعى الماشية
flimsy, tenuous *adj* رقيق	care for *v* رعى بإهتمام
bank *n* رُكام	desire, will *n* رغبة
fabricate *v* ركب	goodwill *n* رغبة حسنة
dispense *v* ركب الادوية	craving *n* رغبة ملحّة
condense *v* ركز	though *c* رَغْمَ ذَلِكَ
pace *v* ركض	foam *n* رغوة
kneel *v* ركع	loaf *n* رغيف
stagnation *n* ركود	bracket *n* رف
pillar *n* ركيزة	shelf, shelves *n* رَفّ
ash, cinder *n* رماد	luxury *n* رفاهية
spear *n* رمح	flutter, hover *v* رفرف
character, symbol *n* رمز	denial, refusal, rejection *n* رفْض
symbolic *adj* رمزيّ	elevate *v* رفع

رَمْل sand n	رّي irrigation n
رمم refurbish v	رياضة exercise, sport v
رمى discard, cast v	رياضة الكَارَاتيه karate n
رمىى إلى drive at v	رياضي athletic adj
رمية put v	رِيّان chubby adj
رهان bet n	ريح wind n
رِهْبانيّ monastic adj	ريشة feather n
رَهّن mortgage n	ريفيّ rural, rustic adj
رهيب lurid, dire adj	رئة lung n
رهينة hostage n	رئيس boss, chef n
رواسب residue n	رئيسُ الجلسة chairman n
رواق corridor, hallway n	رئيس دير للرهبان abbot n
رواق porch n	رئيسي foremost, main adj
رواقيّ stoic adj	زاحِف reptile n
رواية novel n	
روتين red tape n	
روث dung n	
روح spirit n	
روحيّ spiritual adj	
روسي Russian adj	
روسيا Russia n	
رَوْع awe n	
روعة splendor n	
رؤيا vision n	
رؤيا نبوئية apocalypse n	
رؤية view n	

ز

embitter v زاده مرارة	زَرْكَشَة n trimmings
sightseeing v زار معالم	زَرْنيخ n arsenic
pass away v زال	زعنفة السمك n fin
corner, angle n زاوية	زعيم n elder
phoney, sham adj زائف	زعيم فتنة n ringleader
transient adj زائل	زغبي adj hairy
clientele n زبائن	زفافيّ adj bridal
lather n زَبَد	زفت n asphalt
butter n زُبدة	زفير n expiration
bowl n زُبْدية	زُقاق n lane
customer n زبون	زقاق بحري n fjord
raisin n زبيب	زلة n trip, slip; lapse
bottle n زجاجة	زلزال n earthquake
snub n زَجْر	زَلِق adj slippery
enrich v زخرف	زمرد n emerald
décor n زخرفة	زميل n fellow
decorative adj زخرفي	زنّاً n adultery
button n زرّ	زنبور n wasp
agriculture n زراعة	زنجبيل n ginger
agricultural adj زراعيّ	زنْديق adj heretic
giraffe n زرافة	زنزانة n dungeon
pliers n زَرديّة	زُهْديّ adj ascetic
grow up v زرع,	زهرة n flower
	زهرة اللؤلؤ n daisy
	زواج n matrimony
	زواج أحادي n monogamy

س

سابع seventh adj
سابق past, previous adj
سابق لأوانه premature adj
سابقا formerly, previously adv
سابقة precedent n
ساجد magical adj
ساحق crushing adj
ساحل coast n
ساحلي coastal adj
ساخط discontent adj
ساد prevail v
سادي sadist n
ساذج gullible adj
سارية mast, post n
سارِيَةُ العَلَم flagpole n
ساعة hour n
ساعة كبيرة clock n
ساعي courier n
ساعي البريد postman, mailman n
سافر voyage v
سافر متطفلا hitchhike n
ساق stalk n
ساقُ النبات stem n

زواجي conjugal adj
زوبعة cyclone n
زوج pair n
زوج اثنان couple n
زوج الأمّ stepfather n
زوج قرين husband n
زوجة wife, wives n
زوجة الأب stepmother n
زوجة الكونت countess n
زوجي marital adj
زود equip v
زود بالوقود fuel v
زورق طويل canoe n
زي fad, fashion n
زيادة increase n
زيت oil n
زيتون olive n
زينة ornament n
زيني ornamental adj
زئبق mercury n

calm, still *adj* ساكن	curtain, drape *n* ستارة
bereaved *adj* سالِب	six *adj* ستّة
former *adj* سالف	sixteen *adj* ستّة عشر
sideburns *n* سالف الشعر	coat *n* سترة
unharmed *adj* سالِم	jacket *n* سِتْرة , جاكيت
poisonous *adj* سامّ	sixty *adj* ستّون
sublime *adj* سامٍ	carpet, rug *n* سجادة
forgive *v* سامح	rhyme *n* سَجْع
haggle *v* ساوم	sausage *n* سُجُق
prevalent *adj* سائد	mark down *v* سجل
driver *n* سائق	log *n* سجل طائرة
chauffeur *n* سائق السيّارة	matriculate *v* سجل للجامعة
trucker *n* سائق سيارة نقل	goal *n* سجل هدف
inquire *v* سأل	imprison, jail *v* سجن
coma *n* سبات	jail *n* سِجْن
swimming *n* سباحة	intern *v* سجن
cause *n* سبب	prison *n* سِجْن
September *n* سبتمبر	cloud *n* سجابة
rosary *n* سُبْحة	magic, sorcery, witchcraft *n* سِحر
probe *v* سبر	hermetic *adj* سحري
seven *adj* سبع	abysmal *adj* سحِيق
seventeen *adj* سَبع عشرة	generosity *n* سخاء
seventy *adj* سبعون	grime *n* سخام
anticipation *n* سَبْق	debunk *v* سخر
chalkboard *n* سبورة	guy *n* سخر
way *n* سبيل	ridicule *v* سخر من

سُخْرِيّ sarcastic adj	سُرعة velocity, speed n
سخرية mockery, sarcasm n	سرق sack v
سَخِيّ sumptuous adj	سرق السلع shoplifting n
سخيف absurd, ridiculous adj	سَرقة theft n
سد floodgate, dam n	سرمدي timeless adj
سد دينه pay off v	سروال trousers n
سِدادة plug n	سروال قصير shorts n
سدة blockage n	سِرّي clandestine, covert adj
سدد الدين pay back v	سرير bed n
سدد ضربات strike out v	سرير ذو طابقين bunk bed n
سدس revolver v	سريع fast, quick adj
سَدُودٌ للهواء airtight adj	سريع الإهتياج fussy adj
سديم haze n	سريع الأشتعال flammable adj
سِرّ secret n	سريع الغثيان squeamish adj
سر مقدس sacrament n	سريع الغضب hasty adj
سِرّا secretly adv	سريع الفهم apprehensive adj
سراب mirage n	سطا على burglarize v
سراويل briefs n	سطح flatten v
سَرج saddle n	سَطح surface n
سرداب cellar n	سطحي external adj
سرداب الموتى catacomb n	سطوة ascendancy n
سرطان cancer n	سُعال cough n
سرطان البحر lobster n	سَعة capacity n
سَرطانِيّ cancerous adj	سعر frenzy n
سرع hurry up v	سُعْر calorie n
سرعة expedition n	سِعْر price n

blissful, fortunate *adj* سعيد	hush *n* سكوت
hoodlum *n* سفاح	calm *n* سكون
embassy *n* سفارة	ingot *n* سكيبة
frostbite *n* سفح الجليد	alcoholic *adj* سكّير
scale *n* سَفَطة	knife *n* سكّين
sunburn *n* سَفْعَة	weapon *n* سلاح
downstairs *adv* سفلى	airfare *n* سلاح الطيران
ambassador *n* سفير	breed *n* سلالة
ship *n* سفينة	dynasty *n* سلالة حاكمة
warship *n* سفينة حربيّة	stairs *n* سَلالِم
shipwreck *n* سفينة غارقة	peace *n* سلام
ark *n* سفينة نوح	integrity *n* سلامة
fail *v* سقط	sanity *n* سلامة العقل
ceiling, roof *n* سقف	plunder *v* سلب
downfall *n* سقوط	unfavorable *adj* سلبيّ
booth *n* سقيفة	basket *n* سلّة
mint *v* سك العملة	waste basket *n* سلة المهملات
cutlery *n* سكاكين	trash can *n* سلة النفايات
household *n* سكان البيت	tortoise *n* سُلَحْفاة
infusion *n* سكب	turtle *n* سُلَحفاة
railroad *n* سكة حديدية	series, sequence *n* سلسلة
cardiac arrest *n* سكتة قلبية	ancestry *n* سلسلة النسب
sugar *n* سُكّر	ridge *n* سلسلة تلال
intoxicated *adj* سكران	bowl *n* سلطانية
secretary *n* سكرتير	authority *n* سلطة
inhabit *v* سكن	salad *n* سَلَطة

س

groceries n سـلع	grace n سـمو
seller n سلعة رائجة	سُمّي adj toxic
predecessor n سَلَفٌ	thick adj سميك
wire n سِلْك	corpulent, fat adj سمين
string n سِلك	tooth n سِنّ
ladder n سـلم	minority n سنّ القصور
stair n سُلّم	thread n سنّ اللولب
peaceful adj سلمي	menopause n سِنّ اليأس
attitude n سـلوك	senator n سـناتور
manners n سُلُوك	stake n سِناد
descendant n سـليل	hump, hunch n سـنام
intact adj سـليم	leap year n سنةٌ كبيسةٌ
sane adj سـليم العقل	cent n سنت
poison n سُمّ	hence adv سنتين من الأن
compost, manure n سـماد	bear v سند
audience n سـماع	anvil n سِـندان
headphones n سماعة الرأس	sandwich n سـندويتش
celestial adj سـماوي	annual adj سنويّ
type n سِـمَة	yearly adv سنويًّا
brunette adj سـمراء	dental adj سِنّي
reputation n سـمعة	ease, facilitate v سـهل
fish n سـمك	easy, plain adj سـهل
swordfish n سمك أبو سيف	frail adj سـهل الإنقياد
clam n سمك صَدَفيّ	affordable adj سـهل المأخذ
plumbing n سـمكرية	attainable adj سـهل المنال
fatten v سـمن	arrow n سَهْم

سَيّد n mister

سيدة n lady, madam

سيّدي n sir

سَيْر n course

سِيْرْك n circus

سيطر v dominate

سيطرة n domination

سَيْف n sword

سِيْكار n cigar

سَيْل n torrent

سيماء n countenance

سينما n cinema

سُيَيْر n asteroid

ش

شابّ n youngster

شابه v resemble

شاحب adj livid, pale

شاذ adj eccentric, abnormal

شارب n drinker

شارب القط n whiskers

شارَة n badge

سهم قصير n bolt

سوء التغذية n malnutrition

سواء adj alike

سواء c whether

سواد n blackness

سوار n bracelet

سوّد v denigrate

سُوْر n wall

سَوْط n scourge, whip

سوف v ought to

سوفياتيّ adj soviet

سُوق n market

سوق خيرية n bazaar

سوى v equate

سويدي adj Sweedish

سُويسرا n Switzerland

سويسريّ adj Swiss

سؤال n question, request

سياج n rail

سيادة n supremacy

سيادة مشتركة n condo

سيّارة n automobile

سيّارة إسعاف n ambulance

سيّارة مقفلة n wagon

سياسة n policy

سيجارة n cigarette

street n شارع	شِبْرٌ span n
lawn n شاشٌ	شبك v staple
share v شاطر	شبكة net, network n
beach, shore n شاطئ	شبكية العين mesh n
seashore n شاطئ البحر	شِبْه جزيرة peninsula n
conscious adj بـ شاعرٌ	شتت v disperse
riot v شاغب	شجار brawl n
unoccupied adj شاغر	شجاع brave adj
arduous adj شاقّ	شجاعة bravery n
thankful adj شاكر	شجب condemnation n
mole n شامة	شجر الصّفصاف willow n
comprehensive adj شامل	شجرة tree n
behold v شاهد	شجرة الدّردار ash n
eyewitness n شاهد عيان	شجرة عيد الميلاد X-mas n
steep, towering adj شاهق	شجع encourage v
tea n شاي	شجيرة shrub, plant, bush n
trendy adj شائع	شحّاذ beggar n
thorny adj شائك	شحذ sharpen v
disgraceful adj شائن	شحم grease n
affair, concern n شأن	شحم lubricate v
clarinet n شبّابة	شحم الخنزير lard n
February n شباط	شحن البطارية recharge v
box office n شباك التذاكر	شحن السريع express n
ghost, apparition, phantom n شبح	شِحنَة charge n
spooky adj شبحي	شَحْنة shipment n
span v شبر	شحوب paleness n

ش

stingy *adj* شـحيح	sort out *v* شرح
person *n* شخص	condition, prerequisite *n* شَرْط
drifter *n* شخص غير مستقر	cop, policeman *n* شرطي
somebody, someone *pro* شخص ما	legislate *v* شرع
eager *adj* شخص متحمس	lawful *adj* شرعيّ
respective *adj* شخصيّ	validity *n* شرعية
personality *n* شخصية	balcony *n* شُرْفَة
effigy *n* شخصية مكروهة	east *n* شرق
enthrall *v* شدّ	easterner *n* شرقى
adversity *n* شدّة	eastward *adv* شرقي
emphasize *v* شدد	snare *n* شَرَكٌ
boisterous *adj* شديد	company *n* شركة
telling *adj* شديد الأثر	firm *n* شركة تجارية
fragrance *n* شذا	greed *n* شره
oddity *n* شذوذ	artery *n* شِريان
evil *n* شر	slice *n* شريحة
purchase *n* شراء	steak *n* شريحة من لحم
beverage *n* شراب	wicked *adj* شرّير
liquor *n* شراب كحوليّ	tape *n* شريط
booze *n* شراب مسكر	tag *n* شريط الحذاء
spark *n* شرارة	cordon *n* شريط زينيّ
bedding *n* شراشف	partner *n* شريك
sail *n* شراع	accomplice *n* شريك في جريمة
partnership *n* شراكة	cross *v* شطب
toast *n* شُرْب النخب	cancellation *n* شَطْب
rectum *n* شرج	halve *v* شطر

ش

chess n شِطرنج	sister n شـقيقة
hamburger n شطيرة لحم	doubt, scuples n شك
shrapnel n شظايا	doubt, inkling v شك
fragment, splinter n شظية	scrupulous adj شكّ
emblem n شعار	thanks n شكرا
ray n شُعاع	formality n شكلانية
nation n شعب	grievance n شكوى
popular adj شَعْبِيّ	paralyze v شل
hair n شعر	chute, cataract, waterfall n شلال
hairpiece n شعر مستعار	cascade n شلال صغير
feeling n شعور	paralysis n شَلَل
barley n شَعير	northeast n شَمالٌ شَرْقِيٌّ
disturbance, riot, tumult n شغب	northern adj شَمالِيّ
activate, preoccupy v شغل	solar adj شَمْسِيّ
occupation n شُغْل	wax n شَمْع
vacancy n شغور	candle n شمعة
transparent adj شفّاف	spark plug n شمعة الإشعال
orally adv شِفَاهًا	candlestick n شَمْعِدان
medicinal adj شفائيّ	lump together v شمل معا
lip n شَفَة	beet n شَمَنْدَر
twilight n شفق	trigger v شن
pity n شفقة	open up v شن هجوما
compassionate adj شَفُوق	hang up v شنق
incision, cleft, split n شق	outrageous adj شنيع
disunity n شقاق	meteor n شهاب
apartment n شقّة للسكّن	testimony n شهادة

ش

شهر العسل honeymoon n	شيوعيّ communist adj
شهر مارس march n	شَيْئًا فَشَيْئًا little by little adv
شهر مايو May n	
شهرة celebrity n	
شهريًّا monthly adv	# ص
شَهوانيّ lustful adj	
شهوة lust n	صات blow v
شهيّ delicate adj	صاحب العمل employer n
شهية appetite n	صاحب مقام رفيع dignitary n
شهيد martyr n	صاخب gusty adj
شهير illustrious adj	صادر expropriate v
شوش dislocate v	صادق truthful adj
شوش mix-up n	صارخ flamboyant adj
شوكولا chocolate n	صارم severe, strict adj
شوه pervert v	صاروخ rocket n
شوه شيئا disfigure v	صاعقة bolt n
شوى grill v	صاغ من جديد remodel v
شيءٌ ما something pro	صافٍ clear, lucid adj
شيء نافع asset n	صالح valid adj
شَيْخوخة old age n	صالح للأكل edible adj
شيخوخيّ senile adj	صالح للسكن inhabitable adj
شيد put up v	صالح للشرب drinkable adj
شيطان demon n	صالون lounge, saloon n
شيطانيّ diabolical adj	صامت mute, silent adj
شيعة sect n	صامدٌ للماء waterproof adj
شيك أجر العمل paycheck n	صان keep v

صائغ الفضّة silversmith n	صدمة قوية bump n
صَبْر patience n	صدى echo n
صبغ color v	صديق friend, pal n
صبور patient adj	صديق حميم crony n
صبيانيّ childish, puerile adj	صديقة girlfriend n
صحراء desert n	صَدِئٌ rusty adj
صحّي wholesome adj	صَرَاحَة candor n
صحيح correct, accurate, just adj	صُراخ cry n
صحيفة, مجلة journal n	صراع hassle n
صخب boulder n	صرامة fortitude, rigor, severity n
صخر rock n	صُرّة package n
صخريّ rocky adj	صرح declare v
صد fend off, repulse v	صرخة scream, shriek n
صدّ rebuff n	صرْخة yell v
صدار bra n	صرع cut down v
صدارة forefront n	صرف النظر dismiss v
صداع headache n	صريح frank adj
صداع نصفي migraine n	صرير creak n
صداقة friendship n	صعب difficult adj
صَدأ rust n	صعد escalate v
صُدْرة vest n	صُعُداً uphill adv
صدع split, crevice, rift n	صعوبة difficulty n
صَدَفة shell n	صغير small, little adj
صِدق truth n	صغير جدًّا tiny adj
صدقة bounty, alms n	صف rank n
صَدمة shock n	صفّ range n

صَفّارة whistle n	صناعة يدوية handmade adj
صفّارة الإنذار siren n	صنبور nozzle n
صفة adjective n	صندوق box, chest n
صفحة page n	صُنْدُوق بَريد mailbox n
صِفْر zero n	صندوق للخزن bin n
صفعة slap n	صنع make n
صَفْقة bargain n	صنع ثانية remake v
صفقة cuff n	صنع مقدما prefabricate v
صفى filter v	صِنف species n
صفيحة can n	صنوبرة pine n
صقر hawk n	صه heist n
صقل polish v	صهر fusion n
صقيع frost n	صِهْريج cistern n
صكّ charter n	صواب reason n
صلابة stiffness n	صُوان cupboard n
صلاة prayer n	صوت sound n
صُلْب callous, adamant adj	صَوْت voice n
صلب cross, crucifixion n	صوْتُ لِيْن vowel n
صلب crucify v	صَوْتِي acoustic adj
صلة tie, link n	صورة image, picture n
صلصة اللحم gravy n	صُورَةٌ جانِبيّة profile n
صِمام valve n	صورة زيتيّة painting n
صمد outlast v	صورة فوتوغرافية photo n
صَمَمّ deafness n	صُوْف wool n
صناعة industry n	صوفيّ woolen adj
صناعة البيت homemade adj	صولجان verge n

crying n صياح	foggy, hazy, blurred, misty adj
hunter n صياد	ضبابي
fisherman n صياد سمك	accuracy n ضَبْط
conservation n صيانة	frame v ضبط
call, shout n صيحة	hyena n ضبع
drugstore n صيدلية	boredom, tedium n ضَجَرّ
formula n صيغة	fed up, restless adj ضجر
gerund n صيغة الفعل	noise n ضَجِيج
tray n صينيّة	giggle v ضحك
	laughter n ضَحِكّ
	laugh n ضَحكة
	shallow adj ضَحْل
ض	victim n ضَحِيّة
	colossal adj ضخم
noisy adj ضاجّ	burly adj ضخم الجسم
outskirts n ضاحية	versus, with pre ضدّ
ferocious, pernicious adj ضار	ferocity n ضراوة
grayish adj ضارب الى الرمادي	battery n ضَرْب
double v ضاعف	mint v ضرب العملة
pressing adj ضاغط	beat, strike, stroke n ضربة
astray v ضالّ	kickoff n ضربة الإفتتاح
stray adj ضالّ	heatstroke n ضربة الحر
disturb v ضايق	knock n ضربة عنيفة
missing adj ضائع	bounce n ضربة قوية
fog n ضباب	coup n ضربة موفقة
	molar n ضِرس

ص
ض

necessity *n* ضرورة	**ط**
indispensable, necessary *adj* ضروري	
contribution *n* ضريبة	printer *n* طابع
frailty *n* ضعف	ground floor *n* طابق أرضي
impotent *adj* ضعيف	windmill *n* طاحونة هوائية
pressure, force *v* ضَغْط	pursue *v* طارد
stress, pressure *n* ضَغْط	emergency *n* طارئ
rancor *n* ضغينة	docility *n* طاعة
frog *n* ضفدع	pest *n* طاعون
queue *n* ضفيرة	adrift, afloat *adv* طافٍ
rib *n* ضِلْع	manpower *n* طاقة البشرية
gauze *n* ضمادة خفيفة	crew *n* طاقم
warranty *n* ضمانة	applicant *n* طالب الوظيفة
ensure *v* ضمن	table *n* طاولة
inclusive *adv* ضمنا	dummy *n* طاولة بريدج
implicit *adj* ضمني	aeroplane *n* طائرة
pronoun *n* ضمير	helicopter *n* طائرة عامودية
his *adj* ضمير الغائب المتصل	frivolous *adj* طائش
light, lighting *n* ضوء	cardiology *n* طب القلب
gleam *n* ضوء ضعيف	gynecology *n* طب النساء
spotlight *n* ضوءٌ كشّاف	psychiatry *n* طبّ النفس
guest *n* ضيف	chalk *n* طباشير
cramped, narrow *adj* ضيق	printing, press *n* طباعة
trouble *n* ضِيق	normalize *v* طبع
insignificant *adj* ضئيل	naturally *adv* طَبْعًا

ض
ط

print *n* طبعة	طرف الكم *n* cuff
reprint *n* طبعة ثانية	طرفٌ مستدقّ *n* tip
dish *n* طبق	طرق *n* beating
according to *pre* طبقا	طرق الحديد *v* forge
category *n* طَبَقة	طرى *v* flatter
layer *n* طبقة	طريّ *adj* tender
class, caste *n* طبقة اجتماعية	طريدة *n* quarry
film *n* طبقة رقيقة	طريق *n* way, path
turf *n* طبقة عشب	طريق تحتية *n* underpass
drum *n* طبل	طريق جانبي *n* bypass
drum *n* طبلة	طريق خاصة *n* driveway
eardrum *n* طبلة الأذن	طريق سريع *n* highway
handgun *n* طَبَنْجَة	طريق مسدود *n* dead end
doctor *n* طبيب	طشت *n* basin
dentist *n* طبيب الأسنان	طعام *n* food
veterinarian *n* طبيب بيطريّ	طعام شهيّ *n* delicacy
psychiatrist *n* طبيب نفساني	طُعْم *n* bait
nature *n* طبيعة	طَعْم *n* smack
natural *adj* طبيعيّ	طعنة *n* stab
physically *adj* طَبِيعِيًّا	طغيانيّ *adj* despotic
freshness *n* طُحْلُب	طفح جلدي *n* rash
tenderness *n* طراوة	طفر *v* skip
lay *v* طرح	طفل *n* child, children
expel *v* طرد	طَفَلٌ *n* baby, infant
expulsion *n* طرد	طِفل *n* kid
embroider *v* طرز	طفلٌ مزعج *adj* brat

ط

toddler n طفل يبدأ المشي	evolve v طور
infancy n طفولة	phase n طَوْر
drop in v طفيلية	willingly adv طوعا
rite n طَقْس	flood v طوفان
crack n طقطقة	encircle v طوق
liturgy n طقوس دينيّة	length n طول
divorce n طلاق	fold v طوى
demand n طلبٌ	lengthy adj طويل
overcharge v طلب ثمنا أعلى	long-term adj طويل الأجل
come up v طلع	goodness n طيب القلب
vanguard n طليعة الجيش	pleat n طيّة
tomato n طَماطِم	bird n طَيْر
avid adj طمّاع	flight n طيران
reassure v طمأن	indiscretion n طيش
menstruation n طمث	manageable adj طيِّع
surge n طُمُوّ	shade n طيف
ambitious adj طَموح	
ton n طنّ	
buzz n طنين	
chastity n طهارة	
disinfect v طهر	
concoction n طهو	
cooking n طَهْو	
during pre طوال	
overnight adv طوالَ الليل	
canonize v طوب	

ط

ظهور اليابسة landfill *n*

ظ

injustice *n* ظالم

thirsty *adj* ظامئ

phenomenon *n* ظاهرة

outward *adj* ظاهري

allegedly, apparently *adv* ظاهريًّا

deer *n* ظبي

circumstance *n* ظَرْف

envelope *n* ظرف مغلف

circumstancial *adj* ظرفى

pretty *adj* ظريف

fingernail *n* ظفر

toenail *n* ظفر الرجل

shadow *n* ظِلّ

overshadow *v* ظلل

unfairness *n* ظلم

unfairly *adv* ظُلمًا

obscurity, darkness *n* ظلمة

shade *n* ظليل

distrustful *adj* ظنان

back *n* ظَهْر

loom *v* ظهر

deck *n* ظَهْر المركب

appearance *n* ظهور

ع

fleeting *adj* عابر

passer-by *n* عابر سبيل

ivory *n* عاجّ

incapable *adj* عاجز

normally, ordinarily *adv* عَادَةً

custom *n* عادةٌ

unbiased *adj* عادل

ordinary, normal *adj* عاديّ

nude, bare, naked *adj* عار

beam *n* عارضة

unmarried *adj* عازب

pianist *n* عازف البيانو

stormy *adj* عاصف

tempest, storm *n* عاصفة

thunderstorm *n* عَاصِفَةٌ رعْدِيّة

understanding *adj* عاطف

emotion *n* عاطفة

sentimental *adj* عاطفيّ

unemployed *adj* عاطل عن العمل

hinder v عاق	threshold n عَتَبة
ungrateful adj عاقّ	moldy, old adj عتيق
barren adj عاقر	outmoded adj عتيق الزي
handle v عالج موضوعا	old-fashioned adj عتيق الطراز
learned adj عالِم	omelette n عُجّة بيْض
botany n عالم النبات	disability n عجز
worldwide adj عالميّ	deficit n عجز بشكل عام
year n عام	calf, veal n عجل
public adj عامّ	wheel n عَجَلة
factor, agent n عامل	wheelbarrow n عجلة اليد
parameters n عامل متغير	elderly adj عجوز
help v عاون	weird adj عجيب
standardize v عايرن إختبر بمعيار	dough n عجين
nitpicking adj عائب	count n عدّ
disadvantage n عائق	besides pre عدا
family n عائلة	gallop v عدا بسرعة
surcharge n عِبء ثقيل	feud n عداء
cloak n عباءة	odometer n عداد المسافات
phrase n عبارة	justice n عدالة
wind up v عبأ الساعة	enumerate v عدد
mess up v عبث	death toll n عدد الضحايا
vainly adv عَبَثاً	lentil n عَدَس
across pre عَبْر	lense n عدسة
overseas adv عَبْر البحار	fairness n عدل
bondage n عبودية	instability n عدم استقرار
crossing, transit n عبور	insecurity n عدم الأمان

ع

عُرْف الديك	crest n
عرفان بالفضل	gratitude n
عَرَق	sweat n
عروة	buttonhole n
عري	nudity n
عريس	groom n
عريض	broad adj
عريضة	petition n
عرين	den n
عزاء	solace n
عَزَب	celibate adj
عزز	enhance v
عزل	insulation, isolation n
عزلة	loneliness n
عُزوبة	celibacy n
عزيز	dear adj
عسر	distress n
عسر الهضم	indigestion n
عشّ	nest n
عشب	grass, pasture n
عشبة ضارّة	weed n
عَشَرة	ten adj
عشرون	twenty adj
عَشْري	decimal adj
عَشْوائيّا	blindly adv
عشية العيد	vigil n

عدم معرفة	disclaim v
عدم نضوج	immaturity n
عدو	enemy, foe n
عَدْو	run v
عُدْوان	aggression n
عُدْواني	aggressive adj
عدوى	infection n
عدى	infect v
عديد	numerous adj
عديم الجدوى	useless adj
عديم الحس	blunt adj
عُذْرة	virginity n
عربة الموتى	hearse n
عربة نقل	truck n
عربيّ	Arabic adj
عَرْج	limp n
عُرْس	wedding n
عرش	throne n
عرض	expose v
عَرْض	breadth, width n
عَرَض	symptom n
عرض للخطر	endanger v
عرض مسبّق	preview n
عرضا	incidentally adv
عَرَضيّ	accidental, casual adj
عرف	figure out v

ع

clan n عَشِيرة

staff, cane n عصا

bandage n عِصابة

blindfold n عِصابة للعينين

neurotic adj عُصابيّ

succulent adj عصاري

nerve n عَصَب

jumpy, uptight, nervous adj عصبي

epoch, era n عصر

up-to-date, modern adj عصري

insurgency n عصيان

hectic adj عصيبي

juice n عصير

cider n عصير التفاح

bite n عضّ

muscle n عَضَلة

member, limb, organ n عضو

membership n عُضويّة

embalm v عطر

aromatic adj عِطريّ

sneeze n عَطْسة

hold up v عطل

gratuity n عطية

homily n عظة دينية

bone n عَظْم

magnitude n عِظَمّ

greatness n عظمة

gigantic adj عظيم

abstinence n عِفّة

putrid adj عفِن

pardon n عَفو

amnesty n عفو عام

spontaneous adj عَفْوي

chaste adj عفيف

penalty n عِقاب

drug n عقار

hook n عقاف

dogmatic adj عقائدي

hurdle, setback n عقبة

decade n عقد

contract n عَقْد

necklace n عِقد

lease n عقد الإيجار

knob n عُقْدة

knot n عُقْدة

scorpion n عقرب

curl n عقصة

wit n عقل

mental adj عقليّ

mentally adv عقليا

mentality n عقلية

futility n عقم

creed *n* عقيدة	lay *n* علمانيّ
futile, sterile *adj* عقيم	scientific *adj* عِلْميّ
crutch *n* عكاز	upper *adj* عُلْويّ
reverse *n* عكس	on, upon *pre* على
remedy *n* علاج	likely *adv* على الأرجح
rapport *n* علاقة	mainly *adv* على الغالب
mark *n* علامة	lift-off *n* على بعد
trademark *n* علامة تجارية	along *pre* على طول كذا
bonus *n* علاوة	reluctantly *adv* على كره
furthermore, moreover *adv* علاوة على ذلك	aboard *adv* على متن سفينة
canister *n* علبة صغيرة	badly *adv* على نحو رديء
leech *n* عَلَقة	hurriedly *adv* على نحو سريع
instruct, know *v* علم	grossly *adv* على نحو فادح
standard *n* عَلَم	abruptly *adv* عَلَى نَحْو مُفَاجِئ
biology *n* علم الأحياء	widely *adv* على نحو واسع
ethics *n* علم الأخلاق	notably *adv* على نحو وجيه
ecology *n* علم البيئة	detriment *n* علي حساب
chronology *n* علم التاريخ	reputedly *adv* علي ما يقال
anatomy *n* علم التشريح	attic *n* عِلّية المنزل
astrology *n* علم التنجيم	aunt *n* عمة
arithmetic *n* علم الحساب	purposely, willfully *adv* عمداً
zoology *n* علم الحيوان	age *n* عُمر
hygiene *n* علم الصحة	heyday *n* عمر الشباب
astronomy *n* علم الفَلَك	deed *n* عَمَل
geometry *n* علم الهندسة	employment, work *n* عمل
layman *n* علماني	housework *n* عمل البيت

ع

عمل بطولي feat n	component n عنصر
عمل روتيني chore n	racist adj عنصري
عمل قوادا pander v	racism n عنصرية
عمل مسرحيّ revue n	heating n عنف
عمل ورقي paperwork n	neck n عنق
عملة currency, coin n	bunch, cluster n عنقود
عمليّ workable adj	spider n عنكبوت
عملية process n	tarantula n عنكبوت ذئبي
عمم generalize v	address n عنوان
عمود column n	subtitle n عنوان فرعيّ
عمود الإنارة lamppost n	address v عنون
عموديّ upright adj	stubborn adj عنيد
عُمُومًا overall adv	assurance, seal n عَهْد
عمومي common adj	testament, pledge n عهد
عمّى blindness n	return n عودة
عميد rector n	remunerate v عوض
عميد كلية dean n	float v عوم
عميق deep adj	backing n عَوْن
عميق التفكير thoughtful adj	howl v عوى
عميق جدا bottomless adj	lament, wail n عويل
عناد obstinacy n	falter v عى في الكلام
عناق hug n	clinic n عيادة
عِنان rein n	blemish n عَيب
عنب grape n	shortcoming n عيب
عند at, near pre	holiday n عيد
عنزة goat n	Easter n عيد الفصح

ع

عيد الميلاد n Christmas

عِيدٌ مِئَويّ n centenary

عين n eye

عيّنة n specimen, sample

عينهُ adj same

غ

غابة n forest

غابة كثيفة n jungle

غادر v hop

غار n grotto

غارة n raid

غاز n invader

غازل v flirt

غاضب adj angry, furious

غاضب جدا v writhe

غافل adj oblivious

غال adj pricey, costly

غالون n gallon

غالي السعر adj expensive

غامض adj fuzzy, vague

غاية n purpose

غائب adj absent

غائر adj hollow

غائم adj cloudy

غبيّ adj mindless

غثيان n disgust, nausea, qualm

غجر n gypsy

غداً adv tomorrow

غَدَاء n dinner

غداء n lunch

غدة n gland

غِذاء n diet

غرا v glue

غراء n glue

غراب n crow

غراب أسود n raven

غرام n gram

غرامة n penalty

غرانيت n granite

غربيّ adj western

غرز v stick

غرس v implant, instil

غرض n destination

غرغرينا n gangrene

غرفة n room

غرفة التدريس n classroom

غرفة أطفال n nursery

غ
غ

snore n غطيط	drown v غرق
cassock n غفارة	fine v غرم
excuse, pardon v غفر	evening n غروب
absolution, remission n غفران	pride n غرور
shackle n غُلّ	bizarre, queer adj غريب
wrapping n غلاف	instinct n غريزة
boy n غُلام	invasion n غزو
kettle, boiler n غلّاية	dishwasher n غسالة الأواني
drop off v غلبه النعاس	bath n غَسْل
yield n غلّة	brainwash v غسل دماغ
lapse v غلط	membrane n غشاء
slam v غلق بعنف	mist n غشاوة
gloom, chagrin n غمّ	trance n غَشْيَة
immerse v غمر	branch, bough n غُصْن
dump v غمر الاسواق	spur n غصن ناتئ
wink v غمز	displease, enrage v غضب
wink n غمزة	displeasing adj غضب
mystery n غموض	anger n غضبّ
song n غناء	crease n غَضَن
wealth n غنى	snore v غط
rich, wealthy adj غنيّ	coat, lid n غطاء
colorful adj غنيّ بالألوان	bedspread n غطاء السرير
booty, loot n غنيمة	pillowcase n غطاء الوسادة
sink in v غور	handkerchief n غطاء لرأس المرأة
diving n غوص	diver n غطاس
absence n غياب	plunge n غَطْس

ع

غير أمّيّ literate adj	غير مرغوب فيه undesirable adj
غير جدير بالثقة unreliable adj	غير مستوجب undeserved adj
غير حساس insensitive adj	غير مقاوم unprotected adj
غير خبير inexperienced adj	غير ملائم inadequate adj
غير دقيق imprecise adj	غير ملحوظ unnoticed adj
غير رسمي informal adj	غير ملحوم seamless adj
غير شرعي illegal adj	غير منتبه irrespective adj
غير شعبيّ unpopular adj	غير منطقي illogical adj
غير شفاف opaque adj	غير مؤلم painless adj
غير ضار unhurt adj	غير واقعى unrealistic adj
غير ضرورى needless adj	غَيْرَة ardor, jealousy n
غير ضروري undue, undue adj	غيظ rage n
غير عاقل unreasonable adj	غيور ardent, jealous adj
غير عملي impractical adj	
غير كفؤ misfit, unfit adj	
غير مألوف uncommon adj	
غير مباشر indirect adj	
غير متبلور amorphous adj	
غير متساو unequal adj	
غير متصل unrelated adj	# ف
غير مثقّف uneducated adj	
غير مجهز unfurnished adj	فاتح للشهية aperitif n
غير محتمل improbable adj	فاتر lukewarm, tepid adj
غير مدخن nonsmoker n	فاتن adorable adj
غير مُربح unprofitable adj	فاتورة bill, invoice n
غير مرتاب unsuspecting adj	فاحش obscene adj
	فاحشة misconduct n
	فاحم pitch-black adj

غ
ف

luxurious *adj* فاخر	interlude *n* فترة فاصلة
gross *adj* فادح	go through *v* فتش
mice *n* فارة	rupture *n* فَتْق
knight *n* فارس	enchant *v* فتن
vain *adj* فارغ	apathy *n* فتور الشعور
nuance *n* فارق بسيط	immature *adj* فج
corrupt; vicious *adj* فاسد	sudden, unexpected *adj* فُجائيّ
immoral, lewd *adj* فاسق	suddenly *adv* فجأةً
authoritarian *adj* فاشِسْتِي .	dawn *n* فجر
interval *n* فاصل	radish *n* فِجْلَة
bean *n* فاصوليا	gap, cavity *n* فجوة
green bean *n* فاصوليا خضراء	merely, only *adv* فحسب
effectiveness *n* فاعلية	obscenity *n* فُحْش
surpass *v* فاق	survey, inspection *n* فحص
outnumber *v* فاقه عددا	double-check *v* فحص مجدد
fruity *adj* فاكهي	porcelain *n* فخار
benefit, profit *n* فائدة	thigh *n* فَخِذ
superfluous *adj* فائض	imposing *adj* فخم
mouse, rat *n* فأر	acre *n* فَدّان
ax *n* فأس	federal *adj* فدرالي
omen *n* فأل	get off *v* فر
girl *n* فتاة	stampede *n* فرارٌ جماعيّ
chick *n* فتاة جميلة	mattress, bed *n* فِراش
hernia *n* فتاق مرض	deathbed *n* فراش الموت
conquest *n* فَتْح	butterfly *n* فراشة
period *n* فترة	emptiness *n* فراغ

ف

raspberry n فراولة	annulment n فسخ
single n فرد	disintegrate v فسد
singlehanded adj فردي	explain, interpret v فسر
bay n فرسٌ	immorality n فسوق
furniture n فرش	vast adj فسيح
paintbrush n فرشاة الدهن	mosaic n فُسَيْفُساء
hairbrush n فرشاة للشعر	flop n فشل
occasion n فرصة	eloquence n فصاحة
enjoy v فرض	disconnect v فصل
premise n فَرْض	segregation, seperation n فَصْل
supposition n فرضية	season n فصل
excess n فرط	chapter n فَصْل من كتاب
finish, end v فرغ	quarterly adj فصليّ
deflate v فرغ الهواء	platoon n فصيلة
brake n فرملة	unwrap v فض
furnace, oven n فرن	dissolution n فض البرلمان
France n فرنسا	unpack v فضا
French adj فرنسي	silver n فِضّة
fur n فرو	baggy, loose adj فضفاض
scalp n فرَوة الرأس	favor, kindness n فضل
furry adj فروي	aside from adv فضلا عن
prey n فريسَة	curiosity n فضول
team n فريق	nosy, curious adj فضولي
shift n فريق مناوبة	furor n فضيحة
decay n فساد	virtue n فضيلة
space n فُسحة	pastry n فطائر

ف

fungus n فطر	pepper n فُلفُل
innate adj فطري	bell pepper n فُلفُل أَسْوَد
pie n فطيرة	astronomic adj فَلَكِيّ
impolite, brusque adj فظ	mouth n فم
discourtesy n فظاظة	art n فنّ
shocking adj فظيع	architecture n فن العمارة
efficient adj فعال	caricature n فنّ الكاريكاتور
efficiency n فعالية	sculpture n فنّ النحت
verb, action n فعل	courtyard, patio n فِنَاء
chill v فِعْل	dying adj فناء
quit v فعلًا	farmyard n فناء المزرعة
vertebra n فَقارَة	disprove v فند
bubble n فُقّاعة	Finland n فنلندا
forfeit v فقد	Finnish adj فنلندي
amnesia n فَقْد الذاكرة	artistic adj فنّي
lack n فقدان	exterminate v فني
poverty n فَقْر	contents n فِهْرِسْت
clause, paragraph n فقرة	grasp v فهم
small print n فقرة صغيرة	phobia n فُوبيَا
breed v فقس	immediately adv فورا
indigent, needy adj فقير	instant n فوري
poorly adv فَقيرًا	entrust v فوض
jaw n فَكّ	anarchist n فوضوي
concept, idea n فكرة	anarchy, mess n فوضى
humorous adj فكه	upstairs adv فوق
philosophy n فلسفة	muzzle n فُوّهة

ق

فُوَّهة البركان crater n	قابل meet v
فى within pre	قابلٌ لـِ capable adj
فى الواقع actually adv	قابل للاحتراق combustible n
فى هذه الايام nowadays adv	قابلٌ للتصديق believable adj
في in pre	قابل للتعليم docile adj
في الأغلب mostly adv	قابل للتمدد elastic adj
في الخلاء outdoors adv	قابل للحسم deductible adj
في الداخل inland adv	قابل للشفاء curable adj
في المائة percent adv	قابل للعطب vulnerable adj
في المُتَناوَل accessible adj	قابل للقسمة divisible adj
في الهواء الطلق outdoor adv	قابل للكَسْر breakable adj
في الواقع really adv	قابلٌ للمقارنة بـ comparable adj
في أحسن حال fine adv	قابلية aptitude n
في أي وقت whenever adv	قاحل infertile adj
في تمام الصحة healthy adj	قاد lead, mastermind v
في حالة سيئة disrepair n	قادر able adj
في حينه timely adj	قادم forthcoming adj
في غضون meantime adv	قارّة continent n
في ما يتّصل بـ regarding pre	قارس shrewd adj
في ما يتعلق بـ concerning pre	قارّيّ continental adj
في مكان آخر elsewhere adv	قاس austere n
فيض flooding n	قاس firm, hard adj
فيل elephant n	قاسٍ relentless, ruthless, severe adj
فَيْلَق legion n	
فيلم movie n	
فيما بعد later adv	

ف ق

قاصد إلى bound adj	قائمة كلمات glossary n
قاضٍ judge n	قبة dome n
قاضى prosecute v	قَبَّةُ الثَّوْب collar n
قاطع sharp adj	قَبْتاريخي prehistoric adj
قاطع بالكلام heckle v	قبر grave, tomb, burial n
قاطع تيار fuse n	قَبْض contraction n
قاطع طريق gangster n	قبض الامعاء constipate v
قاعة الرقص ballroom n	قبض على grasp, grip v
قاعة المحاضرات auditorium n	قبضة fist, grip n
قاعة رياضية gymnasium n	قبعة hat n
قاعدة principle n	قبلُ before adv
قاعدة أساس foundation n	قُبلة kiss n
قاعده بيانات database n	قبول admittance, acceptance n
قافلة caravan n	قبيلة tribe n
قالب shape, mold n	قتال combat n
قام بصيانته service v	قتل dock n
قام ثانية ب redo v	قتْل murder, killing n
قامة setup n	قتل غير متعمد manslaughter n
قامر gamble v	قحط drought n
قانط despondent adj	قحل potent adj
قانون law n	قد قوام figure n
قانونيّ legal, lawful adj	قداسة holiness n
قانونيّة legality n	قِدْر pot n
قاوم hold out v	قدر بسرعة sum up v
قائد leader n	قدر غاشم doom n
قائمة list, schedule n	قدرة capability n

ق

charisma *n* قدرة خارقة	pirate *n* قُرصان
foot, feet *n* قدم	piracy *n* قرصنة
apply for *v* قدم طلبا	dislike *n* قرصي الشكل
be born *v* قدم للحياة	gnaw *v* قرْض
come forward *v* قدم نفسه	loan *n* قرْض
saint *n* قِدّيس	tap into *v* قرع
ancient, archaic *adj* قديم	toll *n* قرْع الناقوس
crappy, squalid *adj* قَذِر	pumpkin *n* قرْعَة
dirt, filthy *n* قذر	cinnamon *n* قرفة
eject; shoot *v* قذف	tile *n* قرميدة
libel *n* قذف	pink *adj* قرنفليّ
bombing *n* قذف بالقنابل	medieval *adj* قروسطي
grenade, missile *n* قذيفة	impending *adj* قريب
reading *n* قراءة	soon *adv* قريباً
kinship *n* قرابة	village *n* قرية
decision *n* قرار	hamlet *n* قرية صغيرة
verdict *n* قرار محكمة	dwarf, midget *n* قزم
read *v* قرأ	chaplain *n* قَسّ
beside *pre* قرب	installment *n* قسط
vicinity *n* قُرْب	department *n* قِسْم
sore *n* قرْح	divide *v* قسم
ulcer *n* قرْحَة	oath *n* قَسَم
ape *n* قِرد	portion *n* قسمة
pinch *v* قرص	hardness, austerity *n* قسوة
dial *n* قرص الساعة	pastor, priest *n* قسيس
tablet *n* قرص دواء	priestess *n* قِسّيسة

ق

coupon *n* قسيمة	munch *v* قضم
sale slip *n* قسيمة الشراء	execute *v* قضى
straw *n* قشّ	bar *n* قضيب
cream *n* قِشْدَة	issue *n* قضية
creamy *adj* قِشْدِيّ	lawsuit *n* قضيّة
peel *n* قشرة	train *n* قطار
crust *n* قشرة الرغيف	sector *n* قِطاع
crusty *adj* قشري	frown *v* قطب
chill *n* قُشَعريرَة	polar *adj* قُطْبيّ
clipping *n* قَصّ	drip *v* قطر
drive away *v* قصا	tar *n* قطران
scrap *n* قُصاصة	diagonal *adj* قُطْريّ
cane *n* قَصَب	chop *n* قطْع
fiction, story *n* قصة	discontinue *v* (قطع (عن
intend *v* قصد	slice *v* قطع الى شرائح
intention *n* قصد	switch off *v* قطع تيار
tin *n* قَصْدير	lump, chunk *n* قطعة
bleach *v* قصّر	log *n* قطعة خشب
mansion *n* قصر	firearm *n* قطعة سلاح
brevity *n* قِصَر	spare part *n* قطعة غيار
malfunction *v* قَصَر عَنْ	artwork *n* قطعة فنية
poem *n* قصيدة	cut *n* قطعة لحم
short *adj* قصير	cotton *n* قطن
shortlived *adj* قصير الاجل	flock, group *n* قطيع
brittle *adj* قصيم	floor *n* قعر
fate *n* قضاء	glove *n* قفاز

cloth n قماش	waste n قَفْر
canvas n قماش القنّب	flier n قفز
apex, top n قمة	jump n قفز
wheat n قَمْح	cage n قفَص
satellite n قمر صناعيّ	lock, padlock n قفل
cabin n قمرة	snooze v قفى
lice, moth n قمل	hive n قفير خلية نحل
louse n قملة	fries n قلا
shirt n قميص	fry v قلا
aqueduct, canal n قناة	pendant n قلادة
sniper n قناص	essence n قلب
disguise, mask n قناع	downtown n قلب المدينة
bomb n قنبلة	hearty adj قلبي
cauliflower n قُنبيط	cardiac adj قلبيّ
consul n قنصل	indecency n قلة إحتشام
consulate n قنصلية	imitate, mime v قلد
arch n قَنطرة	reduce v قلص
legalize v قنن	castle n قلعة
overwhelm v قهر	anxious adj قلِق
compelling adj قهري	uneasiness, worry, anxiety n قلِق
armaments n قوّات حربية	pen n قلم
grammar n (قواعد (اللغة	pencil n قلم رصاص
etiquette n قواعد التشريفات	crayon n قلم ملون
agency n قوّة	hood, cap n قلنسوة
intensity n قوّة	little bit n قليل
strength n قوّة	green adj قليل الخبرة

ق

ك

كاب n cape

كابح n nightmare

كاتدرائية n cathedral

كاتم السر n confidant

كاثوليكي adj catholic

كادّ adj diligent

كادح adj industrious

كارّة n cart

كارثة n catastrophe

كاره adj averse

كاريكاتور n cartoon

كاف adj due, competent, adequate

كافأ v match

كافح v strive

كافيتيريا n cafeteria

كافيين n caffeine

كاكاو n cocoa

كامل adj absolute, entire

كامن adj potential

كاميرا n camera

كان v be

كاهن n clergyman

كائن adj located

قوةٌ عسكرية n convoy

قوت n sustenance

قَوْس n arc

قوس قُزَح n rainbow

قوض v undermine

قول n saying

قوى v beef up, fortify

قوى كالفولاذ adv sternly

قوي adj forceful, powerful, strong

قويم adj right

قَيْء n vomit

قيادة n drive, lead

قياس n measurement

قيافة n setup

قيثار n harp

قيثارة n guitar

قَيْح n pus

قَيْد n band, bond

قيد v handcuff

قَيْد n limit

قيلولة n nap

قيم n guardian

قيمة n rate, value

ق
ك

chalice *n* كأس	Catholicism *n* كثلكة
bumper *n* كأس مترعة	many *adj* كثير
as *c* كأن	seedy *adj* كثير البزور
grief *n* كآبة	nutty *adj* كثير الجوز
repress *v* كبح	juicy *adj* كثير العُصارة
check, restraint, repression *n* كبح	demanding *adj* كثير المطالب
enlarge *v* كبر	dearly *adv* كثيراً
glory *n* كبرياء	often *adv* كثيراً ما
ram *n* كبش	dense, intensive *adj* كثيف
scapegoat *n* كبش الفداء	exertion, dillegence *n* كد
big *adj* كبير	heap, pile up *v* كدس
foreman *n* كبير العمال	bruise *n* كدمة
book *n* كتاب	deceitful *adj* كذاب
writing *n* كتابة	lie *n* كَذِبٌ
documentary *n* كتابى	falsehood *n* كذبة
linen *n* كَتّان	brochure, pamphlet *n* كراسة
write *v* كتب	dignity *n* كرامة
shoulder *n* كِتِف	antipathy *n* كراهية
chick *n* كتكوت	agony, anguish *n* كَرْب
mass, lump *n* كتلة	ball, sphere *n* كرة
block *n* كتلة خشبية	football *n* كرة القدم
hush up *v* كتم	afresh *adv* كرَّة أخرى
battalion *n* كتيب	bullet *n* كرة صغيرة
handbook, manual, booklet *n* كتيب	cardboard *n* كرتون
tight *adj* كتيم	duplicate *v* كرر
consistency *n* كثافة	chair *n* كرسيّ

ك

confessional *n* كرسيّ الاعتراف	payslip *n* كشف الراتب
crane *n* كُركيّ	disclose *v* كشف عن
hospitality; vineyard *n* كرم	kiosk *n* كشك
grapevine *n* كرمة اشاعة	newsstand *n* كُشْك الصحف
dislike *v* كره	heel *n* كعب
unwillingly *adv* كرها	cake *n* كعكة
globule *n* كرية دم	bun *n* كعكة محلّاة
cricket *n* كريكيت	cookie *n* كعكة مُحلّاة
gracious, good *adj* كريم	twist *n* كعكة هلاليّة
sunblock *n* كريمة	paw *n* كف الحيوان
repulsive *adj* كريه	desist *v* كف عن
apparel *n* كِساء	struggle *n* كفاح
harvest *v* كسب	expiation *n* كفارة
chestnut *n* كستناء	penance *n* كفّارة
break *v* كسر	guarantee *n* كفالة
fraction, break *n* كسر	scale *n* كِفّة الميزان
fracture *n* كسر العظم	infidelity *n* كفر
crumb *n* كِسْرَة	expiate *v* كفر عن
casserole *n* كسرولة	ingratitude *n* كفران
laziness *n* كسل	guarantee *v* كفل
eclipse *n* كسوف	shroud *n* كَفَن
idle, lazy *adj* كسول	each, every, all *adj* كل
lame *adj* كسيح	everyone *pro* كل شخص
mug *v* كشر	everything *pro* كل شيء
grimace *n* كشرة	whoever *pro* كلّ مَن
payroll *n* كشف الأجور	everyday *adj* كل يوم

ك

كِلا both adj	كَنِيس synagogue n
كلاسيكيّ classic adj	كنيسة church n
كلب dog n	كهرب electrify v
كلب صيد hound n	كهرباء electricity n
كلس lime n	كهربائي electrician n
كلف cost v	كَهْف cave, cavern n
كلفن galvanize v	كهنوتيّ clerical adj
كَلِمَاتٌ مُتَقَاطِعَة crossword n	كوب glass, cup n
كلمة word n	كوخ hustle n
كلمة المرور password n	كوز cone n
كلمة مركّبة compound n	كولسترول cholesterol n
كلّيّ القدرة almighty adj	كولونيا cologne n
كلية college n	كولونيل colonel n
كُلْية kidney n	كومبيوتر computer n
كليل dull adj	كَوْمَة stack n
كُمّ sleeve n	كومة قش haystack n
كما يعتقد reportedly adv	كَوْنيّ cosmic adj
كما ينبغي duly adv	كَيْ that adj
كُمّاشة pincers n	كياسة elegance n
كِمامة muzzle n	كيان existence n
كمان fiddle n	كَيْد intrigue n
كميّة quantity n	كيس graceful, elegant adj
كن له owe v	كيس bag, sack n
كنز treasure n	كيس المرارة gall bladder n
كنغر kangaroo n	كيس صغير cyst n
كُنْية surname n	كيميائي chemical adj

being *n* كينونة

depressing *adj* كئيب

لا يُدْحَض *adj* irrefutable

لا يزال *adv* still

لا يصدق *adj* incredible, unbelievable

لا يُطاق *adj* unbearable

لا يُعَدّ *adj* countless

لا يُقاوَم *adj* irresistible

لا يقلب *adj* irreversible

لا يُقْهَر *adj* unbeatable

لا يمس *adj* untouchable

لا يمكن التنبّؤ به *adj* unpredictable

لا يُنْسى *adj* unforgettable

لا ينفذ *adj* staunch

لا يُوصَف *adj* unspeakable

ل

لا احد *pro* no one

لا اساس له *adj* unfounded

لا أحد *pro* nobody, none

لا أخْلاقِي *adj* amoral

لا أساس له *adj* baseless

لا شيء *n* nothing

لا طعم له *adj* insipid

لا عقلاني *adj* irrational

لا فقاري *adj* spineless

لا مبالاة *n* carelessness

لا معنى له *adj* meaningless

لا مكان *adv* nowhere

لا واع *adj* unconscious

لا يتجزأ *adj* indivisible

لا يُتَصَوّر *adj* unthinkable

لا يتعب *adj* tireless

لا يُجْحَد *adj* undeniable

لا يحتمل *adj* intolerable

لاءم *v* match

لاأخلاقي *adj* promiscuous

لاتوازن *n* imbalance

لاحِق *adj* later, subsequent

لاذع *adj* harsh

لاسلكيّ *adj* wireless

لاصق *adj* adhesive

لاصقة *n* sticker

لاطف *v* fondle

لافتّ للنظر *adj* noticeable

لامبال *adj* indifferent

لامع *adj* shiny, glossy

لانهائيّ *adj* boundless

لحم مكور n meatball	insoluble adj لايذوب
لحن n melody	innumerable adj لايعد
لحنى adj melodic	indisputable adj لايقبل الجدل
لحية n beard	menu n لائحة الطعام
لخص v epitomize, recap	for pre لأجل
لدن adj flexible	behalf (on) adv لأجل مصلحة
لَذْع n pinch	because c لأنّ
لذلك adv therefore	heart, marrow n لب
لذيذ المَذاق adj tasty	pulp n لُبّ
لَزج adj sticky	gown, dress n لباس
لزم v stick to	tactful adj لَبق
لسان n tongue	milky adj لبنيّ
لَسْعَة n sting	lioness n لَبُوءة
لصّ n robber, burglar, thief	litre n لتر
لصوصيّة n robbery	gum n لثة
لَصُوق n paste	bridle n لِجام
لطافة n gentleness	committee n لجنة
لطخة n blot, smear, soil	bark n لِحاء
لطف n courtesy	quilt n لِحَاف
لطيف adj caring, polite	moment n لحظة
لظُّهْر n midday	flesh, meat n لحم
لُعاب n saliva	beef n لحم البقر
لِعِب n play	pork n لحم الخنزير
لَعُوب adj playful	venison n لحم الطرائد
لُغَة n language	bacon n لحمُ خنزير مملَّح أ
لغز n puzzle	mincemeat n لحمُ مفروم

wrap up v لف	newlywed adj لمتزوج حديثا
scarf n لِفاع	imply, hint v لمح
spill n لفافة ورقية	glance, glimpse n لمحة
floss n لفة حرير	shine v لمع
rivet v لفت الانتباه	gloss n لمعان
emit v لفظ	gasp v لهث
verbally adv لفظيًّا	dialect, accent n لهجة
fake v لفق	eagerness n لهفة
pollen n لَقَاح	amusement n لهو
vaccine n لِقاح	distract v لهى
nickname n لقب	if c لو
vaccinate v لقح	brigade n لواء
shot n لقطة	kidney bean n لوبياء
snapshot n لقطة فوتوغرافيّة	discredit v لوث
morsel n لقمة	slab n لوح
indoctrinate v لقن	board n لوح خشب
yours pro لكَ	keyboard n لوحة المفاتيح
as adv لكذا	tablet n لوحة تذكارية
apiece adv لكلّ	lord n لورد
punch v لكم	almond n لوز
punch n لكمة	but c لولا أنَّ
however c لكن	thread v لولب
momentarily adv لِلَحْظة	winding adj لَولبيّ
ham n للحم خنزير مدخن	reproach, blame n لوم
not adv لم	color v لون
why adv لِمَا	color n لون

لون البشرة complexion n	ماسك المفاتيح key ring n
لؤلؤة pearl n	ماضٍ sharp adj
لي my adj	ماكر foxy, sly, wily adj
لياقة decorum n	مالح salty adj
ليس للنشر off-the-record adj	مالك owner n
ليكيور liqueur n	مالك الأرض landlord n
لَيْل night n	مالكة الأرض landlady n
ليليّ nocturnal adj	مالي financial adj
ليمون lemon n	مانع hindrance n
ليمون الجنة grapefruit n	مائج wavy adj
ليمُونادَة lemonade n	مائع fluid n
	مائيّ aquatic, watery adj
	مأثرة exploit n
	مأدُبة banquet n
	مأزق dilemma, predicament n
م	مألوف familiar adj
	مبادرة initiative, lead n
ما يساوي كذا worth adj	مبادئ basics n
ماء water n	مباراة tournament n
مات expire v	مبارزة duel n
مَاخُور brothel n	مبارزة بالسيف fence, fencing n
مادة material n	مُبَارَك blessed adj
مادة الصَّفراء bile n	مباركة blessing n
مادة غذائية foodstuff n	مباشر eve n
ماديّ bodily adj	مباعة sold-out adj
ماسّ diamond n	مبتدئ beginner n

stale *adj* مبتَذَل		mutually *adv* متبادل
trivial *adj* مبتذل		contestant *n* متباري
racketeering *n* مبتز للأموال		estranged *adj* مُتَباعِد
elated, joyful *adj* مبتهج		remaining *adj* متبق
precept *n* مبدأ		congenial *adj* متجانس
creative *adj* مُبدِع		shop *n* مَتْجر
sharpener *n* مِبْراة		shoestore *n* متجر أحذية
programmer *n* مبرمج		supermarket *n* مَتْجر كبير
envoy *n* مبعوث		southbound *adv* متجه جنوبا
dairy farm *n* مبقرة		westbound *adv* متجه نحو الغرب
precocious *adj* مبكر		gloomy, grim *adj* متجهِم
untimely *adj* مبكّر		challenging, defiant *adj* متحد
early *adv* مبكرا		allied *adj* مُتحد
amount, sum *n* مبلغ		broadminded, open-minded *adj* متحرر
building *n* مَبْنى		museum *n* مُتْحَف
delicious *adj* مُبهج		aloof *adj* متحفّظ
flashy *adj* مبهرج		hot *adj* متحمس
pesticide *n* مبيد الحشرات		zealous *adj* متحمّس
labyrinth *n* متاهة		unlike *adj* متخالف
belated, overdue *adj* متأخر		bumpy *adj* متخبط
late *adv* متأخّرا		wooden *adj* متخشّب
ingrained *adj* متأصل		replete *adj* مُتْخَم
brilliant *adj* متألّق		trainee *n* متدرب
suffering *n* متألّم		gradual *adj* متدرج
bossy *adj* مُتأمّر		vibrant *adj* مُتذبذب
nice *adj* متأنّق		grouchy *adj* متذمر

متراس barricade n	مُتعاقِب consecutive adj
متراكز concentric adj	متعاون collaborator n
مترجم interpreter n	متعب disturbing adj
متردد ambivalent, undecided adj	مُتعَب tired, tiresome adj
مِتْريّ metric adj	متعة enjoyment n
متزامن simultaneous n	متعجرف overbearing adj
متزايد increasing adj	متعدّد multiple adj
متزعزع shaky adj	متعدّد الجوانب versatile adj
متزن grave adj	متعذر inexcusable adj
متزوّج married adj	متعذر إصلاحه irreparable adj
متساهل indulgent adj	متعذر بلوغه inaccessible adj
مُتّسع ample, roomy adj	متعذر تفسيره inexplicable adj
متسكع prowler n	متعصب fanatic adj
متسم بالاحترام respectful adj	متعفن mouldy adj
متشابك criss-cross v	متعلق related adj
متشابك twisted adj	متعنت opinionated adj
متشَابه similar adj	متغطرس insolent adj
متشائم pessimistic adj	متفاخر ostentatious adj
متصفح browser n	مُتفادي avoidable adj
متّصل continuous adj	متفائل optimistic adj
متصلّب stark adj	متفتت crunchy adj
متضادّ opposite adj	متفرّق sparse adj
متضارب incompatible, conflicting adj	متفشٍ rampant adj
متطابق coincidental adj	متفق عليه concurrent adj
متطاير volatile adj	متفوق superior adj
متطرف extreme adj	متقدّما ahead pre

م

sporadic *adj* متقطّع	edgy, tense *adj* متوتر
fickle, variable *adj* متقلب	bound for *adj* متوجه
precarious *adj* متقلقل	loner, alone *adj* متوحد
exact *adj* متقن	savage *adj* متوحّش
arrogant, proud *adj* متكبّر	involved *v* متورّط
frequent *adj* متكرر الحدوث	swollen *adj* متورم
adaptable, adjustable *adj* متكيّف	mediocre *adj* متوسّط
inseparable *adj* متلازم	indisposed *adj* متوعك
concrete *adj* متماسك	deceased *adj* متوفى
rebel *n* متمرّد	dependent *adj* متوقّف على
conventional *adj* متمسّك بالعُرْف	flame *n* متوهج
versed *adj* متمكّن	when *adv* متى
crispy *adj* متموج	stiff *adj* متيبس
distinct *adj* متميز	durable *adj* متين
debatable *adj* مُتَنازَعٌ عليه	persistent *adj* مُثابر
incoherent *adj* متنافر	bladder *n* مَثانة
alternate *adj* متناوب	proven *adj* مُثْبت
varied, various *adj* متنوّع	exemplify *v* مثل
dissolute *adj* متهتك	instance *n* مثل
elusive, evasive *adj* متهرب	like *pre* مثل
jubilant *adj* متهلّل	parable, proverb *n* مَثَلٌ
impetuous *adj* متهور	such *adj* مِثل
equal *adj* متوازٍ	triangle *n* مُثلّث
parallel *n* متوازِ	ice-cold *adj* مثلج
incessant *adj* متواصل	fruitful *adj* مثمر
modest *adj* متواضع	exciting, breathtaking *adj* مثير

م

مثير للإعجاب impressive *adj*	مجموعة قوانين code *n*
مجاز allegory *n*	مجنّد recruit *n*
مجازاة repayment *n*	مجنون mad, lunatic *adj*
مجاعة famine *n*	مجنون بالشك paranoid *adj*
مجال reach, scope *n*	مجهر binoculars *n*
مجال جوي airspace *n*	مجهول anonymous *adj*
مجالد gladiator *n*	مجيء coming *n*
مُجامِل complimentary *adj*	مجيد glorious *adj*
مجاور adjacent, adjoining, nearby *adj*	محا erase *v*
مجبر obliged *adj*	محادثة conversation *n*
مُجْتَمَع community *n*	محارب belligerent *adj*
مِجذاف oar *n*	محاسَبَة account *n*
مجرة فضائية galaxy *n*	محاضرة lecture *n*
مجرد deprived, abstract *adj*	محاط بالأرض landlocked *adj*
مِجْرَفة shovel *n*	محافظ conservative *adj*
مجرم felon *n*	محاولة endeavor *n*
مجروح hurt *adj*	محاولة اعتداء attempt *n*
مجرى نهر channel *n*	محايد neutral *adj*
مَجزر shambles *n*	محب fond, affecionate *adj*
مِجَسّ tentacle *n*	مُحبّب lovable *adj*
مجفف dryer *n*	محبة charity, love *n*
مَجْلِس council *n*	محبوب beloved *adj*
مجلس الشيوخ senate *n*	مُحْتَشِم decent *adj*
مجلس الوزراء cabinet *n*	محتقر scornful *n*
مجمد frozen *adj*	مُحْتَمَل contingent, probable *adj*
مجموع كلّي totality *n*	مُحْتَمَل bearable, tolerable *adj*

م

محتوم inevitable *adj*	مُحمَّل loaded *adj*
محدّد definite *adj*	مِحنة ordeal *n*
مُحْدَوْدِب hunched *adj*	محور hub *n*
محرق المباني arsonist *n*	مِحْوَر axis *n*
محرقة يهود أوروبا holocaust *n*	محور الدولاب nave *n*
محرك engine *n*	محوِر العجلة axle *n*
محرم illicit, unlawful *adj*	مُحيِّر confusing *adj*
محروم من destitute *adj*	محيط circuit *n*
مُحْزن pathetic *adj*	مخ العظم bone marrow *n*
مُحسِن charitable *adj*	مخادع misleading, tricky *adj*
محسوس palpable *adj*	مخاط mucus *n*
مَحْشُوّ loaded *adj*	مخاطرة risk *n*
محصور stranded *adj*	مخالفة disagreement *n*
محصور crop, fruit *n*	مخبأ cover *n*
محضر proceedings *n*	مخبر informer *n*
مَحْضَر record *n*	مَخْبَز bakery *n*
مَحْظُوظ lucky *adj*	مخبّل crazy, demented *adj*
محفظة wallet *n*	مخبول insane *adj*
مَحْفَظَةُ purse *n*	مختبر lab *n*
مَحْفُور bored *adj*	مختصر outline *n*
مِحقنة syringe *n*	مختل deranged *adj*
محكمة tribunal *n*	مختلِط chaotic *adj*
محكمة ألاستئناف court *n*	مختلف different, diverse *adj*
محل بجوهرات jewelry store *n*	مختَلى closet *n*
محمر fried *adj*	مُخْجِل shameful *adj*
مِحْمَصة toaster *n*	مخدِّر narcotic *n*

 م

painkiller *n* مخدِّر	grisly *adj* مخيف
opium *n* مخدِّر	awesome *adj* مُخيف
dope *n* مخدرات	camp *n* مُخيم
devastating *adj* مخرِب	orbit *n* مَدار
wasteful *adj* مخرِّب	defender *n* مُدافِع
exit, outlet, way out *n* مخرج	medal *n* مَدالية
dishonorable, shameless *adj* مخز	medallion *n* مَدالية كبيرة
depot, storage *n* مخزن	raid *n* مداهمة
supplies, store *n* مخزون	therapy *n* مداواة
sketch *n* مُخطَّط	housekeeper *n* مدبرة المنزل
striped *adj* مخطَّط	tanned *adj* مدبوغ
manuscript *n* مخطوطة	compliment *n* مَدْح
mistaken *adj* مخطئ	complimentary *adj* مَدْحِيّ
attenuating *adj* مُخَفِّف	access *n* مَدْخَل
unsuccessful *adj* مخفق	doorway *n* مدخل
clutch, claw *n* مخلب	smoked *adj* مدخن
faithful *adj* مخلص	amphitheater *n* مُدَرَّج
scrambled *adj* مخلوط	school *n* مدرسة
shaken *adj* مخلوط بالهز	sensible *adj* مُدرِك
creature *n* مخلوق	deliberate *adj* مدروس
velvet *n* مُخْمَل	fireplace, heater *n* مدفأة
sissy, ladylike *adj* مخنث	cannon *n* مِدْفَع
dreaded *adj* مَخُوف	gun *n* مدفع
cerebral *adj* مُخّي	payee *n* مدفوع له
disappointing *adj* مخيب للأمل	hammer *n* مدقة
batter *v* مَخِيض	choosy *adj* مدقق في الاختيار

مُدَمَّج compact adj	مرارة bitterness n
مُدْمِن addicted adj	مراسم ceremony n
مدنس soiled adj	مراسيم إحتفالية festivity n
مَدَنيّ civil adj	مرافق escort n
مدهش wonderful, ashtonishing adj	مراقبة oversight n
مدهن greasy adj	مراقبة المطبوعات censorship n
مدوس بالاقدام downtrodden adj	مُراهِق adolescent n
مدى extent n	مراوغة evasion n
مدير directory n	مرآة mirror n
مدينة city n	مربط الجواد stall n
مَدَينيّ civic, urban adj	مربع square adj
مذبحة massacre, slaughter n	مربك staggering adj
مِذْراة pitchfork n	مربية nanny n
مذكر masculine adj	مرّة once adv
مذكّرات memoirs n	مرتّب tidy adj
مذكرة memo, notebook n	مرتبة rank n
مذكرة إحضار subpoena n	مرتبك uneasy adj
مذل degrading adj	مرتجل impromptu adv
مذنب guilty adj	مُرْتَش corrupt adj
مذهب doctrine n	مرتفع loud adj
مذهب العُرْي nudism n	مرتين twice adv
مذهل prodigious, amazing adj	مَرْج meadow, prairie n
مذيع announcer n	مَرْجع reference n
مر pass v	مرجل generator n
مرّ bitter adj	مرجل تسخين geyser n
مراجعة rehearsal n	مرح cheerful, jovial, merry adj

مرحاض n toilet	مَرْكبة الجليد n sleigh
مرحلة الحمل n gestation	مركز n center
مردود n output	مركزيّ adj central
مِرْساة n anchor	مرمدة n ashtray
مرسة n cable	مرمي n goal
مُرْسِل n sender	مرن adj resilient, pliable
مرسوم n decree	مرهق adj strained
مَرْسَى n berth	مرهق للأعصاب adj stressful
مرشح n candidate	مَرْهَم n ointment
مرشد n guide	مِروحة n van
مَرْصَد n observatory	مروع adj ghastly, scary
مرصص adj leaded	مريب adj questionable
مرصع adj inlaid	مريح adj convenient
مرض n disease, sickness	مُريح adj restful
مُرْضٍ adj satisfactory	مريح adj soft
مرض الجُديْري n chicken pox	مرير adv bitterly
مرض الحَصْبة n measles	مريض adj ill, sick
مرعب adj alarming, daunting, appaling	مرئيّ adj apparent, visible
مرفق n elbow	مزاج n mood, temper
مرفوض adj inadmissible	مزاد علنيّ n auction
مَرَقّ n broth	مزارع n farmer
مرق التوابل n dressing	مزبلة n dump
مركب n assembly	مَزْج n mixture
مُرَكّب adj complex	مَزْحَةٌ n prank
مركب شراعي n sailboat	مزخرف adj fancy
مركبة n coach, vehicle	مزدحم adj crowded

مساهمة n input	مزدهر prosperous adj
مساو tantamount to adj	مزدوج double adj
مساواة n equality	مزراب gutter n
مساومة n bargaining	مزرعة farm n
مسألة n affair, matter	مزرعة كبيرة ranch n
مِسْبَر n probing	مزعج disagreeable, bothersome adj
مسبك n foundry	مُزَعْزَع unstable adj
مستاء dissatisfied adj	مزق rip apart v
مستبد domineering adj	مزكوم stuffy adj
مستجد bum n	مِزْلاج latch n
مستجيب responsive adj	مزلج skate n
مستحِق deserving adj	مِزْمار pipe n
مستحق ل worthy adj	مُزْمِن chronic adj
مستحق للعقاب punishable adj	مزود supplier n
مستحيل impossible adj	مزيج blend n
مستدل عليه unjustified adj	مزيف counterfeit adj
مستدير circular adj	مس touch n
مسترخ relaxing adj	مسابقة race n
مُسْتَرَق stealthy adj	مسار trajectory n
مستشار chancellor n	مسار الرحلة itinerary n
مستشفى hospital n	مساعد conducive adj
مُسْتَصْوَب advisable adj	مُساعِد subsidiary adj
مستطيل oblong adj	مساعَدة assistance n
مستطيلي rectangular adj	مسافة distance n
مستعار fake adj	مسافر voyager n
مستعدّ ready, willing adj	مسامّي porous adj

م

مسْتعرض cross adj	مسحوق powder n
مستعمرة colonization n	مسخن مائى waterheater n
مُسْتَعْمَريّ colonial adj	مسدس colt n
مستغلق illegible adj	مُسَدَّس pistol n
مستقبل future n	مسدل downcast adj
مستقرّ stable adj	مسرح dramatize v
مُسْتَقرّ whereabouts n	مسرح theater n
مستقل independent, unattached adj	مسرحى مفاجئ dramatic adj
مستقيم straight, direct adj	مسرف extravagant, lavish adj
مستكشف explorer n	مسرور happy adj
مستمع listener n	مسعور frantic adj
مُسْتَنْقِع pond n	مسقط رأس hometown n
مستنقَع bog n	مسل funny, amusing adj
مستنقع quagmire n	مُسلّح armed adj
مستنقع swamp n	مَسْلَخ butchery n
مستهلك consumer n	مَسْلَك route n
مستو plain n	مُسْلِم Muslim adj
مستودع warehouse, depot n	مسلم به undisputed adj
مُسْتَودَع الجُثَث mortuary n	مسلي entertaining adj
مستودع أسلحة arsenal n	مسمار nail n
مستوى level n	مسموع audible adj
مُسجّل patent adj	مسند subject n
مُسَجّى shrouded adj	مُسْهِلٌ laxative adj
مِسْحاة spade n	مسؤول responsible, accountable adj
مَسْحَة trait n	مسؤوليّة responsibility n
مِسْحَقَة stamp n	مسيحي christian adj

March n مسيرة	مُشْمس sunny adj
sovereign adj مسيطر	مشنقة gallows n
watertight adj مَسِيْك	مشهد spectacle n
altercation n مشاحنة	مشهد مسرحيّ scene n
tumultuous adj مشاغِب	مُشَهَّر notorious adj
contentious adj مشاكس	مشهور famous adj
paperclip n مشبك	مشهيات appetizer n
suspicious adj مشبوه	مشواة grill, broiler n
ablaze adj مشتعل	مشوش disorganized, muddy adj
alight adv مشتعلاً	مشويّ roast n
derivative adj مشتقّ	مشؤوم disastrous, ominous, unlucky adj
aghast adj مشدوه	مَشْي walk n
homeless adj مشرد	مشيئة pleasure n
outlook n مَشْرَف	مصاب بفقر الدم anemic adj
clear adj مشرق	مصادرة confiscation n
oriental adj مَشْرقيّ	مُصادفة chance, accident n
drink n مشروب	مُصارع wrestler n
conditional adj مَشْروط	مصارع ثيران bull fighter n
enterprise n مشروع	مصارعة الثيران bull fight n
comb n مُشْط	مصاريف spending n
torch n مشعل	مَصّاص sucker adj
swindler n مشعوذ	مصافحة handshake n
busy adj مشغول	مصب النهر estuary n
problematic adj مُشْكِل	مصباح bulb, lamp n
problem n مشكلة	مصباح الشارع streetlight n
doubtful adl مشكوك فيه	مصداقية credibility n

مصدر origin n	مضرب التنس racket n
مصرف drainage n	مِضرب الكرة club n
مصطلح idiom n	مَضْروب beaten adj
مصطنَع unreal adj	مَضْغ chew v
مصعد elevator n	مضلل misguided adj
مصغر miniature n	مضيف host n
مصفاة filter, strainer n	مضيفة stewardess n
مُصْمَت solid adj	مضيفة طيران hostess n
مصمم draftsman n	مضيق bottleneck n
مصمِّم resolute adj	مَضيق strait n
مصنع factory n	مطابقة conformity n
مصنع الجعة brewery n	مطاردة hunting, chase n
مصنع الخمرة winery n	مطاط rubber n
مصنَّف assorted adj	مطالبةٌ بـ claim n
مصون secure adj	مطاوع compliant adj
مصيبة casualty n	مطاوعة compliance n
مصيري fatal, fateful adj	مطبخ cuisine, kitchen n
مضادّ contrary adj	مِطحنة mill n
مضادّ للجراثيم antibiotic n	مَطَر rain n
مضاعفة multiplication n	مطران archbishop n
مضايق irritating adj	مَطْعَم restaurant n
مُضْجِر tedious adj	مَطلَب requirement n
مَضْجع couch n	مطلق full adj
مضحك ludicrous adj	مُطلَق unlimited adj
مِضَخّة pump n	مطلق الحرية free adj
مضر hurtful adj	مطلى بالفضة silverplated adj

م

مَطْمَح ambition n	معاملة سيئة mistreatment n
مطهر detergent n	معاهدة pact, treaty n
مِطْواع supple adj	معاون help n
مَطْوِيّ pleated adj	معاونة aid n
مطيّة mount n	معبد chapel n
مُطيع للقانون law-abiding adj	معبود idol n
مِظَلّة umbrella n	معتاد customary, usual adj
مِظَلّة هبوط parachute n	معتدل moderate adj
مظلم dark, murky adj	مُعْتَرِفّ avowed adj
مظلمة gripe n	معتزلّ solitary adj
مظلي paratrooper n	معتقد faith n
مع أنّ although c	معتل ailing adj
مَعَ ذَلِكَ nonetheless c	معتم dim, overcast, somber adj
معًا jointly, together adv	معتوه cranky adj
مُعادٍ adverse adj	معجب fan n
معاد hostile adj	معجزة prodigy n
معادة replay n	مُعجزة miracle n
معادل equivalent adj	مُعْجَم dictionary n
معارضة opposition n	معد infectious, contagious adj
معاصرّ لِـ contemporary adj	مُعْدٍ catching adj
معاق disabled adj	مَعِدَة stomach n
معاقبة chastisement n	معدّل varied adj
معاقرة addiction n	معدم penniless adj
معاكس opposite adv	مَعْدِن metal, mineral n
معالجة treatment n	معدن النيكل nickel n
معاملة treatment n	مَعْدِنيّ metallic adj

معلومات n information, data	معدي gastric adj
معنى n meaning	معدية n ferry
معهِد v institute	مَعْذُور forgivable adj
مَعْهد n academy	معرض n exhibition
معوز v lack	معرفة n awareness
معوق عن discouraging adj	معرفة n acquaintance
معيار n criterion, norm	معرفة n knowledge
مغال overdone adj	معركة n battle
مغال في الصوت n ultrasound	معروف well-known adj
مغالطة n fallacy	معزّ comfortable adj
مغامرة n adventure	معصوم impeccable adj
مغبر dusty adj	مِعْطف n overcoat
مغتصب n rapist	معظم most adj
مغث sickening adj	معفى exempt adj
مُغَذٍّ nutritious adj	معقد intricate adj
مُغْر alluring adj	معقل n fortress
مغرم fond adj	معقوف crooked adj
مغرور cocky, haughty adj	معقول plausible, credible adj
مَغزَى n tenor	معكوس n counter
مغسلة n laundry	معلّب canned adj
مَغْص n colic	معلف n manger, crib
مغطاء n cover	معلّق outstanding adj
مغفرة n forgiveness	معلم n instructor
مُغْلَق close adj	مَعْلَم n milestone
مغمور swamped adj	مَعْلَم n sight
مُغمَّى عليه senseless adj	معلم خصوصيّ n tutor

مُغَن singer n	hopeful adj مفعم بالأمل
مغناطيس magnet n	مِفَكّ screwdriver n
مغناطيسي hypnosis n	مُفْلِس broke adj
مغنطيسيّ magnetic adj	beneficial, profitable adj مفيد
مغو enticing adj	مقابلة encounter n
مغير raider n	مُقاتِل combatant n
مفاجأة surprise n	مقاتل militant adj
مفاجئ unforeseen adj	مقارن comparative adj
مُفَارَقَة paradox n	مقارَنة comparison n
مفتاح key n	مقاطعة enclave n
مفتاح الرموز key n	مَقام shrine n
مفتاح العلب can opener n	مقاول entrepreneur n
مفتاح رَبْط wrench n	مُقَاوِم reluctant adj
مُفْتَرَق parting n	مقاومة fight n
مُفْتَرَق الطُّرُق crossroads n	مقايضة swap n
مفتش inspector n	مقبرة cemetery n
مفتوح open adj	مقبض grasp n
مفتوح جزئيًّا ajar adj	مقبض الة handle n
مفحم convincing adj	مقبوض الأمعاء constipated adj
مُفْرَد odd adj	مقبول acceptable adj
مفرط excessive adj	مقبول admissible adj
مفرق طرق fork n	مقت aversion n
مفرقعة نارية firecracker n	مُقْتَرَحّ proposition n
مِفْرَمة chopper n	مقتصد economical adj
مفزع dreadful adj	مقتطفات excerpt n
مفصلة hinge n	مقدارّ deal n

مقدار lot adv	مُقيت detestable adj
مقدار volume n	مقيم inhabitant n
مقدماً beforehand adv	مكافأة incentive n
مقدّمة introduction n	مكافئ rewarding adj
مقدّمة preface n	مكان lieu, place n
مقدمة prelude, prologue n	مكان خطر death trap n
مقدمة المركب prow n	مِكَبّ reel, spool n
مقر بالجميل grateful adj	مكبّر الصوت loudspeaker n
مُقْرف nasty adj	مكبوت pent-up adj
مِقَص scissors n	مكبوح subdued adj
مَقْصِف canteen n	مكتب desk n
مقصلة guillotine n	مكتب البريد post office n
مقصورة compartment n	مكتب فرعي branch office n
مقصورة الطيار cockpit n	مكتبة library n
مَقْطَع section n	مكتظ overcrowded adj
مَقْطَع لَفْظِيّ syllable n	مكتفٍ content adj
مقعد bench, pew, seat n	مَكْتُوب written adj
مُقعَد lame adj	مكر guile n
مِقْلاة pan n	مكرّس sacred adj
مقلق worrisome adj	مُكْرِه compulsive adj
مُقْلْقَل unsteady adj	مكروه discomfort n
مقلي frying pan n	مَكْس toll n
مُقمّل lousy adj	مكشاف detector n
مُقْنِع persuasive adj	مكشوف exposed adj
مقو tonic n	مكعّب cubic adj
مقياس للحطب cord n	مكعب ثلجى ice cube n

enable v مكن	مُلِحّ urgent adj
let out v مكنه من الفرار	ملحد godless adj
electric adj مكهرب	مُلْحَق annex n
device n مكيدة	مُلْحَق attached adj
adapter n مُكَيِّف	ملحم plump adj
spoonful n مِلْء ملعقة	ملحمة الأوديسة odyssey n
expediency n ملاءمة	ملحوظ noteworthy adj
clothes, garment n ملابس	ملخص overview n
remark n ملاحظة	مُلْزِم binding adj
hideaway n ملاذ	مِلْزم clamp n
malaria n ملاريا	ملعب field n
collateral adj مُلازم	مَلْعَب playground n
lieutenant n ملازم أول	مِلعَقة spoon n
caress n مُلاطَفة	ملعقة المائدة tablespoon n
angel n مَلاك	ملعقة شاي teaspoon n
angelic adj مَلائِكِيّ	ملعون evil adj
feasible adj ملائم	ملف file, folder n
uncertain adj ملتبس	ملفوف cabbage n
shelter n مُلْتَجَأ	مِلْقاط صغير tweezers n
bearded adj مُلْتَح	مِلقَط tongs n
coherent adj ملتحم	مِلِك king n
corner n ملتقى شارعين	مَلِكَة queen n
red-hot adj ملتهب	مِلْكُكَ your adj
warped adj ملتو	مِلكنا ours pro
refuge n ملجأ	مِلكي mine pro
salt n مِلح	مَلَكِيّ royal adj

 م

ownership n ملكية	aisle n ممشى
monarchy n ملكية مطلقة	rainy adj مُمْطِر
fatigue n ملل	possible adj ممكن
tangible adj ملموس	approachable adj مُمْكِنّ بُلُوغُهُ
majestic adj ملوكيّ	detachable adj ممكن فصلها
milligram n مليغرام	boring adj مُمِلّ
tycoon n مليونير	kingdom n مملكة
below pre مما لا يليق بـ	lethal, deadly adj مُميت
identical adj مماثل	distinctive, specific adj مميز
practising adj ممارسة	from pre من
bully adj ممتاز	of pre مِنْ
conformist adj ممتثل	who, whom pro من
widespread adj ممتدّ	sideways adv من الجَنْب
absorbent adj ممتص	orangutan n من القَرَدة
enjoyable adj ممتع	afar adv مِن بُعْد
comedian n ممثّل هزليّ	remote adj من بعد
eraser n ممحاة	again adv من جديد
outstretched adj ممدود	since then adv من قبل
passage n ممرّ	further adv من ناحية أخرى
gap n ممر ضيق	climate n مُناخ
crosswalk n ممر مسمر	climatic adj مُناخي
nurse n مُمرضة	calling n مناداة
ragged adj مُمزّق	beacon n منارة
card n مِمْشَطة للصوف	fitting adj مناسب
slim adj ممشوق	opportunity n مناسَبة
alley n مَمْشى	landscape n مناظر الطبيعة

م

مناظرة dispute n	منح donate v
مناعة immunity n	مَنْح البَرَكة benediction n
منافسة competition n	منحة pension n
منافق hypocrite adj	منحة تعليمية scholarship n
مناقشة discussion n	منحة جامعية fellowship n
مَنامة pajamas n	مُنحدَر slope n
مناورة maneuver n	منحرف slanted, oblique adj
مناوشة skirmish n	مُنْحَلّ degenerate adj
مِنْبر pulpit n	مُنحنى curve n
منبع source n	منخفض low adj
منبهر dazed adj	مندفع dashing adj
منبوذ outcast adj	مندهش astounding adj
منتبه mindful adj	مندوب delegate n
منتِج productive adj	منديل napkin n
مُنْتَج product n	منذ since pre
منتصِر triumphant, victorious adj	مُنْزرِع arable adj
مُنتصف middle n	منزل lodging n
منتصف الصّيف midsummer n	منزلة grade, status n
منتصف الليل midnight n	منزلة اجتماعية class n
منتظم even adj	منزلي domestic adj
منتفخ swelling, bloated n	منسجم compatible adj
منتن stinking adj	منسحبّ outgoing adj
منتهى السعادة bliss n	منسق coordinator n
مِنْجَل sickle n	منسوج woven adj
مَنْجم mine n	مِنشار saw n
مَنْح concession n	منشار المنحنيات jigsaw n

م

chainsaw n منشار ألي	passive adj منفعل
towel n مِنْشَفة	beak n مِنقار
lyrics n منشود	extinct adj منقرض
founder n منشئ	method n منهج
office n منصب	methodical adj منهجيّ
springboard n مِنصّة الوثب	exhausting adj منهك
bureau n منضدة	engrossed adj منهمك
balloon n مُنطاد	immune adj منيع
aircraft n مُنطاد أو طائرة	emigrant n مهاجر
logic n منطِق	attacker n مهاجم
area, district, zone n منطقة	attack n مهاجمة
logical adj منطقيّ	know-how, skill n مهارة
scene n منظر	airstrip n مَهْبط طائرات
perspective n منظور	emotional adj مهتاج
inhibit v منع	interested adj مهتم
secluded adj منعزل	cubicle n مهجع
refreshing adj منعش	deserted adj مهجور
crisp adj منعش أو بار	cradle n مهد
benefactor, donor n منعم	dowry n مهر
conditioner n منعم الشعر	emaciated adj مهزول
effusive adj منفتح القلب	broken adj مُهشّم
outlet n مَنْفَذ	destructive adj مُهْلِك
single adj منفرد	sleazy adj مهلهل
apart adv منفرداً	regardless adv مهما يكن
several adj منفصل	spur n مِهماز
usefulness n منفعة	assignment, errand n مهمة

task, mission *n* مهمّة	sloppy *adj* مُوْحِل
commission *n* مهمةمأمورية	intimacy *n* مودة
negligent *adj* مهمِل	resource *n* مورد
business *n* مهنة	banana *n* موز
engineer *n* مهندس	feast *n* موسِم
professional *adj* مِهْنيّ	seasonal *adj* موسِمِيّ
maniac *adj* مهووس	meticulous *adj* مُوَسْوَس
confrontation *n* مواجهة	razor *n* موسى الحلاقة
livestock *n* مواش	music *n* موسيقى
citizen *n* مواطن	prism *n* مَوْشور
compatriot *n* مواطن المرء	relative *adj* موصول
citizenship *n* مُواطَنة	custom-made *adj* موصى عليه
times *n* مواعيد	vogue *n* موضة
approval *n* موافقة	position *n* موضع
partisan *n* مُوالٍ	depth *n* موضع عميق
death *n* موت	local *adj* موضعيّ
dependable *adj* موثوق	subject, theme *n* موضوع
wave *n* موجة	topic *n* موضوع مقالةٍ
microwave *n* موجة الصغرى	officer *n* موظّف
tidal wave *n* موجة عارمة	receptionist *n* موظف الإستقبال
outline, summary *n* موجَز	sermon *n* موعظة
agonizing *adj* موجِّع	stove *n* مَوْقِد
leading *adj* موجّه	location, site *n* موقع
oriented *adj* موجه	garrison *n* موقع عسكري
assets *n* موجودات	stand, station *n* مَوْقِف
suggestive *adj* مُوْحٍ	parking *n* موقف سيارات

موكب procession n

مول finance v

مولد birthday n

مولود born adj

مولود حديثا newborn n

مومياء mummy n

موهبة genius, gift n

موهوب gifted adj

مؤامرة plot, web n

مؤيد everlasting adj

مؤثر mind-boggling, touching adj

مؤجر lessor n

مُؤَخَّرة rear n

مؤدب gallant adj

مؤدب gentleman n

مؤذ damaging, detrimental adj

مؤرخ historian n

مؤرق watchful adj

مؤسسة institution n

مؤسف regrettable adj

مؤقّت provisional, temporary adj

مؤلف author n

مؤلم distressing, sore adj

مَيّال إلى prone adj

مياه البوالع sewage n

مَيْت dead, lifeless adj

مَيْتَم orphanage n

ميراث legacy n

ميراثٌ patrimony n

ميز discriminate v

ميزان balance n

ميزان البناء level n

ميزة feature n

مِيفاء solvent adj

ميكروب microbe n

ميل gusto n

مَيْل propensity n

ميمون auspicious adj

ميناء harbor, port n

ميناء جوّي airport n

مِئْزَر apron n

ن

ن us _pre_

ناءٍ devious _adj_

ناب fang, tusk _n_

نابض graphic _adj_

نابض بالحياة live _adj_

ناتئ prominent _adj_

ناجح effective _adj_

ناجي survivor _n_

نادر exceptional, rare _adj_

نادرآ rarely, seldom _adv_

نادم penitent _n_

نادم جدا remorseful _adj_

نادى call out _v_

نادي رجال fraternity _n_

نار campfire _n_

ناري fiery _adj_

نازل engaged _adj_

ناسب fit _v_

ناسف dynamite _n_

ناشئ عن consequent _adj_

ناضج mature _adj_

ناطحة سحاب skyscraper _n_

ناظر caretaker _n_

نافذة window _n_

نافع useful _adj_

ناقش discuss _v_

ناقص deficient, faulty _adj_

ناقِه convalescent _adj_

ناقوس الغروب curfew _n_

نائم asleep _adj_

نبات vegetable _v_

نبات الكَرَفْس celery _n_

نبات الهِلْيون asparagus _n_

نباتى vegetarian _v_

نُباح bark _n_

نبالة nobility _n_

نَبْرَة tone _n_

نبض beat, throb _v_

نبض القلب heartbeat _n_

نبضة beat _n_

نبع spring _n_

نبوة prophecy _n_

نبيّ prophet _n_

نِتاج production, produce _n_

نتانة filth _n_

نَتانة stench _n_

نتأ emboss _v_

نتن fetid _adj_

نَتِن rotten _adj_

نَتَنٌّ stink n	ندَمّ contrition n
نتيجة result n	نَدىً dew n
نتيجة مباشرة corollary n	نَدِيّ soggy adj
نثر disseminate v	نذير portent n
نثى female n	نرويجي Norwegian adj
نجاح success n	نزاع conflict, strife n
نجح succeed v	نزع السلاح disarm v
نجدة relief n	نزع القابس unplug v
نجز encounter, fulfill v	نزع ملكية evict v
نجم star n	نزعة tendency n
نحاس copper n	نَزْف bleeding n
نَحْلَة bee n	نزل get down v
نَحْنُ we pro	نزل في الفندق check in v
نَحْوَ towards pre	نزل من السفينة disembark v
نحو خاص extra adv	نزهَة outing n
نحو وضع أدنى downhill adv	نزهة promenade n
نحيل lean, slim adj	نزوة whim n
نُخالة الرأس dandruff n	نزول descent n
نخس punch v	نزيف دم hemorrhage n
نخعة jolt n	نزيل inmate n
نَخْعة , رجّة jerk n	نزيه impartial adj
نخلة palm n	نِساء women n
ندّ match n	نسبة ratio, proportion n
ندامة remorse n	نسبة مئوية percentage n
نُدرة scarcity n	نَسْج العنكبوت web n
نُدْفةُ الثَّلج snowflake n	نسخ engulf v

نُسْخَة copy n	نُصُب statue n
نسخة counterpart n	نُصُب تذكاري trophy n
نسخة صورة photocopy n	نصب فخا snare v
نسر eagle n	نُصْبيّ monumental adj
نَسْر vulture n	نصح بالعدول dissuade v
نُسْغُ sap n	نَصْر triumph n
نسق ordain v	نصف half n
نسى forget v	نصف القطر radius n
نسيان oblivion n	نصف سنة semester n
نسيج texture, tissue n	نصف شهري bimonthly adj
نسيج القماش fabric n	نصفى half adj
نسيم breeze n	نصيب allowance n
نَشاء starch n	نصيحة advice n
نُشادر ammonia n	نضال contest n
نشاز dissonant adj	نُضْج maturity n
نشاط activity n	نَطْحَة butt n
نشر edition n	نظارات glasses n
نشرة الأخبار newscast n	نظارات للوقاية goggles n
نشرة إعلانية flier n	نَظَّارَةٌ شَمْسِيَّة sunglasses n
نشط quicken v	نظارة طبية eyeglasses n
نشوة ecstasy n	نظافة cleanliness n
نَشَويّ starchy adj	نظام system n
نَشيج sob n	نِظاميّ systematic adj
نَشِيط bustling adj	نَظَرٌ look n
نشيط energetic, lively adj	نظرا لأن inasmuch as c
نَصًّا verbatim adv	نظرة look, looks n

نظرية theory n	نفقة expense n
نظم dispose v	نُفُوذ leverage n
نظير match n	نفور distaste n
نظيف clean, spotless adj	نفي banishment n
نعامة ostrich n	نَفيس invaluable adj
نعس doze v	نفيس precious adj
نعسان drowsy adj	نقابة guild n
نعمل yes adv	نَقّال mobile adj
نعناع mint n	نقب piercing n
نعومة smoothness n	نقح file v
نفاذ صبر impatient adj	نقد money, cash n
نفاق hypocrisy n	نقد review n
نفايات litter n	نقديّ critical adj
نفاية garbage, refuse, trash n	نقر peck n
نفخ inflate v	نقرس gout n
نفخة puff n	نقش engrave v
نَفَس breath n	نقش على ضريح epitaph n
نَفْس soul n	نقص flaw, shortage, deficiency n
نفسك yourself pro	نَقْض breach n
نفسُنا ourselves pro	نقض veto v
نفسه oneself pre	نقطة dot, point n
نفسيّ psychic adj	نقطة تحول watershed n
نَفْطة blister n	نقع بالخل marinate v
نفعي expedient adj	نقع فى soak in v
نَفَقٌ subway n	نقل الدم transfusion n
نفَق tunnel n	نقل العربة cart v

captain n نقيب	fit n نوبة
spite n نِكاية	نَوْبَة غَضب tantrum n
calamity n نكبة	gull n نورس
gag v نكت	sort n نوع
gag, joke n نكتة	quality n نوعيّة
snitch v نمّ	November n نوفمبر
come up v نما	loom n نَوْل
outgrow v نما بسرعة	rest, sleep n نوم
growth n نماء	doze n نوم خفيف
gossip n نمام	hypnotize v نوم مغناطيسيا
panther, leopard n نَمِر	nuclear adj نَوَوِيّ
freckle n نمش	mean v نوى
ant n نملة	raw adj نَيْء
model, type n نموذج	bright adj نَيِّر
typical adj نَموذَجيّ	crossfire n نيران متقاطعة
day n نهار	
terms n نهايات	
end, term n نهاية	
weekend n نهاية الأسبوع	
final, irrevocable adj نهائي	
sack n نهب	
river, stream n نهر	
glacier n نهر الجليد	
rebirth n نهضة	
insatiable adj نهم	
glutton n نهمة	

ه	هُبوط landing n
	هبوط slump n
هاتف phone v	هجاء satire n
هاتف خلوي cellphone n	هجر disuse n
هاجر immigrate v	هجرة جماعية exodus n
هاجس obsession n	هجوم offense n
هاجسّ premonition n	هجوم مفاجئ holdup n
هادٍ leading adj	هجوميّ offensive adj
هادئ cool adj	هدأ pacify v
هارب fugitive n	هدب الجفن eyelash n
هارب من الجندية deserter n	هدر growl v
هالك perishable adj	هدف target n
هامّ considerable adj	هَدْم destruction n
هامّ جداً momentous adj	هدنة truce, armistice n
هامش footnote n	هدوء quietness n
هامشيّ marginal adj	هدير roar n
هاو fan n	هدئ أعصابك chill out v
هاوَن mortar n	هذب file v
هاوية gulf, abyss n	هذه الليلة tonight adv
هائل formidable adj	هِر cat n
هب blow v	هراء nonsense n
هبة donation n	هراوة club n
هَبّة blast n	هَرَم pyramid n
هبط slump v	هُرَيْرة kitten n
هبوط descent n	هريس puree n
	هز كتفيه shrug v

هزأ v mock	هورمون n hormone
هَزّة n concussion	هُولَنْدَا n Netherlands
هزلي adj comical	هولندة n Holland
هزم v foil	هولندي adj Dutch
هزيل adj lean	هُولِيّ adj monstrous
هزيمة n overthrow	هؤلاء adj these
هستيري adj hysterical	هي pro she
هستيريا n hysteria	هياج adj turmoil
هش adj fragile	هيبة n prestige
هضبة n plateau	هيجان n eruption
هضميّ adj digestive	هيدروجين n hydrogen
هطول المطر n rainfall	هيدروليكي adj hydraulic
هَفوة n lapse	هيكل n frame
هكذا adv thus	هيكل السفينة n hull
هلوس v hallucinate	هيئة n guise
همّ n care	هيئة n form
همجيّ adj barbaric	هيئة المحلّفين n jury
همجيّة n barbarism	
همز v goad	
هَمْس n whisper	
همهم v hum	
هناك adv there	
هو من pro he	
هواء n air	
هوائي n antenna	
هوّة n chasm	

واقعيًّا virtually adv	**و**
واهن feeble adj	
واو العطف and c	و لا واحد من neither adj
وإذ ذاك whereupon c	واثق confident adj
وإلّا otherwise adv	واجب obligation n
وباء epidemic n	واجب دفعه payable adj
وبخ rebuke v	واجهة مبنى frontage n
وبين amid pre	واحة oasis n
وتد pin n	واحد one adj
وتر bend v	وادٍ valley n
وترّي uneven adj	واد ضيق canyon n
وثاق bond n	وارث heir n
وثب leap v	وازن offset v
وثبة dart n	واسطة intermediary n
وثنيّ pagan adj	واسع large adj
وثيق الصلة pertinent adj	واصل go on v
وثيقة bill n	واصلة hyphen n
وجار الكلب kennel n	واضح conspicuous adj
وجب have to v	واضحّ obvious adj
وجبة brunch, meal n	واظب keep up v
وجد ecstatic adj	واع aware adj
وجرة pitfall n	واعد favorable adj
وجع distress v	وافر plentiful adj
وجع السنّ toothache n	واقع situated adj
وجه face n	واقعيّ actual adj
وجهة نظر standpoint n	

و

brief *adj* وجيز	devout *adj* وَرِع
facet *n* وجيه	paper *n* ورق
module *n* وحدة	sandpaper *n* ورق الزّجاج
meter *n* وحدة لقياس	parchment *n* ورق نفيس
mile *n* وحدة لقياس	leaf *n* ورقة
liter *n* وحدة مكاييل متريّة	blade *n* ورقة نبات
solely *adv* وحدَهُ	tumor *n* ورم
brutalize *v* وحش	successor *n* وريث
bloodthirsty, inhuman, brutal *adj* وحشيّ	heiress *n* وريثة
atrocity, brutality *n* وحشية	vein *n* وريد
mud *n* وحْل	intravenous *adj* وريدي
revelation *n* وحْي	leaflet *n* وَرَيقَة
sole *adj* وحيد	ministry *n* وزارة كهنوت
pang *n* وخز	distribute *v* وزع
farewell *n* وداع	scale *v* وزن
bow out *v* ودع بالانحناء	weight *n* وزْن
genial *adj* ودي	lightweight *n* وزن خفيف
deposit *n* وديعة	minister *n* وزير
genetic *adj* وراثي	cushion *n* وسادة
inherit *v* ورث	convenience *n* وسائل الراحة
rose *n* ورْد	fair *n* وسط
rosy *adj* ورديّ	among *pre* وسَط
workshop *n* ورْشَة	gimmick *n* وسيلة للتحايل
garage *n* ورشة عمل	fair *adj* وسيم
implicate *v* ورط	ribbon *n* وشاح
deadlock *adj* ورْطة	imminent *adj* وشيك

description n وَصْف	وَغْد n rascal
recipe n وصفة	وفاء n loyalty
prescription n وصفة طبيّة	affluence, abundance, plenty n وفرة
descriptive adj وَصْفِيّ	fender n وقاء
link v وصل	boldness n وقاحة
voucher n وَصْل	prevention n وقاية
junction n وصلة	preventive adj وقائيّ
extension n وصلة تلفون	time n وقت
stain n وصمة	cheeky adj وقح
arrival n وصول	check n وَقْف
regent n وصي العرش	cease-fire n وقف إطلاق النار
illustrate v وضح	fuel n وقود
lay v وضع	standing n وقوف
setting n وَضْع	proxy n وكالة
status n وَضْع	best man n وكيل العريس
clarity n وضوح	nor c ولا
lowly adj وضيع	allegiance n ولاء
homeland n وطن	birth n ولادة
countryman n وطني	lighter n ولاعة
national adj وطنيّ	state n ولاية
function n وظيفة	generate v ولد
container n وعاء	lad n ولد
gut n وعاء جلدي	hack v ولع ب
well n وعاء لسائل	liking, penchant n ولوع
promise n وَعْد	howl n ولولة
preaching n وَعْظ	nod v ومأ

و
يا

nevertheless *adv* ومع ذلك	undertake *v* يباشر
flash *n* وميض	overdo *v* يبالغ
illusion *n* وهم	curtail *v* يبتر
deity *n* وهية	blackmail *v* يبتزّ بالتهديد
woes *n* ويل	smile *v* يبتسم
	dignify *v* يبجّل
	research *v* يبحث
	look for, seek *v* يَبْحثُ عَنْ
	navigate *v* يبحِر

يا

Japanese *adj* يابانيّ	vaporize *v* يبخر
mainland *n* يابسة	start *v* يبدأ
yard *n* يارد	lavish *v* يبدد
jasmine *n* ياسمين	shift, alter *v* يبدّل
ruby *n* ياقوت	look *v* يبدو
lottery *n* يانصيب	get down to *v* يبدي إهتمام
mellow *adj* يانع	sow *v* يَبْذُر الحَبّ
hopeless *adj* يائس	refrigerate *v* يبرد
sin, trespass *v* يأتَمُ	cool *v* يبرّد باعتدال
decimate *v* يأخذ	justify *v* يبرر
despair *n* يأسّ	stand out *v* يبرز
regret *v* يأسف	rivet *v* يبرشم
eat *v* يأكل	master *v* يبرع في
nibble *v* يأكل بتأنٍ	argue *v* يبرهن
command *v* يأمر	whittle *v* يبري
	clear *v* يبرئ
	rise *v* يَبْزغ

simplify v يبسّط	consist v يتألف من
unveil v يبسط	contemplate v يتأمل
spit v يبصق	conspire v يتآمر
annihilate v يُبطل	break off v يتباعَد
nullify v يبطل	boast, show off v يتباهى
vacate v يبطل	contribute v يتبرّع بـ
abrogate v يبطل , يُلغي	adopt v يتبنّى
pad v يبطّن	overstep v يتجاوز
scatter v يبعثر	trail v يتجرجر
dent v يبعّج	belch v يتجشّأ
stain v يبقع	wrinkle v يتجعّد
remain v يبقى	freeze v يتجمد
subsist v يبقى	avert v يتجنّب
survive v يبقى حيّا	wander v يتجوّل
weep v يبكي	converse v يتحدّث مع
notify v يُبلغ	steal v يتحدر
reach v يبلغ	confront, defy v يتحدّى
construct v يبني	crash v يتحطّم
rejoice v يبهج	overrule v يتحكّم
urinate v يبول	afford v يتحمّل
whiten v يبيض	transform v يتحوّل
sell v يبيع	major in v يتخصّص في
auction v يبيع بالمزاد العلني	rid of, put off v يتخلص من
carry on v يتابع	abdicate v يتخلى
traffic v يتاجر بـ	forsake v يتخلى عن
corrode v يتأكّل	dangle v يتدلّى

يتذبذب v vacillate	يتصفّح v browse
يتذكّر v mind	يتصوّر v visualize
يتذمّر v murmur	يتضاءل v wane
يتذوّق v taste	يتضارب v conflict
يترأس v preside	يتطابق v agree
يترجم v translate	يتطفّل v meddle
يتردّد v waver	يتطلّب v require
يترصّد v lurk	يتظاهر v simulate
يَتْرُكُ v let go	يتعاطف v sympathize
يترنّح v stagger	يتعاون v cooperate
يتزامن v concur, synchronize	يتعايش v cohabit
يتزحزح v budge	يتعثر v stumble
يَتَزَحْلَق v ski	يتعفّن v rot
يتزلّج v skate	يتعقّب v tail
يتزوّج v wed	يتعلّق بـ v concern
يتزوّج ثانيةً v remarry	يتعمّد v premeditate
يتسرّب v leak	يَتَعَنْقَد v cluster
يتّسع v broaden	يتغاضى عن v connive
يتسوّق v shop	يتغاير v contrast
يتشاجر v row	يتغدّى v dine
يتشاجر n scuffle	يتفاخر v brag
يتشاور v confer	يتفادى v avoid
يَتَشَقْلَب v tumble	يتفرّع v branch out
يتشمّس v bask	يتقاتل v fight
يتصادم v collide	يتقاذف v toss
يتصرّف v deport	يتقاعد v retire

face up to v يتقبل الأمر	يتنافس مع v compete
distill v يتقطر	يتنبّأ v predict
wear v يتقلّد	يتنبأ بـ v foresee
back up v يَتَقَهْقَرُ	يتنشّق v sniff
vomit v يتقيّأ	يتنفّ v breathe
adhere بـ v يتقيّد	يتنكّر v masquerade
culminate v يتكبّد	يتنهّد v sigh
speak v يتكلّم	يتهجّى v spell
forecast v يتكهن	يتّهم v accuse
vanish, flee v يتلاشى	يتواجد v coexist
twinkle v يتلألأ	يتوافق v correspond
boil down to v يَتَلَخّص فِي	يتوانى v loiter
deign v يتلطّف	يتوب v repent
televise v يُتَلْفِز	يتوّج v crown
dial v يتلفن إلى	يتوسّط v mediate
smack v يتلمّظ	يتوسّل v invoke
recite v يتلو	يتوق v aspire
sway v يتمايل	يتوق إلى v yearn
mumble, stammer v يتمتم	يتولى v assume
lie v يتمدّد	يتولّى الأمر v take over
rebel v يتمرّد	orphan n يتيم
stroll v يتمشّى	persevere v يثابر
complete v يتمّم	retaliate v يثأر
wish v يتمنّى	bounce v يثب
quarrel v يتنازع	affirm v يثبّت
condescend v يتنازل	clench v يثبّت المسمارَ

يُثبّت بِمِشبك clip v

يثخن thicken v

يثرثر babble v

يثق trust v

يثق بـ depend v

يثقب bore, perforate, prick v

يُثقِل burden v

يثمن appraise v

يثني deter v

يثور revolt v

يثير raise v

يجب must v

يجتث uproot v

يجتمع convene v

يجتنب shun v

يجِد come about v

يجدِّد rejuvenate v

يجدِّد renew v

يجدّف على الله blaspheme v

يجدِل twist v

يجذب attract v

يجدّف paddle v

يجرح hurt, wound v

يجرح بطلقة نارية gun down v

يجرُؤ dare v

يجزّ shear v

يجصّص plaster v

يجعله أسوأ worsen v

يجعله مشرقاً clear v

يجفف wind v

يجلب bring v

يجلد lash v

يجلِس sit v

assemble, collect, aggregate v
يجمع

يجمّل beautify v

يجنّ madden v

يجنّد conscript n

يجنّس nationalize v

يجوس prowl v

يجوع starve v

يجيب answer, reply v

يجيز license v

يحاذي adjoin v

يحاصر blockade v

يحاكم try v

يحاول اكتساب كذا court v

يحبّ love v

يحتجّ protest v

يحتجز detain v

يحترس beware v

يحترم regard v

crowd v يحتشد		outlaw v يحرّم	
retain v يحتفظ بـ		afflict v يُحزن	
celebrate v يحتفل ب		compute v يحسب	
commemorate v يحتفل بذكرى		calculate v يحسب رياضيًا	
despise v يحتقر		assemble v يحشد	
contact, rub v يحتك بـ		cram, stuff v يحشُرُ	
monopolize v يحتكر		annotate v يحشّي	
coincide v يحتلّ		mow v يحصد	
necessitate v يحتّم		reap v يحصد	
support v يحتمل		allot v يحصص	
motivate v يحثّ		civilize v يحضّر	
screen v يحجب		wreck v يحطّم	
attach v يحجز		forbid, ban v يحظر	
border on v يحدّ		dig v يحفر	
occur v يحدُث		preserve v يحفظ	
determine v يحدّد		investigate v يحقّق	
stare v يحدّق		arbitrate v يحكّم	
warn v يحذّر		reign v يحكم	
cross out, omit v يَحْذِفُ		bar v يُحكم إقفال باب	
plow, till v يحرّث		refer to v يحكم بين	
deliver v يحرّر		sentence v يحكم على	
attain, obtain v يحرز		loosen, unwind v يحلّ	
scald v يُحرق بُخار		solve v يُحلّ	
cremate v يحرق جثّة ميْت		soar v يحلّق	
stir v يحرّك		analyze v يُحلّل	
deprive v يَحرم		dream v يحلم	

sweeten v يحلّي	seal v يختم
redden v يحمر	circumcise v يختن
blush v يحمّر وجهه	curdle v يخثر
parch v يحمّص	shame v يخجل
toast v يحمّص الخبز	scratch v يخدش
carry v يحمل	defraud, deceive v يخدع
defend v يحمي	minister v يخدم
curve v يحني	serve v يخذل
recline v يحني	ruin, waste v يخرب
modify v يحوّر	scribble v يخربش
deliver v يحوّل	come out v يخرج
relive v يحيا	produce v يخرج
baffle v يحير	step out v يخرج
puzzling adj يحير	store v يخزن
cordon off v يحيط بحبل	confound v يخزي
animate v يحيي	chase away v يخسأ
renovate v يحيي	belong, pertain v يخص
antagonize v يخاصم	specialize v يخصص
bake v يخبز	allow v يخصص لـ
knock v يخبط	succumb, subdue v يخضع
select v يختار	protracted adj يخطط
prove v يختبر	miscalculate v يخطئ التقدير
devise v يخترع	slow down v يخفض السرع
penetrate v يخترق	alleviate v يخفف
stock v يختزن	miss v يخفق
differ v يختلف	mingle v يخلط

يخلع depose v	يدرك perceive v
يخلع القناع unmask v	يُدرك إدراكاً كاملاً appreciate v
يخلف supersede v	يدعم stay v
يَخلق create v	يدّعي allege v
يُخمد muffle, stifle v	يدغدغ tickle v
يخمّر brew v	يدفع defray v
يخنة stew n	يَدْفع push v
يَخنق asphyxiate, choke v	يدفع الى الامام drive v
يخيط sew v	يدفّئ toast v
يخيم camp v	يُدفّئ warm up v
بدأ بيد hand in v	يدقّ maul v
يدافع plead v	يدقّق الحسابات audit v
يدافع عن advocate v	يدلّ على denote v
يدِبّ crawl v	يدلّك massage v
يدبّر procure v	يدلّل pamper v
يدجّن tame v	يدمج compact v
يدحرج roll v	يَدْمج consolidate v
يدخر put aside v	يدمج merge v
يدّخر save v	يدمدم rumble v
يَدخل come in v	يدمّر devastate v
يُدخل introduce v	يدمّر raze v
يُدخّن smoke v	يدنّس desecrate v
يدرّب coach v	يدنو approach v
يدرج schedule v	يُدهِش astonish v
يدرز stitch v	يدهن بمرهم anoint v
يدرس deliberate, thresh v	يدوّخ daze v

circulate v يدور	thaw v يُذيب
circle v يدور حول	publish v يُذيع
stamp v يدوس	sound out v يُذيع
last v يدوم	underwrite v يُذَيِّل
whirl v يدوم	check up n يُراجِع
record v يدوّن	accompany v يرافِق
boom v يدوّي	crouch v يربِض
manual adj يدويّ	tie, connect v يربط
resounding adj يدوّي	knit v يربُط
administer v يدير	articulate v يربِط بمَفصِل
operate v يدير	confuse v يُربِك
turn v يدير	bring up v يربّي
campaign v يدير حملة	nurse, rear v يربّي
screw v يدير لولبيًّا	mistrust, suspect v يرتاب
convict v يدين	arrange, rank v يرتّب
slaughter v يذبح	tremble v يرتجِف
vibrate v يذبذِب	rebound v يرتدّ
wither v يذبُل	shudder v يرتعِد
bow v يذعن	shiver v يرتعش
mention v يذكر	climb, move up v يرتفع
mind v يذكّر	deplore v يرثي ل
recollect, remember, remind v يذكّر	come back v يرجع
go; strike v يذهب	stone v يرجم
bewilder, amaze v يذهِل	welcome v يرحّب بـ
melt v يذوب	depart v يرحل
taste v يذوق	permit v يرخّص

يا

يُرخي v slacken	يركز على v focus on
يرسم v depict, trace	يرمي v throw
يرسم بـ v decree	يرهب v daunt
يرسم كاهناً v consecrate	يرهِق v load
يرشّ v spray	يرهِّن v pawn
يرشِّد v conduct	يروِّع v terrify
يرشُف v sip	يروع فجأة v startle
يرشو v bribe, corrupt, buy-off	يروي v narrate, tell
يرُض v bruise	يروي بتفصيل v detail
يرضي v content	يرى v notice, see
يرطِّب v dampen, moisten	يريد v want
يرعِب v appall	يريق v shed
يرعَى v patronize	يزامِل v associate
يرغب في v desire	يزاول v practice
يرفس v kick	يزجُر v snub
يرفض v reject, refuse	يزحف v march
يرفع v boost, raise	يزخرف v decorate
يرفو v darn	يزداد v augment
يرقّ v relent	يزدرع v transplant
يرقد v rest	يزدري v scorn
يرقُص v dance	يزدهر v prosper
يرقى إلى v date	يزعِج v annoy, bother
يركب v ride, compose	يزقو v peep
يركب في الباص v bus	يزن v balance
يركُد v stagnate	يزِن v weigh
يركِّز v concentrate	يزهر v bloom, blossom

يَسْتر shelter v	يزوّج marry v
يسترخي relax v	يزود provide, supply v
يسترد withdrawn adj	يزور stop by, visit v
يسترد recoup, regain v	يزيّف counterfeit v
يَسْترضي conciliate v	يزيل strip v
يستروح wind v	يزيل التراب eat away v
يستشير consult v	يزيل العشب الضارّ weed v
يستطرد digress v	يزيّن adorn v
يستطلع spy v	يزيّن trim v
يستطيب savor v	يُسابق race v
يستطيع can, may v	يساعد assist v
يستعد prepare v	يسافر travel v
يستعطي beg v	يساند sustain v
يستعمر colonize v	يُسَاهِم lots adj
يستعمل apply v	يساوم bargain v
يَسْتَعْمِل use v	يسأل ask, request v
يَسْتَعيد win back v	يسبّب cause v
يستعير borrow v	يسبح surf v
يستغيث بـ appeal v =	يَسْبَح swim v
يستفيد profit v	يسبق outrun, precede v
يستكمل replenish v	يستأنف الدعوى appeal v
يستمتع relish v	يستبدل replace v
يستمرّ continue v	يستبقي spare v
يستنتج deduce v	يستحثّ arouse v
يستنفد consume v	يستحقّ deserve, merit v
يستهلّ commence v	يستر screen, shield v

يستهلك الدّين v amortize		يسكن (الالام) v sedate
يستوضع v pose		يسلب v pillage, rob, spoil
يستوعب v assimilate		يسلّح v arm
يستوعبُ v take in		يسلخ v skin
يستولي على v capture, seize		يسلك v behave
يستيقظُ v wake up		يسلّم v surrender
يسجّل v register, record		يسلِم إلى v commit
يسجّل إصابة v score		يسلِم إلى v submit
يسحب v retract		يسِيم v sign
يسحر v bewitch		يسمح بـ v admit
يسحق v quash		يسمّم v poison
يسخر v quiz		يسند v back, bolster
يسخر من v deride		يسود v predominate
يسدّ v block, obstruct		يسوّغ v rationalize
يسدّ v plug		يسوّي v adjust
يسدّد v aim		يسوّي في الرتبة v coordinate
يسرد n recount		يسوّي نزاعاً v compromise
يسرع v speed		يسيء الادارة v mismanage
يسطع v brighten		يسيء السلوك v misbehave
يسعف v relieve		يسيء الفهم v misunderstand
يسعُل v cough		يسيء المعاملة v mistreat
يسفح v spill		يسيم n graze
يسفَع v scorch		يشاء v please
يسقط v bring down		يشاهد v view
يسكت v shut up		يشبع v satisfy
يسكّن v mitigate		يشبع بـ v saturate

squander v يُشتّت	curb v يَشكُم
stipulate v يشترط	complain v يشكو
participate v يشترك	smell v يشمّ
collaborate في v يشترك	comprise v يشمل
derive v يشتقّ	strangle v يشنُق
cuss v يشتم	testify v يشهَد
abuse v يشتِم	deface v يشوّه
lust v يشتهي	mangle, maim v يشوّه
denounce v يشجُب	broil, roast v يشوي
cheer v يشجّع	confiscate v يصادر
charge v يشحن بطاريّة	befriend v يصادق
personify v يشخّص	ally v يصاهر بين
strain, tighten v يشُدّ	diffuse v يصبّ
drink v يشرب	paint v يصبغ
slash v يشرُط	correct, rectify v يصحّح
set out في v يشرع	rebuff v يصدّ
sprout v يشطأ	rust v يَصدأ
cancel v يشطب	export v يصدّر الى الخارج
rinse v يشطف	certify, ratify v يصدّق على
splinter v يشظّي	shock v يصدم
dilute v يشعشِع	creak, squeak v يصِرّ
turn on v يشعل	persist v يصِرّ
occupy v يشغَل	press v يصرّ على . يحثّ
cure v يشفي	cry out, scream v يصرخ
rip, slit, split v يشُقّ	conjugate v يصرّف الأفعال
thank v يشكر	clash v يصطدم

يصطدم بـ run into v	يُصيب come over v
يصعد ascend v	يصيبه بالعَرج cripple adj
يَصْعَق astound v	يصيبه بالعَرج cripple v
يصغر belittle v	يصيح call, shout v
يصغي listen v	يصيح الديك crow v
يصف describe v	يضادّ counteract v
يصفّ acclaim v	يضاعف multiply v
يُصُفّ align v	يضايق molest v
يصفح عن spare v	يضحك laugh v
يصفِر wheeze, whistle v	يضحك ضحكاً خافتاً chuckle v
يصفع clap, slap, spank v	يضحّي victimize v
يصفّق applaud v	يضخّ pump v
يصفّي clarify v	يضرب bludgeon v
يَصْقُل brush up v	يضرب بالسّوط switch v
يصقل varnish v	يضرب بعنف bang v
يصِل arrive v	يضرب بهراوة club v
يُصْلِح mend, patch v	يضطهد oppress v
يصلي pray v	يَضَع جانبًا brush aside v
يُصِمّ deafening adj	يُضعف weaken v
يصِمّ deafen v	يضغط squeeze v
يصنع perform v	يضغط على depress v
يصنّف classify v	يضِلّ stray v
يصوّت sound v	يضلّل beguile, betray v
يصوّر picture, portray v	يَضُمّ إلى affiliate v
يصوغ mold, shape v	يَضْمُر atrophy v
يصون conserve, secure v	يضمن warrant v

يُضيف add v	يطوف في البحر cruise v
يطابق conform v	يطوّق circle, ring v
يطارد chase v	يطوي turn down v
يطالب بـّ claim v	يطير fly v
يطأ trample v	يطيع comply v
يطبع print v	يُطِيْل lengthen v
يطبّق عمليًا apply v	يظلم darken v
يطحن grind v	يظمأ thirst v
يطّرح put away v	يُظْهِر manifest, attest v
يطرد oust v	يُظهِر بوضوح demonstrate v
يُطري praise v	يُظْهِر للعيان appear v
يطعم feed v	يعارض oppose, thwart v
يطعن pierce, stab v	يعاف loathe v
يطفئ quench v	يعاقب penalize, punish v
يُطَقْطِق crack v	يعاكس counter v
يطلّ overlook v	يعالج remedy, tackle v
يطلب ask, demand v	يُعامل process v
يُطْلِع acquaint v	يعانق cuddle v
يطْلُع spring v	يعاني suffer v
يُطلِق launch, release, shoot down v	يعاني من suffer from v
يطمر bury v	يعاود recur v
يطمس obliterate v	يعاون aid v
يطِنّ buzz v	يُعايِر calibrate v
يطهِّر purge, purify v	يعبث play v
يطهو cook v	يعبئ في زجاجات bottle v
يطوف roam v	يَعْتَبِر deem v

يا

reckon v يعتبر	isolate v يَعزِل
apologize v يعتذر	console v يعزّي
object v يعترض	bandage v يعصِب
confess v يعترف	blindfold v يعصِب العينين
acknowledge بـ v يعترف بـ	crush v يعصِر
meditate v يعتزم	modernize v يعصِّر
suppose, think v يعتقد	wring v يعصر
apprehend, seize v يعتقل	bite v يعضّ
look after بـ v يعتني بـ	sneeze v يعطس
wonder v يعجب	break down v يعطّل
admire بـ v يعجب بـ	suspend v يعطّل موقّتا
dent n يعجة	give v يعطى
accelerate v يعجّل	preach v يعظ
count v يعدّ	acquit v يعفي
concoct v يعدّ شراباً بالمَزج	complicate v يعقّد
list v يعدّد	contract v يعقد
amend, reform v يعدّل	tie v يعقد
agonize, torture, torment v يعذّب	curl v يعقص الشّعر
limp v يعرج	sterilize v يعقم
offer, show v يعرض	reversible adj يعكّس
subject v يعرّض	pack v يعلّب
jeopardize v يعرّض للخطر	comment v يعلّق على
air v يعرّض للهواء	advertise v يعلم
perspire, sweat v يعرق	coach, teach v يعلّم
uncover, undress v يعرّي	announce v يعلِن
cherish v يعزّ	baptize, christen v يعمِّد

outlive v يُعمِّر	plant v يغرس
deepen v يُعمِّق	sink v يغرق
operate v يعمِل	lure, tempt v يُغري
work v يعمل	spin v يَغْزِل
boss around v يعنف	invade v يغزو
direct v يُعَنوِن	bathe v يغسِل
signify v يُعني	wash v يَغْسِل
accustom v يُعوِّد	washable adj يُغسَل
return, revert v يعود	anger, irritate v يُغْضِب
charm v يُعوِّذ	crease v يُغَضِّن
compensate, atone v يُعوِّض	plunge v يُغطِّس
clog v يُعوِّق	wrap v يُغطِّي
prevent v يعوق	canvas v يُغطِّي بالقما
lament, moan v يُعْوِل	absolve, remit v يَغْفِر
malign v يعيب	overpower v يغلب
bring back v يُعيد	envelop v يُغلِّف
restore v يعيد	close, shut v يُغْلِق
reprint v يعيد الطبع	boil v يَغْلي
live v يعيش	simmer v يغلي برفق
appoint v يُعيِّن	inundate v يَغْمِر
venture v يغامر	submerge v يغمر
assassinate v يغتال	pass out v يُغْمى علَيه
assault, usurp v يغتصب	sing v يغني
rape v يَغْتصِب	change, commute v يُغيِّر
nourish, nurture v يُغذِّي	raid v يغير على
seduce v يُغَرِّر	surprise v يفاجئ

aggravate v يفاقم	decay v يَفسُد
negotiate, treat v يفاوض	deteriorate v يُفسِد
crumble v يفتّت	demoralize v يُفسِد الأخلاق
open, unlock v يفتَح	deprave adj يُفسِد الأخلاق
break open v يفتح قفلاً	account for v يفسّر
redeem v يفتدي	deplete v يَفْصِد
presume v يفترض	segregate v يفصل
part v يفترق	separate, sever v يَفصِل
defame v يفتري على	prefer v يفضّل
search v يفتّش	undo, untie, loose v يفكّ
ransack v يفتّش بتدقيق	decipher v يفكّ المغالق
misjudge v يفتقد	reason v يفكّر
warp v يَفْتِل	consider v يفكّر في
captivate v يفتِن	take apart v يفكّك
detonate v يفجِر	cultivate v يفلح
scan v يفحص بِدِقّة	bankrupt v يُفلِس
char v يفحم	crash v يُفلِس
run away v يفرّ	refute v يفنّد
cheer up v يفرح	catalog v يفهرس
levy v يَفْرِض	comprehend v يفهم
assess v يَفْرِضُ ضريبة	understand v يَفْهم
unload v يُفرّغ الحمولة	win v يفوز
brush, scrub v يفرك	authorize v يفوّض
mince v يَفْرِم	recommend v يفوّض أمرَه إلى
scare v يُفْزِع	benefit v يفيد
admit v يفسح مجالاً لـ	avail v يفيد

يا

يا

combat, battle v يقاتل	loan v يُقرض
compare v يقارن بين	knock v يقرع
litigate, sue v يقاضي	click v يقرقع
resist, withstand v يقاوم	swear, vow v يقسم
barter, swap v يُقايض	skim v يقشد
apprehend v يقبض على	peel v يقشر
accept v يقبل	clip v يقص
kiss v يقبّل	abridge v يقصر
quote v يقتبس	shorten v يقصر
burst into v يقتحم	bite v يقضم
break in v يقتحم بيتاً	trickle v يقطر
suggest v يقترح	decapitate v يقطع الرأس
vote v يقترع	chop v يقطع بفأس
deduct v يقتطع	behead v يقطع رأسه
kill v يقتل	pick v يقطف
pluck, pull v يقتلع	dwell v يقطن
appreciate v يقدّر شيئاً	attentive adj يقظ
sanctify v يقدّس	wary adj يقظ
contribute v يقدّم	alert n يقظ
report v يقدّم تقريراً	awake adj يقظان
send v يقذف	awakening n يقظة
bomb v يقذف بالقنابل	set v يقعد
dash v يقذف بعنف	rattle v يقعقع
sanction v يقرّ	stand v يقف
decide v يقرر	jump v يقفز
nip v يقرص	lock v يقفل

lessen v يَقِلّ	unearth v يكتشـف
upset, worry v يَقْلِب	live off v يكتفي
diminish v يقلّل	agglomerate v يكتّل
prune v يقلّم	conceal v يكْتُم
quash, quell v يقمع	abound v يَكْثُرُ
suppress v يقمَع	toil v يكدَح
persuade v يُقْنِع	accumulate v يكدّس
convince v بـ يقنع	contradict v يكذّب
overcome v يقهِر	reiterate, repeat v يكرّر
mine v يقوّض	devote, bless v يكرّس
say v يقول	coerce v يكره
strengthen v يقوّي	break up v يُكَسِّر
turn up v يقوّي	scrape, shave v يَكْشِط
confine v يقيّد	unfold v يكشِف
constrain, chain v يقيد	bail out v يَكْفُل
measure v يقيس	muzzle v يكمّم
assess v يقيم	ambush v لـ يكمن
undoubtedly adv يقيناً	sweep v يكنس
wrestle, struggle v يكافح	stack v يكوّم
cope v يكافح بنجاح	iron v يكوي
reward v يكافئ	adapt v يُكيِّف
rein, restrain, check v يكبح	dejected adj يُكْئِب
magnify v يكبّر	notice, observe v يلاحظ
squeeze v يكبس على	caress, coax v يلاطف
subscribe v يكتتب	find v يلاقى
overrun v يكتسـح	accommodate v يلائم

clothe, wear v يُلبس	feel, touch v يَلمِس
abide by v يلتزم	amuse v يُلهِي
bog down v يلتصق	defile, pollute v يلوّث
pick v يلتقط	blame, reproach v يَلوم
pick up v يَلْتَقِطُ	screw v يلوي
crave v يلتمس	soften v يُلَيّن
solicit v يَلْتَمِس	practice v يمارس
blaze v يلتهب	procrastinate v يماطل
devour v يلتهم	stall v يُماطِل
resort v يلجأ	obey v يمتثل
urge v يُلحّ	absorb v يمتصّ
solder, weld v يَلحُم	ride v يمتطي
shuffle v يُلَخبِط	toughen v يمتن
summarize v يُلخّص	represent, act v يمثّل
obligate v يُلزم	appear v يَمْثُل أمام القضاء
sting v يَلسَع	zap v يمحو يحذف
affix, paste v يُلصق	prolong v يمدّ
smear, blot v يلطّخ	stretch v يمدد
play v يلعب	adulterate v يمذُق
lick v يلعق	sicken v يُمرض
curse v يلعن	centralize v يُمَركز
mystify v يُلغِز	blend, mix v يمزج
annul, abolish v يلغي	mixed-up adj يمزج
utter v يلفظ	shred, tear v يمزّق
concoct v يلفّق	claw v يمزّق
invent v يلفّق	wipe v يَمسح

ي

يُمسِك abstain v	يُناوب alternate v
يُمَسْمِر mesmerize v	ينبثق proceed v
يمشّط comb v	ينبح bark v
يمشّط tease v	ينبذ throw away v
يمشي walk v	ينبض pulsate, throb v
يمشي بتشامخ stalk v	يَنْبَعِث مِنْ come from v
يمصّ suck v	ينبه stimulate v
يمقت abhor, detest v	ينبهر dazzle v
يُمَكِّن mechanize v	ينبوع fountain, spring n
يملأ ثانية refill v	ينبوع معدني spa n
يملّس smooth v	ينتبه watch v
يملك hold, own v	ينتدب delegate v
يُملي dictate v	ينتزع tear v
يمنح bestow, award v	ينتظر await, wait v
يمنح براءة charter v	ينتعش revive v
يموت die v	ينتفخ swell v
يمول ثانية refinance v	ينتقد criticize v
يموّه camouflage v	ينتقم avenge v
يميز recognize v	يُنتِن stink v
يُميل tilt v	ينتهي terminate, run out v
يمين right n	ينثر الحَبّ broadcast v
يناصر champion v	يُنجِب procreate v
يناضل contend v	يُنجِد relieve v
يناقش debate v	يُنجِز accomplish v
ينال get v	ينحت carve v
ينام sleep v	ينحرف decline v

advise, counsel v ينصح	attenuate v يُنْجِل
ripen v يَنْضَج	unravel v ينحلّ
water v ينضح	bend down v يَنْحَني
rejoin v ينضم ثانيةً	prod, spur v يَنْخَس
ram v ينطح	jolt v يَنْخَع
bolt, strike v ينطلق	sift v يَنْخُل
look v ينظر	mourn v يندب
look at v يَنْظُرُ إلى	rush v يندفع
clean, mop v ينظف	dampen v يندّي
compose v يَنْظِم	take off v ينزع
organize, arrange v ينظّم	defuse v ينزع الفتيل
recreate v ينعش	come down v يَنْزِل
refresh v ينعش	land v ينزل إلى اليابسة
resuscitate v ينعش	demote v ينزل درجته
turn in v ينعطف ويدخل	degrade v ينزل رتبتهُ
reflect v ينعكس	slide, slip v ينزلق
bloat v يَنْفَخ	spin, weave v ينسج
blow up v يَنْفُخ	retire, withdraw v ينسحب
carry out v يَنْفِّذ	copy, transcribe v يَنْسَخ
do v ينفذ يفعل	sneak v يَنْسَلّ
serve v ينفع	derive v ينشأ عن
yawn v يَنْفَغِر	sob v يَنْشِج
spend v يَنْفِق	deploy, spread v يَنْشُر
banish v ينفي	set about v ينشر إشاعةً
save, rescue v يَنْقُذ	originate v ينشئ
peck v يَنْقُر	install, set up v ينصب

ينقش carve v	يهدر roar v
ينقص decrease v	يهدم destroy v
ينقّط spot v	يهدي conduct v
ينقع soak v	يهدي convert v
ينقل remove v	يهدّئ appease, soothe v
ينقل transport, convey v	يهذي rave v
ينقلب overturn, topple v	يهرس mash v
ينكر deny v	يهزّ thrill v
ينمو grow v	يهزّ بعنف convulse v
ينهار collapse v	يهزأ scoff v
ينهب loot, ravage v	يهزم overthrow v
ينهمر pour v	يهلك perish v
ينهي conclude v	يهمّ concern v
ينهي log off v	يهمد deaden v
ينوّع vary v	يهمس whisper v
يهاجر migrate v	يهمل neglect v
يهاجم attack, assail v	يهنئ congratulate v
يهب yield v	يهوديّ Jewish adj
يهبط cave in v	يهويّ air, ventilate v
يهبط concede v	يهين affront v
يهبط على الأنف nosedive adv	يوافق consent v
يهتز quake, shake v	يوافق على approve v
يهتم care v	يوافق على assent v
يهجر abandon, waive v	يوبّخ chide, scold v
يهدأ calm down v	يوثّق authenticate v
يهدد threaten v	يوثق moor v

يا

trouble v يُوجِع	Greece n يونان
unify, unite v يُوحِّد	Greek adj يوناني
like v يودّ	vandalize v يونلد
commend v يُودِّع	June n يونيو
bequeath v يورث بوصيّة	react v يُؤَثِّر
involve v يورط	lease, rent v يُؤجِر
allocate v يوزِّع	postpone v يُؤجِّل
cushion v يوسِد	chastise v يؤدب
widen, amplify v يوسِّع	frostbitten adj يؤذي بالصقيع
settle v يوطِّد	swing v يُؤرجِح
time v يوقِّت	date v يُؤرِخ
adore v يوقِر	acclimatize v يُؤقلِم
arouse v يوقظ	assert, vouch for v يُؤكِّد
cease, stop v يُوقِف	believe v يؤمن بـ
affect v يولَع بـ	qualify v يُؤهِّل
July n يوليو	lodge v يؤيّ
someday adv يوماً	corroborate v يد
daily adv يوميّ	stiffen v بس
beckon v يومئ	